S. S. Hayter

Introduction To The Theory Of
Finite-State Machines

Introduction To The Theory Of Finite-State Machines

ARTHUR GILL

Assistant Professor of Electrical Engineering
University of California, Berkeley

McGRAW-HILL BOOK COMPANY

New York   San Francisco   Toronto   London

INTRODUCTION TO THE THEORY OF FINITE-STATE MACHINES

23243

3 4 5 6 7 8 9 – M P – 9 8

PREFACE

Recent years have witnessed the rapid emergence of a new scientific discipline, commonly known as *system theory*. The advent of this discipline was largely motivated by the acute need for a theoretical framework within which investigators of different fields of science and engineering could find a common language. The aim of this theory was to build up an arsenal of ideas and tools which would be of equal usefulness to specialists in a wide variety of fields, such as electrical engineering, mechanical engineering, physiology, and linguistics. This was achieved by viewing a *system* (which could be a living organism, an industrial establishment, a guided missile) not via its internal structure, but through the mathematical laws which govern its observable behavior. Employing this "black-box" approach, it was found that systems exhibiting completely dissimilar physical compositions could still be characterized in similar terms and analyzed through the same set of rules.

Although the conception of system theory as an independent discipline is fairly recent, most of its component areas are well-established bodies of knowledge. The theory of information, the theory of linear systems, the theory of control, and the theory of finite-state machines may well be regarded as some of the essential building blocks of system theory, inasmuch as they cut across many different fields of scientific and engineering interest. Of these four areas, the theory of finite-state machines represents the youngest addition and the only area which, thus far, has not been integrated and summarized in any single textbook. With the widening use of discrete-state systems in general, and digital computers in particular, the need for such a textbook has been continuously increasing in both academic and industrial research circles. The purpose of this book is to abate this need by presenting an introductory exposition of the concepts and techniques underlying the theory of synchronous, deterministic, finite-state machines.

As an introductory text on the theory of finite-state machines, the present volume covers only a small segment—but a very basic one—of what is commonly known as the "theory of automata." Thus, the book confines itself to the fundamental system-theoretic aspects of finite-state machines, such as machine characterization, transition matrices, state and machine equivalence, machine minimization, identification experiments for states and machines, and fault identification, and also of information-lossless machines and finite-memory machines. The material is largely based on the work done in the past decade by Huffman, Moore, Mealy, Aufenkamp, Hohn, Ginsburg, Zadeh, Simon, Paull, and Unger (more detailed references are distributed in footnotes throughout the book). Special emphasis is placed on analysis techniques, while synthesis aspects of finite-state machines are not discussed. The reason is that synthesis methods are inherently specialized and require thorough knowledge of the particular system under investigation and of the components available for realization; the analysis methods, on the other hand, may be made quite general and applicable to any system (e.g., a nerve cell, a mathematical algorithm, an electronic computer) which can be modeled by a finite-state machine. Also omitted is a general discussion of modular sequential machines (although linear binary machines are treated in detail), because of the extensive mathematical background required for such a discussion. Finally, it was decided to avoid the topics of Turing machines and Markov chains, since these topics, although closely related to the subject of finite-state machines, constitute separate and independent mathematical disciplines, which are adequately covered in other textbooks.

The bulk of this book was originally written as class notes for a course on finite-state machines, taught at the University of California, Berkeley, during the Spring semester of 1961. Although the course was offered by the Department of Electrical Engineering, the material is not directed specifically to the electrical engineer, but is addressed to any specialist —be he an econometrician or a traffic engineer, a mathematician or a network designer—whose interests lie within the realm of system theory. At the same time, the material in this book is especially recommended for electronics engineers and applied mathematicians, whose area of specialty is control, communication, or digital computation. For students who plan to specialize in computer technology and applications, the material can provide useful preparation for courses in logical design and programming. The book does not assume any advanced mathematical background on the part of the reader, although "mathematical maturity" gained through previous studies is certainly advantageous. The level of presentation corresponds to that of an advanced undergraduate or beginning graduate course. The reader is strongly encouraged to tackle the problems which accompany each chapter, as these problems serve both to illustrate and to complement the material in the text. As a matter of principle, however, the text itself is entirely independent of the problems.

The author is deeply indebted to Dr. L. A. Zadeh of the University of

California, whose seminar on discrete-state systems and automata (taught in Berkeley during the Spring semester of 1960) contributed a great deal to the point of view adopted in this book, as well as to its contents. Thanks are also due to Dr. D. A. Huffman of MIT for some stimulating discussions during his visit in Berkeley in the Spring of 1961.

Arthur Gill

CONTENTS

Preface   v

CHAPTER 1. THE BASIC MODEL   **1**

    1.1.   Introduction   1
    1.2.   The Multiterminal Black Box   1
    1.3.   Time Discreteness   2
    1.4.   Alphabet Finitude   3
    1.5.   States   6
    1.6.   Definition of the Basic Model   7
    1.7.   Examples of Finite-state Machines   8
    1.8.   Determination of State Set from Internal Structure   9
    1.9.   An Alternative Model   12
    1.10. Prediction of Machine Behavior   13
    Problems   15

CHAPTER 2. TRANSITION TABLES, DIAGRAMS, AND MATRICES   **17**

    2.1.   Introduction   17
    2.2.   The Transition Table   17
    2.3.   Enumeration of Machines   19
    2.4.   Isomorphic Machines   20
    2.5.   The Transition Diagram   21
    2.6.   Classification of States and Submachines   24
    2.7.   Machine Decomposition and the Disjunction Machine   27
    2.8.   The Transition Matrix   31
    2.9.   Higher-order Transition Matrices   34
    2.10. Proper Paths   36
    2.11. Determination of Minimal Paths and Complete Cycles   38
    2.12. The Skeleton Matrix   40
    2.13. Partial Construction of Matrices   43
    Problems   44

CHAPTER 3. EQUIVALENCE AND MACHINE MINIMIZATION   **49**

    3.1.   Introduction   49
    3.2.   State Equivalence   49
    3.3. k-equivalence   52
    3.4. k-equivalence Partitions   54
    3.5.   Equivalence Partitions   57
    3.6.   Partitioning by P_k Tables   60
    3.7.   Partitioning by Pairs Table   62
    3.8.   Matrix Method of Partitioning   65

3.9.   Machine Equivalence   67
3.10.   Equivalence Partitioning of Sets of Machines   69
3.11.   The Minimal Form   72
3.12.   Properties of the Minimal Form   75
3.13.   Machine Reduction by Successive Merging   78
3.14.   The Class of Minimal Machines   81
        Problems   82

CHAPTER 4.   STATE IDENTIFICATION EXPERIMENTS   87

4.1.   Introduction   87
4.2.   Classification of Experiments   87
4.3.   Diagnosing and Homing Experiments   89
4.4.   Pairwise Diagnosing Experiments   90
4.5.   Ramifications of the Pairwise Diagnosing Problem   95
4.6.   The Successor Tree   97
4.7.   The Diagnosing Tree   100
4.8.   Simple Preset Diagnosing Experiments   103
4.9.   Simple Adaptive Diagnosing Experiments   105
4.10.   Multiple Preset Diagnosing Experiments   110
4.11.   Multiple Adaptive Diagnosing Experiments   115
4.12.   The Homing Tree   118
4.13.   Simple Preset Homing Experiments   120
4.14.   Simple Adaptive Homing Experiments   121
4.15.   Regular Preset Homing Experiments   123
4.16.   Regular Adaptive Homing Experiments   125
4.17.   Corollaries Regarding State Identification Experiments   129
        Problems   131

CHAPTER 5.   MACHINE IDENTIFICATION EXPERIMENTS   136

5.1.   Introduction   136
5.2.   The General Machine Identification Problem   137
5.3.   Identification of Machines of a Known Class   139
5.4.   The Fault Identification Problem   142
5.5.   Strongly Connected Machines   145
5.6.   Some Properties of Strongly Connected Machines   147
5.7.   Identification of Strongly Connected (n, p, q) Machines   148
5.8.   Information-lossless Machines   149
        Problems   153

CHAPTER 6.   FINITE-MEMORY MACHINES   156

6.1.   Introduction   156
6.2.   Representation of Finite-memory Systems   157
6.3.   Properties of Finite-memory Machines   160
6.4.   Determination of Machine Memory   164
6.5.   The Minimal x-z Function   166
6.6.   Linear Binary Machines   169
6.7.   Time Response of Linear Binary Machines   174
6.8.   Identification of Linear Binary Machines   177
6.9.   Output-independent Machines   179
        Problems   182

CHAPTER 7. INPUT-RESTRICTED MACHINES   **185**

    7.1.   Introduction   185
    7.2.   State Compatibility   186
    7.3.   Quasi-equivalent Machines   188
    7.4.   Determination of Minimal Forms   190
    7.5.   A Reduction Method for Input-restricted Machines   194

    Problems   197

Bibliography   199
Index   203

THE BASIC MODEL

1.1. Introduction

Like other theories motivated by science and engineering needs, the theory of finite-state machines is concerned with mathematical models which serve as approximations to physical or abstract phenomena. The significance of this theory is that its models are not confined to any particular scientific area, but are directly applicable to problems in practically every field of investigation—from psychology to business administration, and from communication to linguistics. One can find the ideas and techniques of the theory of finite-state machines employed in such seemingly unrelated problems as the investigation of the human nervous activity, the analysis of the English syntax, and the design of electronic computers. In an era when the rate of scientific progress greatly depends on interdisciplinary cooperation, the unifying nature of this theory is of apparent value.

In this chapter we shall introduce the so-called "basic model" of the finite-state machine, discussing in detail all its underlying assumptions, and illustrating how it can be utilized in problems of widely differing areas.

1.2. The Multiterminal Black Box

Most problems encountered in scientific and engineering investigations fall into one of the following two categories: *analysis* problems, where one wishes to predict the behavior of a specified system, and *synthesis* problems, where one wishes to construct a system with specified behavior. In this book we shall focus our attention on analysis problems, rather than synthesis problems. From both the analysis and synthesis points of view, it is convenient to separate the variables which characterize the system into (1) *excitation variables*, which represent the stimuli generated by systems other than the one under investigation, and which influence the system behavior; (2) *response variables*, representing those aspects of system behavior which are of interest to the investigator; (3) *intermediate variables*, which are neither excitation nor response variables.

Schematically, a system can be depicted by a "black box," with a finite number of accessible "terminals." The *input terminals* represent the excitation variables and are identified by arrows pointing toward the box. The *output terminals* represent the response variables and are identified by arrows pointing away from the box. The intermediate variables, which are of no direct interest, are assumed to be embedded inside the box. The input and output terminals, as well as the box itself, need not have any physical significance; they merely serve to place in evidence those system variables which are pertinent to the problem at hand.

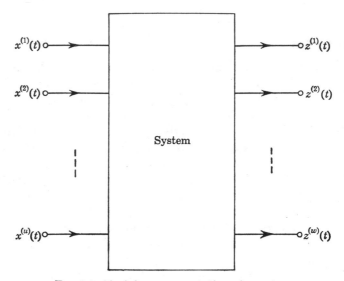

FIG. 1.1. Black-box representation of a system.

Figure 1.1 shows the black-box representation of a system having u input variables and w output variables, all assumed to be time-dependent. $x^{(i)}(t)$, $i = 1, 2, \ldots, u$, denote the input variables, and $z^{(j)}(t)$, $j = 1, 2, \ldots, w$, denote the output variables.

1.3. Time Discreteness

Every system representable by the basic finite-state model is assumed to be controlled by an independent *synchronizing source*, in the following fashion: The system variables are not measured continuously, but only at the discrete instants of time at which a certain specified event, called a *synchronizing signal*, is exhibited by the source. These instants of time are called *sampling times*, the νth sampling time being denoted by t_ν ($\nu = 1, 2, \ldots$). An additional assumption is that the behavior of the system at any sampling time t_ν is independent of the interval between t_ν and the previous sampling time $t_{\nu-1}$. Thus, the true independent quantity, against which every system variable is measured, is not time, but the ordinal number associated with the sampling times. A system variable $v(t)$, therefore, can be written as v_ν, which designates the value of v at the νth sampling time.

It should be emphasized that the foregoing assumptions do not imply that the time intervals between two successive synchronizing signals are uniform; neither does it imply that a system variable, within such interval, exhibits some specific mode of behavior (say, remains constant). The only implication is that, whatever the interval is, and whatever the system variations within the interval are, the values of the variables *at the νth sampling time* depend on the number ν and not on the value of t_ν.

Systems which conform with the time-discreteness assumption made above are said to be *synchronous*. Systems in which this assumption is not valid are called *asynchronous* systems; such systems will not be discussed in this book. In practice, many systems which are inherently asynchronous may be, for purpose of analysis, treated as synchronous. As an example, consider a system composed of a switch controlling a light bulb. The input variable is the position of the switch (on or off), and the output variable is the condition of the bulb (lighted or not lighted). The synchronizing source in this case is the operator of the switch, and the synchronizing signal is the switch-throwing action. To the extent that the value of each variable at the νth sampling time (i.e., when the switch is thrown for the νth time) is independent of the intervals between the sampling times (i.e., between one switch-throwing operation and the next), the described system may be regarded as synchronous. Strictly speaking, however, the system is an asynchronous one, since the operation of physical switches and bulbs does depend on the interval between successive switchings: when the switching frequency becomes too high, one can no longer assert, for example, that the light is always on when the switch is on. Nevertheless, when the switching frequency is known to be sufficiently low (this knowledge may be based on the specified characteristics of the synchronizing source), the system may be safely regarded as a synchronous one. It may be remarked that the analysis of most digital computers encountered in practice can be adequately conducted under the assumption that these devices constitute synchronous systems.

Figure 1.2 shows the system of Fig. 1.1, with the notation modified in accordance with the time-discreteness assumption. $x_\nu^{(i)}$, $i = 1, 2, \ldots,$ u, and $z_\nu^{(j)}$, $j = 1, 2, \ldots, w$, are the input and output variables, respectively, at time t_ν.

1.4. Alphabet Finitude

The next assumption to be made for the basic finite-state model is that each variable can assume only a finite number of distinct values (which may or may not be numerical in nature). The set[1] of values which the variable v can assume is called the v *alphabet* and denoted by V; each element in V is called a v *symbol*.

Let $K^{(1)}$, $K^{(2)}$, . . . , $K^{(m)}$ be finite sets, with representative elements $\kappa_i^{(1)}$, $\kappa_i^{(2)}$, . . . , $\kappa_i^{(m)}$, respectively, and let the set $K^{(1)} \otimes K^{(2)} \otimes \cdots \otimes$

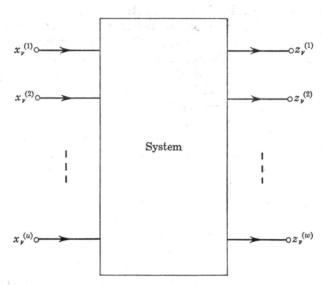

FIG. 1.2. Black-box representation of a system under the time-discreteness assumption.

$K^{(m)}$ denote the set of all ordered m-tuples $(\kappa_i^{(1)}, \kappa_i^{(2)}, \ldots, \kappa_i^{(m)})$. If the excitation variables of a given system are $x^{(1)}$, $x^{(2)}$, . . . , $x^{(u)}$, the *input alphabet* of this system is denoted by X and defined by

$$X = X^{(1)} \otimes X^{(2)} \otimes \cdots \otimes X^{(u)} \tag{1.1}$$

where $X^{(i)}$, $i = 1, 2, \ldots, u$, is the $x^{(i)}$ alphabet. Similarly, if the response variables of the system are $z^{(1)}$, $z^{(2)}$, . . . , $z^{(w)}$, the *output alphabet* of the system is denoted by Z and defined by

$$Z = Z^{(1)} \otimes Z^{(2)} \otimes \cdots \otimes Z^{(w)} \tag{1.2}$$

where $Z^{(j)}$, $j = 1, 2, \ldots, w$, is the $z^{(j)}$ alphabet. If $X^{(i)}$ is of size p_i

---

[1] A *set*, unless otherwise specified, always refers to an *unordered* set. A set with the elements e_1, e_2, . . . , e_r will be written as $\{e_1, e_2, \ldots, e_r\}$. The number of elements r will be called the *size* of the set.

and $Z^{(j)}$ of size q_j, then the sizes p of X and q of Z are given by

$$p = \prod_{i=1}^{u} p_i \tag{1.3}$$

$$q = \prod_{j=1}^{w} q_j \tag{1.4}$$

which are finite.

From the manner in which X is defined, it is seen that a single symbol of the input alphabet, or a single *input symbol*, suffices to describe all u input variables at any given time t_ν. Similarly, from the manner in which Z is defined, it is seen that a single symbol of the output alphabet, or a single *output symbol*, suffices to describe all w output variables at any given time t_ν. Hence, the input variables $x^{(1)}$, $x^{(2)}$, . . . , $x^{(u)}$ may

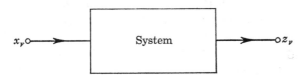

FIG. 1.3. Black-box representation of a finite-state machine.

be replaced by a single input variable x, whose alphabet X is defined by (1.1); the output variables $z^{(1)}$, $z^{(2)}$, . . . , $z^{(w)}$ may be replaced by a single output variable z, whose alphabet Z is defined by (1.2). Accordingly, the u input terminals may be replaced by one input terminal and the w output terminals by one output terminal. The resulting schematic representation is a two-terminal box, as shown in Fig. 1.3, which is the standard representation of the basic finite-state model.

As an illustration, consider a computing device having two input lines $x^{(1)}$ and $x^{(2)}$; line $x^{(1)}$ is fed with the digits 0 and 1, and line $x^{(2)}$ with the digits 1, 2, and 3. At selected times t_ν the device produces the quantities $z_\nu^{(1)} = x_\nu^{(1)} x_\nu^{(2)} + x_{\nu-1}^{(1)} x_{\nu-1}^{(2)}$ and $z_\nu^{(2)} = |x_\nu^{(1)} x_\nu^{(2)} - x_{\nu-1}^{(1)} x_{\nu-1}^{(2)}|$. We thus have

$$X^{(1)} = \{0, 1\} \qquad\qquad X^{(2)} = \{1, 2, 3\}$$
$$Z^{(1)} = \{0, 1, 2, 3, 4, 5, 6\} \qquad Z^{(2)} = \{0, 1, 2, 3\}$$

and hence

$$X = \{(0, 1), (0, 2), (0, 3), (1, 1), (1, 2), (1, 3)\}$$
$$\begin{aligned} Z = \{ &(0, 0), (0, 1), (0, 2), (0, 3), (1, 0), (1, 1), (1, 2), (1, 3), (2, 0), (2, 1), \\ &(2, 2), (2, 3), (3, 0), (3, 1), (3, 2), (3, 3), (4, 0), (4, 1), (4, 2), (4, 3), \\ &(5, 0), (5, 1), (5, 2), (5, 3), (6, 0), (6, 1), (6, 2), (6, 3)\} \end{aligned}$$

1.5. States

While the excitation and response variables are, by choice, quantities which can be observed and measured by the investigator, the intermediate variables are often of obscure nature and their values are often unmeasurable. The importance of the intermediate variables, however, does not lie in their individual behaviors, but rather in their combined effect on the relationship between the input and output variables. This "combined effect," like the variables which cause it, is subject to the time-discreteness and alphabet-finitude assumptions introduced in Secs. 1.3 and 1.4. The effect is called the *state* of the system, the state at time t_ν being denoted by s_ν. The set of states which can be exhibited by a system is called the *state set* of the system and is denoted by S.

The concept of a state can be accurately defined only through the role played by it in the postulation of the basic finite-state model. This role can be described through the following two statements: (1) The output symbol at the present sampling time is uniquely determined by the input symbol and state at the present sampling time. (2) The state at the next sampling time is uniquely determined by the input symbol and state at the present sampling time. Thus, roughly, the state of a finite-state machine at any given sampling time is that variable which, together with the input symbol, enables one to predict the output symbol at this sampling time and the variable at the next sampling time.[1]

As an example, consider a game in which a coin is tossed repeatedly and a point is scored for the first tail in every run of tails and for each head, except the first two heads, in every run of heads. In this case the system is the game, the synchronizing source is the player, and the synchronizing signal is the tossing operation; the input variable is the face of the coin, and the output variable is the score per toss. The input alphabet, then, is {Head, Tail}, and the output alphabet is {Point, No point}. To determine the state set, one looks for a set of conditions

---

[1] The idea of "state" as a basic concept in the representation of systems was first introduced in 1936, by A. M. Turing (On Computable Numbers, with an Application to the Entscheidungsproblem, *Proc. London Math. Soc.*, ser. 2, vol. 42, pp. 230–265, 1936–1937). Later, the concept was employed by C. E. Shannon in his basic work on information theory (A Mathematical Theory of Communication, *Bell System Tech. J.*, vol. 27, pp. 379–423, 623–656, 1948). Still later, the "state" idea was reintroduced by D. A. Huffman (The Synthesis of Sequential Switching Networks, *J. Franklin Inst.*, vol. 257, pp. 161–190, 275–303, 1954), S. C. Kleene (Representation of Events in Nerve Nets and Finite Automata, "Automata Studies," pp. 3–41, Princeton University Press, Princeton, N.J., 1956), and E. F. Moore (Gedanken-Experiments on Sequential Machines, "Automata Studies," pp. 129–153, Princeton University Press, Princeton, N.J., 1956), whereupon it was accepted as one of the most fundamental concepts in the theory of discrete systems.

(which may be expressed verbally, symbolically, numerically, or in any other convenient form) such that the knowledge of the present condition and coin face would uniquely determine the present score and next condition. From the description of the game it can be deduced that, in order to predict the score, one must know the present and two previous coin faces. Tentatively, therefore, consider the state set {Mark first head, Mark two heads, Mark tail}, where "Mark first head" is the state of the system when head follows tail, "Mark two heads" is the state when head follows head, and "Mark tail" when tail follows tail or head. A point is scored each time the system is in state "Mark two heads" and the input is "Head," or when the system is in a state other than "Mark tail" and the input is "Tail." When the present state is "Mark first head" or "Mark two heads," the next state is "Mark two heads" if the input is "Head," and "Mark tail" if the input is "Tail"; when the present state is "Mark tail," the next state is "Mark head" if the input is "Head," and "Mark tail" if the input is "Tail." It has thus been verified that, knowing the present state and input, the present output and next state can be predicted and, hence, that the chosen state set meets all the requirements.

The selection of a state set in any given problem is neither unique nor necessarily simple. Since no general rules are available for this selection, it often calls for a trial-and-error approach. The speed at which the state set is selected and the size of the selected set are, by and large, a matter of "insight" and personal acquaintance with the system at hand.

1.6. Definition of the Basic Model

We are now in a position to provide an exact definition for the class of systems which we shall call *finite-state machines*. For the sake of brevity, a member of this class will henceforth be referred to simply as a "machine."[1]

DEFINITION 1.1. A finite-state machine M is a synchronous system with a finite input alphabet $X = \{\xi_1, \xi_2, \ldots, \xi_p\}$, a finite output alphabet $Z = \{\zeta_1, \zeta_2, \ldots, \zeta_q\}$, a finite state set $S = \{\sigma_1, \sigma_2, \ldots, \sigma_n\}$, and a pair of *characterizing functions* f_z and f_s, given by

$$z_\nu = f_z(x_\nu, s_\nu) \tag{1.5}$$
$$s_{\nu+1} = f_s(x_\nu, s_\nu) \tag{1.6}$$

where x_ν, z_ν, and s_ν are, respectively, the input symbol, output symbol, and state of M at time t_ν ($\nu = 1, 2, \ldots$).

---

[1] The motivation for this term is derived from the fact that the finite-state model finds its widest application in the analysis of digital machines. However, as will become evident from the examples, there need not be anything "mechanical" about a finite-state machine.

Throughout this book we shall assume that M, as postulated in Definition 1.1, is *deterministic*, i.e., its characterizing functions are not subject to any uncertainty. With the exception of Chap. 7, we shall also assume that M is *nonrestricted*, i.e., any input symbol can be applied to M at any time t_ν.

A special case of a finite-state machine arises when

$$f_z(x_\nu, s_\nu) = f_z(x_\nu) \tag{1.7}$$

Such a machine is called a *trivial* machine. The intermediate variables in a trivial machine have no effect on its input-output relationship, and hence the concept of state in this case is redundant. A *nontrivial* machine is one in which

$$f_z(x_\nu, s_\nu) \neq f_z(x_\nu) \tag{1.8}$$

1.7. Examples of Finite-state Machines

To illustrate the variety of situations which lend themselves to representation by the basic finite-state model, we shall present a few examples. With each example, the pertinent input alphabet X, output alphabet Z, and an appropriate state set S will be listed. The names of the states will be so chosen as to convey the system conditions which the states imply. A verbal argument will be enclosed with each example to justify the choice of the state set.

Example 1. Given: An organism excited by stimuli of two types— "positive" and "negative"; the organism shows no reaction to negative stimuli and reacts to *alternate* positive stimuli.

$X = \{$Positive stimulus, Negative stimulus$\}$
$Z = \{$Reaction, No reaction$\}$
$S = \{$Reaction to last positive stimulus, No reaction to last positive stimulus$\}$

If the present state is "Reaction to last positive stimulus" and the input is "Positive stimulus," the output is "No reaction" and the next state is "No reaction to last positive stimulus." If the present state is "No reaction to last positive stimulus" and the input is "Positive stimulus," the output is "Reaction" and the next state is "Reaction to last positive stimulus." When the input is "Negative stimulus," the output is "No reaction" regardless of the present state, and the next state is the same as the present one.

Example 2. Given: An English text, composed of the 26 letters of the alphabet and spaces, scanned with the purpose of counting the number of words starting with "*un*" and ending with "*d*" (such as "understand," "united," etc.). For simplicity, a space will be designated by π and letters other than d, n, and u by λ.

$X = \{d, n, u, \pi, \lambda\}$
$Z = \{$Count, No count$\}$
$S = \{$New word, Wait for new word, Mark u, Mark u-n, Mark u-n-$d\}$

When the input is "π," the next state is "New word," regardless of the present state. If the present state is "Mark u-n-d" and the input is "π," the output is "Count"; under all other conditions the output is "No count." If the present state is "New word" and the input is "u," the next state is "Mark u"; if the input is "d," "n," or "λ," the next state is "Wait for new word." If the present state is "Mark u" and the input is "n," the next state is "Mark u-n"; if the input is "d," "u," or "λ," the next state is "Wait for new word." If the present state is "Mark u-n" or "Mark u-n-d" and the input is "d," the next state is "Mark u-n-d"; if the input is "n," "u," or "λ," the next state is "Mark u-n." If the state is "Wait for new word" and the input is other than "π," the state remains unchanged.

Example 3. Given: A motor-driven wheel whose direction of motion is controlled by a two-position switch; the right and left positions, respectively, cause a clockwise and counterclockwise rotation of the wheel; each time the wheel changes direction, an indicator lamp flashes.

$$X = \{\text{Right, Left}\}$$
$$Z = \{\text{Lamp on, Lamp off}\}$$
$$S = \{\text{Clockwise, Counterclockwise}\}$$

If the present state is "Clockwise" and the input is "Right," or if the present state is "Counterclockwise" and the input is "Left," the state remains unchanged and the output is "Lamp off." If the present state is "Clockwise" and the input is "Left," or if the present state is "Counterclockwise" and the input is "Right," the state changes and the output is "Lamp on."

The above examples and other ones described with the problems at the end of this chapter demonstrate that a "finite-state machine" may be a game, a language, an algorithm, a switching device, a living organism, an organization—in fact, any system in which the present response depends on the present "state" (with the intuitive connotation) as well as on the present excitation and in which the next "state" depends on the present "state" and on the present excitation.

1.8. Determination of State Set from Internal Structure

In the following discussion, the variables which constitute either intermediate or response variables of a system will be called *dependent variables*.

In many cases of practical interest, sufficient information is available on the internal structure of a given system to establish all the variables which determine the system behavior.   In addition, it is possible to predict the value of every dependent variable at any sampling time, if the values of the excitation variables at this sampling time and the values of the dependent variables at the preceding sampling time are known.   In such cases, the compilation of a state set for the system can be carried out methodically, as will be shown below.

Let the excitation variables of a given system be $x^{(1)}$, $x^{(2)}$, $\ldots$, $x^{(u)}$, the response variables be $z^{(1)}$, $z^{(2)}$, $\ldots$, $z^{(w)}$, and the dependent variables be $y^{(1)}$, $y^{(2)}$, $\ldots$, $y^{(r)}$ (the set of dependent variables includes all the response variables).   Suppose that, for each dependent variable $y^{(k)}$, the structure of the system dictates the following relationship:

$$y_\nu^{(k)} = g_k(x_\nu^{(1)}, x_\nu^{(2)}, \ldots , x_\nu^{(u)}, y_{\nu-1}^{(1)}, y_{\nu-1}^{(2)}, \ldots , y_{\nu-1}^{(r)}) \qquad (1.9)$$

Following the procedure described in Sec. 1.4, the excitation variables can be represented by a single variable x, with the alphabet

$$X = X^{(1)} \otimes X^{(2)} \otimes \cdots \otimes X^{(u)} \qquad (1.10)$$

where $X^{(i)}$, $i = 1, 2, \ldots , u$, is the $x^{(i)}$ alphabet; the response variables can be represented by a single variable z, with the alphabet

$$Z = Z^{(1)} \otimes Z^{(2)} \otimes \cdots \otimes Z^{(w)} \qquad (1.11)$$

where $Z^{(j)}$, $j = 1, 2, \ldots , w$, is the $z^{(j)}$ alphabet.   Similarly, the dependent variables can be represented by a single variable y, with the alphabet

$$Y = Y^{(1)} \otimes Y^{(2)} \otimes \cdots \otimes Y^{(r)} \qquad (1.12)$$

where $Y^{(k)}$, $k = 1, 2, \ldots , r$, is the $y^{(k)}$ alphabet.   Equation (1.9), then, yields

$$y_\nu = g_y(x_\nu, y_{\nu-1}) \qquad (1.13)$$

Since every response variable is a dependent variable, we also have

$$z_\nu = g_z(x_\nu, y_{\nu-1}) \qquad (1.14)$$

To transform the above formulations into the standard characterizing functions f_z and f_s of a finite-state machine, a variable s is defined as follows:

$$s_\nu = y_{\nu-1} \qquad (1.15)$$

The alphabet S of s, then, is given by

$$S = Y \qquad (1.16)$$

Equations (1.13) and (1.14) can now be written as

$$y_\nu = f_s(x_\nu, s_\nu) \qquad (1.17)$$
$$z_\nu = f_z(x_\nu, s_\nu) \qquad (1.18)$$

From (1.15) and (1.17) we thus have

$$s_{\nu+1} = f_s(x_\nu, s_\nu) \qquad (1.19)$$

Equations (1.18) and (1.19) are seen to be the desired characterizing functions. Consequently S, as defined above, constitutes an adequate state set for the description of the given system.

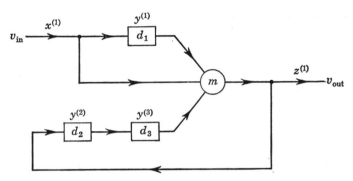

FIG. 1.4. A network with a majority organ.

As an example, consider the network shown in Fig. 1.4. The wire marked v_{in} is connected to a source which generates pulses of values 0 and 1, at the rate of one pulse every T seconds. The sampling times t_ν are taken as the instants at which the pulses are generated. The elements marked d_1, d_2, and d_3 store incoming pulses for T seconds and then transmit them to the next element. The element marked m is a "majority organ," which generates a 0 or a 1 pulse, depending on whether the majority of the incoming pulses are 0 or 1 pulses, respectively. The quantity of interest is the value of the pulse which appears at the wire marked v_{out}. The value of the pulse which appears on v_{in} at time t_ν, then, can be taken as the excitation variable $x^{(1)}$; the value of the pulse which appears on v_{out} at time t_ν can be taken as the response variable $z^{(1)}$. The values of the pulses stored in d_1, d_2, and d_3 at time t_ν can be taken as the dependent variables $y^{(1)}$, $y^{(2)}$, and $y^{(3)}$, respectively. We thus have

$X = \{0, 1\}$
$Z = \{0, 1\}$
$S = \{(0, 0, 0),\ (0, 0, 1),\ (0, 1, 0),\ (0, 1, 1),\ (1, 0, 0),\ (1, 0, 1),\ (1, 1, 0),$
$\qquad\qquad\qquad\qquad\qquad\qquad\qquad\qquad\qquad\qquad (1, 1, 1)\}$

From the network configuration it is seen that $y_\nu^{(1)} = x_\nu^{(1)}$, $y_\nu^{(2)} = z_\nu^{(1)}$, and $y_\nu^{(3)} = y_{\nu-1}^{(2)}$; $z_\nu^{(1)}$ is the majority of the values assumed by $y_{\nu-1}^{(1)}$, $x_\nu^{(1)}$, and $y_{\nu-1}^{(3)}$. Using these relationships, the functions $y^{(1)} = g_1(x_\nu^{(1)}, y_{\nu-1}^{(1)}, y_{\nu-1}^{(2)}, y_{\nu-1}^{(3)})$, $y_\nu^{(2)} = g_2(x_\nu^{(1)}, y_{\nu-1}^{(1)}, y_{\nu-1}^{(2)}, y_{\nu-1}^{(3)})$, and $y_\nu^{(3)} = g_3(x_\nu^{(1)}, y_{\nu-1}^{(1)}, y_{\nu-1}^{(2)}, y_{\nu-1}^{(3)})$ can be computed and tabulated as shown in Table 1.1. From the definition of s it follows that each row in the subtable composed of columns $y_{\nu-1}^{(1)}$, $y_{\nu-1}^{(2)}$, and $y_{\nu-1}^{(3)}$ represents a state s_ν, and each row in the subtable composed of columns $y_\nu^{(1)}$, $y_\nu^{(2)}$, and $y_\nu^{(3)}$ represents a state $s_{\nu+1}$. Noting

TABLE 1.1. g_k FUNCTIONS FOR SYSTEM OF FIG. 1.4

$x_\nu^{(1)}$	s_ν			$s_{\nu+1}$		
	$y_{\nu-1}^{(1)}$	$y_{\nu-1}^{(2)}$	$y_{\nu-1}^{(3)}$	$g_1 = y_\nu^{(1)}$	$g_2 = y_\nu^{(2)}$	$g_3 = y_\nu^{(3)}$
0	0	0	0	0	0	0
1	0	0	0	1	0	0
0	0	0	1	0	0	0
1	0	0	1	1	1	0
0	0	1	0	0	0	1
1	0	1	0	1	0	1
0	0	1	1	0	0	1
1	0	1	1	1	1	1
0	1	0	0	0	0	0
1	1	0	0	1	1	0
0	1	0	1	0	1	0
1	1	0	1	1	1	0
0	1	1	0	0	0	1
1	1	1	0	1	1	1
0	1	1	1	0	1	1
1	1	1	1	1	1	1

that $x_\nu^{(1)} = x_\nu$ and $y_\nu^{(2)} = z_\nu$, it can be seen that Table 1.1 contains the complete description of the characterizing functions for the given network. For example, it can be readily deduced from the table (see fourth row) that if the present state is $(0, 0, 1)$ and the present input 1, the present output is 1 and the next state $(1, 1, 0)$.

1.9. An Alternative Model

Every finite-state machine conforming with the basic model postulated by Definition 1.1 can be transformed into a machine in which the present output symbol is a function of the present state only. The transformation can be carried out by defining a variable s', such that s_ν' is the ordered pair (x_ν, s_ν). The alphabet S' of s' is, therefore, given by

$$S' = X \otimes S \tag{1.20}$$

Using Eq. (1.5), z_ν can be expressed in the form

$$z_\nu = f_z'(s_\nu')$$ (1.21)

From the definition of s' and Eq. (1.6), $s_{\nu+1}'$ is given by

$$s_{\nu+1}' = (x_{\nu+1}, s_{\nu+1}) = (x_{\nu+1}, f_s(x_\nu, s_\nu))$$ (1.22)

or
$$s_{\nu+1}' = f_s'(x_{\nu+1}, s_\nu')$$ (1.23)

Equations (1.21) and (1.23) define an alternative model for a finite-state machine in which the state uniquely determines the response. If the input alphabet of the represented system is of size p and if the size of the state set S is n, the size of S' is seen to be np.

A system represented by the alternative model defined by Eqs. (1.21) and (1.23) can always be represented by the basic model, defined by Eqs. (1.5) and (1.6) of Definition 1.1. This is done by letting $s_\nu = s_{\nu-1}'$; Eq. (1.21) then becomes

$$z_\nu = f_z'(s_\nu') = f_z'(f_s'(x_\nu, s_{\nu-1}'))$$
$$= f_z(x_\nu, s_\nu)$$ (1.24)

From the definition of s_ν and Eq. (1.23),

$$s_{\nu+1} = s_\nu' = f_s'(x_\nu, s_{\nu-1}')$$
$$= f_s(x_\nu, s_\nu)$$ (1.25)

Equations (1.24) and (1.25) can be recognized as the characterizing functions of the basic finite-state model.

Inasmuch as every system representable by one model is representable by the other, and inasmuch as the state set required for the alternative model is often much larger than the state set required for the basic model, there is no special advantage in using the alternative model. In this book, therefore, we shall refrain from using the alternative model, and wherever a reference will be made to the characterizing functions of a finite-state machine, these functions should be taken as those defined by Eqs. (1.5) and (1.6).

1.10. Prediction of Machine Behavior

A succession of input symbols ξ_{i_1}, followed by ξ_{i_2}, . . . , followed by ξ_{i_l}, is called an *input sequence* and written as $\xi_{i_1}\xi_{i_2} \cdots \xi_{i_l}$. A succession of output symbols ζ_{j_1}, followed by ζ_{j_2}, . . . , followed by ζ_{j_l}, is called an *output sequence* and written as $\zeta_{j_1}\zeta_{j_2} \cdots \zeta_{j_l}$. The number of symbols in a sequence is referred to as the *length* of the sequence. As is evident from the time-discreteness assumption, excitations applied to finite-state machines are always in the form of input sequences, and responses are always in the form of output sequences; an input sequence of length l always results in an output sequence of length l.

The state of machine M at time t_1 is called the *initial* state of M. Since t_1 is arbitrary, the initial state of M is commonly taken as the state in which M is found when first presented to the investigator.

THEOREM 1.1.   Let M be a nontrivial machine with the characterizing functions f_z and f_s. Then the response of M, at any initial state σ_{i_0}, to any input sequence $\xi_{j_1}\xi_{j_2} \cdots \xi_{j_l}$ (a) is not predictable if only f_z and f_s are known, (b) is predictable if f_z, f_s, and σ_{i_0} are known.

Proof.   (a) If M is nontrivial, then, by (1.8), M has at least one pair of states σ_u and σ_v and at least one input symbol ξ_h, such that

$$f_z(\xi_h, \sigma_u) \neq f_z(\xi_h, \sigma_v) \tag{1.26}$$

Hence, the response of M to $\xi_h\xi_{j_2} \cdots \xi_{j_l}$ when σ_{i_0} is σ_u differs from the response to $\xi_h\xi_{j_2} \cdots \xi_{j_l}$ when σ_{i_0} is σ_v. Consequently, if only f_z and f_s are known, the response to at least one input sequence cannot be predicted. (b) Consider the inductive hypothesis: "if f_s and σ_{i_0} are known, then the state σ_{i_k} into which M passes when $\xi_{j_1}\xi_{j_2} \cdots \xi_{j_k}$ is applied is also known." When $k = 0$, the hypothesis is trivially true. When the hypothesis is true for k, σ_{i_k} is known, and $\sigma_{i_{k+1}}$ can be found from the knowledge of f_s:

$$\sigma_{i_{k+1}} = f_s(\xi_{j_k}, \sigma_{i_k}) \tag{1.27}$$

Hence, by induction, the hypothesis is true for any $k \geq 0$. If, in addition to f_s and σ_{i_0}, f_z is known, the kth output symbol ζ_{h_k} can be determined by

$$\zeta_{h_k} = f_z(\xi_{j_k}, \sigma_{i_k}) \tag{1.28}$$

where σ_{i_k} is found recursively as indicated by Eq. (1.27). Letting $k = 1$, $2, \ldots, l$, it can be concluded that if f_z, f_s, and σ_{i_0} are known, the response $\zeta_{h_1}\zeta_{h_2} \cdots \zeta_{h_l}$ to any input sequence $\xi_{j_1}\xi_{j_2} \cdots \xi_{j_l}$ can be predicted.

Theorem 1.1 shows that the characterizing functions are not sufficient for the complete description of machine behavior; on the other hand, complete description is always possible when, in addition to these functions, the initial state of the machine is known. This fact can be readily demonstrated with the examples of Sec. 1.7, where the system specifications do not include any initial state information. In Example 1, the response to an input sequence containing "Positive stimulus" is unpredictable; in Example 2, the response to an input sequence starting with "π" is unpredictable; in Example 3, the response to *any* input sequence is unpredictable. All responses, however, become predictable when the initial states in these examples are specified.

The situation is not unlike that encountered in the analysis of linear systems. The relationships f_s and f_z of a finite-state machine are analogous to the equilibrium equations characterizing a linear device, and the initial state of the machine is analogous to the initial energy distribution in the linear device.   The response of the device to any given excitation can be predicted when both the equilibrium equations and the initial energy distribution are known, but it is unpredictable when the initial energy distribution is not specified.

PROBLEMS

1.1. Describe three systems which can be represented as finite-state machines. List the input alphabet, output alphabet, and state set, and justify your choice of state set.

Problems 1.2 to 1.9 contain descriptions of systems which can be represented as finite-state machines.   The input variable x and output variable z are indicated in parentheses at the end of each problem.   For each of the described systems, list the input alphabet, output alphabet, and state set, and justify your choice of state set.

1.2. The binary digits 0 and 1 are fed into a device which counts, modulo 3, the accumulated number of 1's.   (x: input digit. z: cumulative count.)

1.3. A coin is tossed repeatedly, and a point is scored for even tails in a run of tails and for every other head, whether in a run of heads or not.   (x: coin face. z: score per toss.)

1.4. Two chips, each of which has the number "1" marked on one side and "2" on the other, are repeatedly and simultaneously thrown.   After each throw, the sum modulo 2 is computed of the present faces, the faces obtained in the last throw, and the last computed sum.   (x: combination of two chip faces. z: sum per throw.)

1.5. A freight elevator serving a three-story warehouse with a call button on each floor operates according to the following rules: If a single button is pushed, the elevator moves to the floor on which the pushed button is located; if two or three buttons are pushed simultaneously, the elevator moves to the lowest calling floor.   No buttons can be pushed when the elevator is in motion.   (x: calling floor. z: direction of motion to be followed and number of floors to be traversed.)

1.6. An English text composed of the 26 letters of the alphabet and spaces is scanned with the purpose of counting the number of words which rhyme with "art."   (x: letter or space. z: increment to the total count.)

1.7. Figure P 1.1 shows a network N excited by two voltage sources V_1 and V_2. Each source generates a positive or a negative pulse every 1 microsecond.   An element d causes a pulse to be delayed 1 microsecond.   The network N generates a

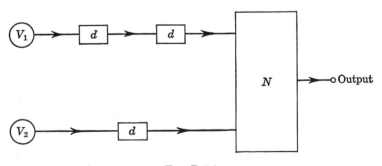

FIG. P 1.1

positive pulse when both pulses arriving at its input terminals are positive; it generates a negative pulse otherwise. (x: combination of input voltages. z: output voltage.)

1.8. Figure P 1.2 represents a neural net, where the fiber marked v_{in} is connected to a source which generates stimuli of values 0 or 1 at times t_ν.† A large circle repre-

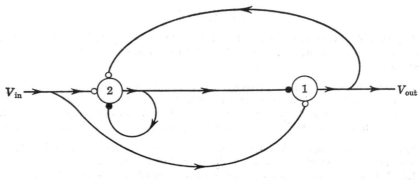

FIG. P 1.2

sents a neuron. The output of a neuron at time t_ν is stimulated (i.e., assumes the value 1) if and only if the number of its stimulated "excitatory inputs" (indicated by heavy dots) minus the number of its "inhibitory inputs" (indicated by small circles) at time $t_{\nu-1}$ equals or exceeds its "threshold" (the integer written inside the large circle). (x: v_{in}. z: v_{out}.)

1.9. The operation of a computing device with the input x and output z is defined through the following equations:

$$z_\nu = x_\nu \oplus z_{\nu-1} \oplus w_{\nu-1}$$
$$w_\nu = x_\nu \oplus w_{\nu-1}$$

where each variable can assume the values 0 or 1 and where $\oplus$ designates modulo-2 addition. (x and z are as defined.)

† This representation is due to J. von Neumann (Probabilistic Logics and the Synthesis of Reliable Organisms from Unreliable Components, "Automata Studies," pp. 43–98, Princeton University Press, Princeton, N.J., 1956).

CHAPTER 2

TRANSITION TABLES, DIAGRAMS, AND MATRICES

2.1. Introduction

Once the input alphabet, output alphabet, and state set of a given system are established, the verbal description of the system can be formalized by means of a table, a diagram, or a matrix. The table, diagram, or matrix are alternative forms of display for the characterizing functions of the finite-state machine which represents the given system. Such a display is indispensable to any precise analysis or synthesis of a finite-state machine, and we shall make extensive use of it throughout this book. Since different display forms are useful under different circumstances, it is advantageous to gain familiarity with all of them. In this chapter, therefore, we shall introduce all three representations, discussing some specific problems in which one representation or another proves to be of special merit.

2.2. The Transition Table

The characterizing functions f_z and f_s, as defined by (1.5) and (1.6), can be displayed in a tabular form referred to as the *transition table*. This table lists the values of the two functions for all possible arguments, i.e., for all possible ordered pairs (x_ν, s_ν), where x_ν ranges over the input alphabet X and s_ν over the state set S. The format of the transition table for a machine whose input alphabet is $\{\xi_1, \xi_2, \ldots, \xi_p\}$, output alphabet is $\{\zeta_1, \zeta_2, \ldots, \zeta_q\}$, and state set is $\{\sigma_1, \sigma_2, \ldots, \sigma_n\}$ is shown in Table 2.1. The table is composed of two adjacent subtables, the z_ν *subtable* and the $s_{\nu+1}$ *subtable*, which display f_z and f_s, respectively. The two subtables have a common stub[1] which lists all possible present states s_ν; the column headings in both subtables are the same and consist of all possible present input symbols x_ν. The rows, then, are labeled σ_1, $\sigma_2, \ldots, \sigma_n$, and the columns $\xi_1, \xi_2, \ldots, \xi_p$. The entry common to row σ_i and column ξ_j is $f_z(\xi_j, \sigma_i)$ in the z_ν subtable (such an entry is called a z_ν *entry*) and is $f_s(\xi_j, \sigma_i)$ in the $s_{\nu+1}$ subtable (such an entry is called an

---

[1] The *stub* is the list of categories appearing in the leftmost column of a table. A row in which the stub is "K" (or whose *stub entry* is "K") will be commonly referred to as "row K."

$s_{\nu+1}$ *entry*).   The z_ν and $s_{\nu+1}$ entries are seen to range over the output alphabet Z and the state set S, respectively, or over any subset thereof.

TABLE 2.1. GENERAL TRANSITION TABLE

s_ν \ x_ν	z_ν					$s_{\nu+1}$				
	ξ_1	ξ_2	$\cdots$		ξ_p	ξ_1	ξ_2	$\cdots$		ξ_p
σ_1 σ_2 . . . σ_n	Entries selected from $\{\zeta_1, \zeta_2, \ldots, \zeta_q\}$					Entries selected from $\{\sigma_1, \sigma_2, \ldots, \sigma_n\}$				

Under the assumption that f_z and f_s are the characterizing functions of a deterministic, nonrestricted machine, these functions must be uniquely defined for every ordered pair (x_ν, s_ν), where x_ν ranges over X and s_ν over S.   Consequently, the z_ν subtable must contain exactly one element of Z and the $s_{\nu+1}$ subtable exactly one element of S at the intersection of every row and column.

While the descriptive state labels (those chosen in the examples of Sec. 1.7) are helpful in the intuitive understanding of the roles played by the various states in the input-output relationships, and in deriving the f_z and f_s functions from the verbal description of the system, once the functions are established, these labels no longer serve any useful purpose.   In the transition table, therefore, the original labels may be replaced by any set of labels which may seem convenient to the investigator.   In most of the examples to be presented in this book, the state labels will be simply the integers 1, 2, 3, etc.

To illustrate the construction of a transition table, Table 2.2 shows the transition table for the system described in Example 2 of Sec. 1.7.   The

TABLE 2.2. MACHINE $A1$

s_ν \ x_ν	z_ν					$s_{\nu+1}$				
	d	n	u	π	λ	d	n	u	π	λ
1	0	0	0	0	0	2	2	3	1	2
2	0	0	0	0	0	2	2	2	1	2
3	0	0	0	0	0	2	4	2	1	2
4	0	0	0	0	0	5	4	4	1	4
5	0	0	0	1	0	5	4	4	1	4

system is referred to as "machine $A1$," and the states "New word," "Wait for new word," "Mark u," "Mark u-n," and "Mark u-n-d" are relabeled as 1, 2, 3, 4, and 5, respectively. The table entries constitute the numerical counterpart to the verbal argument justifying the choice of state set for Example 2. Comparing the verbal argument with the transition table, one can readily appreciate the precise as well as concise nature of the latter as compared with the former.

2.3. Enumeration of Machines

One important application of the transition table is in enumerating the members of various classes of finite-state machines. A class of machines can often be defined through a set of constraints imposed on the distribution of states and output symbols in the transition table. By constructing all possible tables which satisfy these constraints, the specified class can be listed. The size of the class can often be estimated at a glance by counting the number of degrees of freedom which the constraints offer in the construction of the transition table. This application will be demonstrated by estimating the sizes of some machine classes which will be encountered in later chapters.

Class of (n, p, q) *Machines.* An (n, p, q) machine is a machine whose state set is a specified set $S = \{\sigma_1, \sigma_2, \ldots, \sigma_n\}$, whose input alphabet is a specified set $X = \{\xi_1, \xi_2, \ldots, \xi_p\}$, and whose output alphabet is a specified set $Z = \{\zeta_1, \zeta_2, \ldots, \zeta_q\}$ or any subset of Z. Any transition table whose stub entries are $\sigma_1, \sigma_2, \ldots, \sigma_n$, whose column headings are $\xi_1, \xi_2, \ldots, \xi_p$, whose z_ν entries range over Z or a subset of Z, and whose $s_{\nu+1}$ entries range over S or a subset of S characterizes an (n, p, q) machine. The size $N_{n,p,q}$ of the class is, therefore, given by

$$N_{n,p,q} = (qn)^{pn} \tag{2.1}$$

Class of Simply Minimal (n, p, q) *Machines.* An (n, p, q) machine is called simply minimal if for every i and every $j \neq i$ there is at least one k such that $f_z(\xi_k, \sigma_i) \neq f_z(\xi_k, \sigma_j)$. Any transition table in which all the rows in the z_ν subtable are distinct characterizes a simply minimal machine. The size $N'_{n,p,q}$ of the class is, therefore, given by

$$N'_{n,p,q} = n^{pn} \prod_{r=0}^{n-1} (q^p - r) \tag{2.2}$$

where negative values of $N'_{n,p,q}$ are to be interpreted as 0.

Class of Simply Reducible (n, p, q) *Machines.* An (n, p, q) machine is called simply reducible if the following condition exists in its transition table: There is at least one pair of rows, say σ_i and σ_j, which are identical throughout the z_ν and $s_{\nu+1}$ subtables, or which become identical when every σ_i is replaced by σ_j (or every σ_j is replaced by σ_i). If a machine is not simply reducible, it must have a transition table in which all rows (spanning both the z_ν and $s_{\nu+1}$ subtables) are distinct. The number $N''_{n,p,q}$ of machines which are not simply reducible is, therefore, subject to the bound

$$N''_{n,p,q} \leq \prod_{r=0}^{n-1} [(qn)^p - r] \qquad (2.3)$$

From (2.1) and (2.3), the lower bound on the number $N'''_{n,p,q}$ of simply reducible (n, p, q) machines is given by

$$N'''_{n,p,q} \geq (qn)^{pn} - \prod_{r=0}^{n-1} [(qn)^p - r] \qquad (2.4)$$

2.4. Isomorphic Machines

As pointed out in Sec. 2.2, the state labels have no individual significance and may be selected arbitrarily. Machines whose characterizing functions are the same except for possible differences in state labeling are said to be *isomorphic* to each other. Given a finite-state machine M representing a certain system, any machine which is isomorphic to M may serve as a representation of the same system. The representation of a system by a finite-state machine is, therefore, by no means unique.

Let M be an (n, p, q) machine, specified by a transition table such as shown in Table 2.1. Consider another transition table, obtained from the transition table of M by permuting the state labels $\sigma_1, \sigma_2, \ldots, \sigma_n$ among themselves and rearranging the rows so as to restore the original ordering of the stub entries. These operations result in a table which represents a machine isomorphic to M. The set of all different machines resulting from all $n!$ such permutation schemes is called the *permutation family* of M. Clearly, two different permutation schemes do not necessarily result in two different transition tables; the size of a permutation family, therefore, may be smaller than $n!$. It also should be noticed that two machines belonging to two different permutation families cannot be isomorphic to each other. As an example, Table 2.3 represents a machine isomorphic to $A1$ of Table 2.2 obtained by replacing the original state labels 1, 2, 3, 4, and 5 by 5, 4, 3, 2, and 1, respectively.

LEMMA 2.1. The size of the permutation family of a simply minimal (n, p, q) machine is $n!$.

Proof. The rows in the z_ν subtable of a simply minimal machine are, by definition, distinct and remain distinct after the state labels are permuted. Tables resulting from different permutation schemes are, therefore, distinct. Since the number of different permutation schemes is $n!$, the lemma follows.

TABLE 2.3. A MACHINE ISOMORPHIC TO $A1$

x_ν s_ν	z_ν					$s_{\nu+1}$				
	d	n	u	π	λ	d	n	u	π	λ
1	0	0	0	1	0	1	2	2	5	2
2	0	0	0	0	0	1	2	2	5	2
3	0	0	0	0	0	4	2	4	5	4
4	0	0	0	0	0	4	4	4	5	4
5	0	0	0	0	0	4	4	3	5	4

THEOREM 2.1. The size $N_{n,p,q}^{(\mathrm{SM})}$ of the class of simply minimal (n, p, q) machines, such that no two machines are isomorphic to each other, is given by

$$N_{n,p,q}^{(\mathrm{SM})} = \frac{n^{pn}}{n!} \prod_{r=0}^{n-1} (q^p - r) \tag{2.5}$$

where negative values of $N_{n,p,q}^{(\mathrm{SM})}$ are to be interpreted as 0.

Proof. The set of simply minimal (n, p, q) machines is the union[1] of the permutation families of all machines in the class specified in the theorem. Since these permutation families are necessarily disjoint,[2] and since, by Lemma 2.1, each permutation family contains exactly $n!$ different machines, we must have

$$n! N_{n,p,q}^{(\mathrm{SM})} = N'_{n,p,q} \tag{2.6}$$

where $N'_{n,p,q}$ is the size of the class of simply minimal (n, p, q) machines as given by Eq. (2.2). Solving for $N_{n,p,q}^{(\mathrm{SM})}$ yields the theorem.

2.5. The Transition Diagram

The transition diagram is a structure composed of *vertices*, drawn as small circles, and *oriented branches*, drawn as lines between pairs of vertices, with arrow signs pointing from one vertex to the other. A transition diagram describing an n-state machine contains n vertices, each vertex representing a different state; the state represented by a vertex is identified by the label attached to this vertex. The oriented branches are drawn and labeled according to the following rule: Let $X_{ij} = \{\xi_{k_1},$

---

[1] The *union* of the sets $R_1, R_2, \ldots, R_N$ written as $R_1 \cup R_2 \cup \cdots \cup R_N$, is the set which contains all the elements contained in $R_1, R_2, \ldots, R_N$ and no other elements.

[2] The sets $R_1, R_2, \ldots, R_N$ are said to be *disjoint* if no two sets R_i and R_j $(i \neq j)$ contain a common element.

$\xi_{k_2}, \ldots, \xi_{k_r}\}$ be the set of x_ν values for which $f_s(x_\nu, \sigma_i) = \sigma_j$, and let $f_z(\xi_{k_h}, \sigma_i) = \zeta_{l_h}$ for $h = 1, 2, \ldots, r$. If X_{ij} is nonempty,[1] a branch is drawn from the vertex labeled σ_i to the vertex labeled σ_j; the arrow sign of this branch is pointed from vertex σ_i to vertex σ_j, and the branch label is written as $(\xi_{k_1}/\zeta_{l_1}) \vee (\xi_{k_2}/\zeta_{l_2}) \vee \cdots \vee (\xi_{k_r}/\zeta_{l_r})$.[2] Each term (ξ_{k_h}/ζ_{l_h}) contained in a branch label is called an *input-output pair*. The above rule for constructing the transition diagram of a given machine is illustrated in Fig. 2.1. This rule implies a one-to-one correspondence between a transition diagram and a transition table which represent the same machine—given one representation, the other representation can always be constructed. As an example, Fig. 2.2 shows the transition diagram of machine $A1$ specified by Table 2.2.

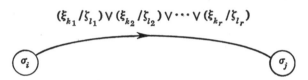

FIG. 2.1. Branch labeling.

By construction, a branch pointing from vertex σ_i to vertex σ_j places in evidence the input symbols which cause the machine to pass from state σ_i into state σ_j and the output symbols which accompany the passage. Since the machine is deterministic and nonrestricted, every input symbol causes every state to pass into exactly one other state; consequently the branches originating from any given vertex are labeled with the total number of p input-output pairs, where p is the size of the input alphabet.

The immediately obvious advantage of the transition diagram is that it facilitates the determination of machine responses to input sequences of arbitrary lengths. Given the initial state σ_i of machine M and an input sequence $\xi_{u_1}\xi_{u_2} \cdots \xi_{u_l}$, the response of M to $\xi_{u_1}\xi_{u_2} \cdots \xi_{u_l}$ can be readily determined by tracing (in the arrow direction) the continuous sequence of l branches which originates at the vertex labeled σ_i and whose kth branch ($k = 1, 2, \ldots, l$) exhibits the input-output pair (ξ_{u_k}/ζ_{v_k}). The output sequence yielded by M when $\xi_{u_1}\xi_{u_2} \cdots \xi_{u_l}$ is applied is then simply $\zeta_{v_1}\zeta_{v_2} \cdots \zeta_{v_l}$; the state into which M passes when $\xi_{u_1}\xi_{u_2} \cdots \xi_{u_l}$ is applied is given by the label of the vertex at which the traced sequence of l branches terminates. For example, the response of machine $A1$ to the input sequence $\pi un\lambda\lambda d\pi$ when the initial state is 3 is readily deter-

[1] A set is said to be *empty* if it contains no elements. An empty set is designated by the symbol 0.

[2] $\vee$ is the standard symbol for the logical "or."

mined from Fig. 2.2 to be 0000001.   The states traversed by $A1$ when the above input sequence is applied are 1, 3, 4, 4, 4, 5, and 1, in that order.

The role played by the transition diagram in the theory of finite-state machines is similar to that played by the circuit diagram in the theory of electric networks.   The diagram transforms an abstract model into a physical picture which enhances the investigator's intuition and enables him to "visualize" various processes and properties which would other-wise remain a series of dry mathematical facts.   As is the case in electric-

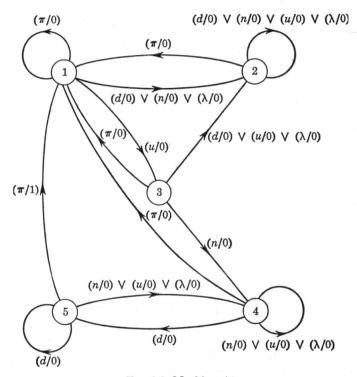

FIG. 2.2. Machine $A1$.

network theory, it is convenient to regard the diagram as the model itself and the symbols which appear in the diagram as the abstract components of which the model is composed.   Thus, we shall often refer to a diagram which represents machine M as "machine M," to a vertex representing state σ_i as "state σ_i," and otherwise identify abstract notions with their geometrical representations, as manifested by the transition diagram.

In terms of the transition diagram, the concept of isomorphism of finite-state machines, introduced in Sec. 2.4, assumes a very simple inter-pretation: Machines are isomorphic to each other if they have identical diagrams, except for possible variations in vertex labeling. Thus, to replace machine M by another machine which is isomorphic to M, simply change one or more vertex labels. Similarly, to produce the permutation family of M, permute, in all possible ways, the vertex labels among themselves.

2.6. Classification of States and Submachines

A branch touching any given state, say σ_i, may be a *converging branch* of σ_i, if it points toward σ_i from another state, or a *diverging branch* of

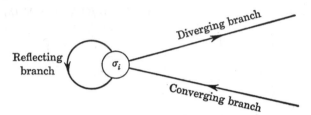

FIG. 2.3. Types of branches.

σ_i, if it points from σ_i toward another state, or a *reflecting branch* of σ_i, if it loops around σ_i. Figure 2.3 illustrates these three types of branches.

A state which lacks converging and/or diverging branches may be one of the following: (1) A *transient state*—a state that has no converging branches but at least one diverging branch; such a state can lead into at least one other state, but cannot be reached once it is abandoned. (2) A *persistent state*—a state that has no diverging branches, but at least one

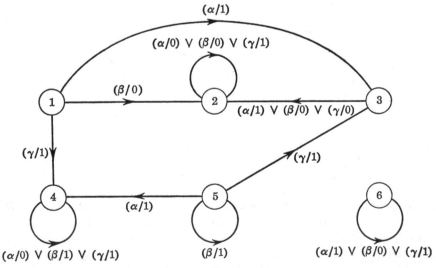

FIG. 2.4. Machine $A2$.

converging branch; such a state can be reached from at least one other state, but cannot be abandoned once it is reached.   (3) An *isolated state*— a state that has neither converging or diverging branches; such a state

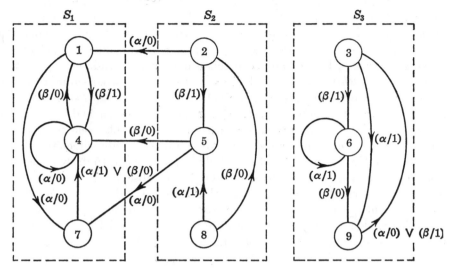

Fig. 2.5. Machine $A3$.

cannot lead into any other state, and cannot be reached from any other state.   Figure 2.4 shows machine $A2$, where states 1 and 5 are transient, states 2 and 4 are persistent, and state 6 is isolated.

Any partition of the state set of a machine into two or more subsets can be placed in evidence by enclosing the states of each subset, as represented by the transition diagram, in a "box," each of which is referred to as a *submachine*.   Figure 2.5 and Table 2.4 represent machine $A3$, whose

TABLE 2.4. MACHINE $A3$

s_ν \ x_ν	z_ν		$s_{\nu+1}$	
	α	β	α	β
1	0	1	7	4
2	0	1	1	5
3	1	1	9	6
4	0	0	4	1
5	0	0	7	4
6	1	0	6	9
7	1	0	4	4
8	1	0	5	2
9	0	1	3	3

state set $S = \{1, 2, 3, 4, 5, 6, 7, 8, 9\}$ is partitioned into $S_1 = \{1, 4, 7\}$, $S_2 = \{2, 5, 8\}$, and $S_3 = \{3, 6, 9\}$; the three submachines are indicated by the boxes labeled S_1, S_2, and S_3.

Regarding each submachine as a single "superstate," transient, persistent, and isolated submachines may be defined in the same manner as transient, persistent, and isolated states, with the word "submachine" replacing "state": (1) A *transient submachine* can lead into at least one other submachine, but cannot be reached once it is abandoned. (2) A *persistent submachine* can be reached from at least one other submachine, but cannot be abandoned once it is reached. (3) An *isolated submachine* cannot lead into any other submachine, and cannot be reached from any other submachine. The transition diagram often enables one to determine by inspection whether specified subsets of the state set constitute transient, persistent, or isolated submachines, and hence to draw conclusions regarding the relative accessibility of these subsets. From Fig. 2.5, for example, it can be readily deduced that S_1 is a persistent submachine, S_2 a transient submachine, and S_3 an isolated submachine.

Let $G_k(S_i)$ denote the set of all states of machine M which are reachable from any of the states in $S_i = \{\sigma_{i_1}, \sigma_{i_2}, \ldots, \sigma_{i_r}\}$ by the application of input sequences of length k or less. In particular: $G_0(S_i) = S_i$. $G_1(S_i)$ is the union of S_i and all the s_{r+1} entries in rows $\sigma_{i_1}, \sigma_{i_2}, \ldots, \sigma_{i_r}$ of the transition table of M. Alternatively, $G_1(S_i)$ can be compiled by inspection of the transition diagram of M. Given $G_{k-1}(S_i)$, $k \geq 1$, $G_k(S_i)$ can be determined through the relationship

$$G_k(S_i) = G_1(G_{k-1}(S_i)) \tag{2.7}$$

When $G_k(S_i) = G_{k-1}(S_i)$, then $G_{k+u}(S_i) = G_{k-1}(S_i)$ for all nonnegative integers u, and hence $G_k(S_i)$ constitutes the set of all states reachable from S_i by input sequences of *any* length. The determination of this set, denoted simply by $G(S_i)$, can now be outlined through the following algorithm:

ALGORITHM 2.1. Given S_i, to find $G(S_i)$: (1) Let $G_0(S_i) = S_i$. Let $k = 1$. (2) Determine $G_k(S_i) = G_1(G_{k-1}(S_i))$. (3) (a) If $G_k(S_i) \neq G_{k-1}(S_i)$, increment k by 1 and return to (2). (b) If $G_k(S_i) = G_{k-1}(S_i)$, then $G_k(S_i) = G(S_i)$.

If $G_k(S_i) \neq G_{k-1}(S_i)$, $G_k(S_i)$ must contain at least one more element than $G_{k-1}(S_i)$. Since the size of $G_k(S_i)$ cannot exceed the total number of states n of M, $G_k(S_i)$ must equal $G_{k-1}(S_i)$ for some $k \leq n - r + 1$, where r is the size of S_i. Hence

$$G(S_i) = G_{n-r}(S_i) \tag{2.8}$$

Algorithm 2.1, therefore, requires at most $n - r$ iterations of step 2.

Table 2.5 illustrates the algorithm for machine $A3$ of Fig. 2.5, with $S_i = \{5, 6\}$, yielding $G(5, 6) = \{1, 3, 4, 5, 6, 7, 9\}$.

TABLE 2.5. ALGORITHM 2.1 FOR $A3$ AND $S_i = \{5, 6\}$

k	$G_k(S_i) = G_1(G_{k-1}(S_i))$
0	5, 6
1	4, 5, 6, 7, 9
2	1, 3, 4, 5, 6, 7, 9
3	1, 3, 4, 5, 6, 7, 9

If S_i consists of a single state σ_i, $G(\sigma_i)$ is called the σ_i-*reachable set* and constitutes the set of all states which can be reached from σ_i.

THEOREM 2.2. Let σ_i and σ_j be two states in an n-state machine. If σ_j is at all reachable from σ_i, it is reachable by applying an input sequence whose length is at most $n - 1$.

Proof. When $S_i = \{\sigma_i\}$, the size r of S_i is 1, and Eq. (2.8) becomes

$$G(\sigma_i) = G_{n-1}(\sigma_i) \tag{2.9}$$

which implies that the σ_i-reachable set is the set of all states reachable from σ_i by the application of input sequences of length $n - 1$ or less.

If the initial state of machine M is known to belong to the nonempty set S_i, which constitutes a persistent or an isolated submachine, M can be simplified by eliminating all states which do not belong to S_i and all the branches which originate from these states. The simplified machine, although not necessarily an adequate representation of the original system at all times, is adequate insofar as *future* behavior is concerned. This follows from the fact that the eliminated states can never be reached from the initial state and hence that their inclusion as part of the representation is redundant. As an example, if the initial state of machine $A3$ of Fig. 2.5 is known to be 1, the analysis of the future behavior of $A3$ can be adequately carried out when states 2, 3, 5, 6, 8, and 9, and the branches which originate from these states, are eliminated from the transition diagram.

2.7. Machine Decomposition and the Disjunction Machine

Let $H_k(S_i)$ denote the set of all states of machine M connected to the states in $S_i = \{\sigma_{i_1}, \sigma_{i_2}, \ldots, \sigma_{i_r}\}$ via k branches or less, where the direction of the branches is immaterial. In particular: $H_0(S_i) = S_i$. $H_1(S_i)$ is the union of S_i, the $s_{\nu+1}$ entries in rows $\sigma_{i_1}, \sigma_{i_2}, \ldots, \sigma_{i_r}$ of the transition table of M, and the stub entries of those rows in which any $s_{\nu+1}$ entry belongs to S_i. Alternatively, $H_1(S_i)$ can be compiled by inspection of the transition diagram of M. Given $H_{k-1}(S_i)$, $k \geq 1$, $H_k(S_i)$ can be determined through the relationship

$$H_k(S_i) = H_1(H_{k-1}(S_i)) \qquad (2.10)$$

When $H_k(S_i) = H_{k-1}(S_i)$, then $H_{k+u}(S_i) = H_{k-1}(S_i)$ for all nonnegative integers u, and hence $H_k(S_i)$ constitutes the set of all states connected to S_i via a chain of branches of *any* length (with branch direction ignored). The determination of this set, denoted simply by $H(S_i)$, can now be outlined through the following algorithm:

ALGORITHM 2.2.   Given S_i, to find $H(S_i)$: (1) Let $H_0(S_i) = S_i$. Let $k = 1$. (2) Determine $H_k(S_i) = H_1(H_{k-1}(S_i))$. (3) (a) If $H_k(S_i) \neq H_{k-1}(S_i)$, increment k by 1 and return to (2). (b) If $H_k(S_i) = H_{k-1}(S_i)$, then $H_k(S_i) = H(S_i)$.

By an argument analogous to that used for Algorithm 2.1, it can be shown that Algorithm 2.2 requires at most $n\text{-}r$ iterations of step 2, where n is the size of the state set S of M and r is the size of S_i. Table 2.6 illustrates the algorithm for machine $A3$ of Fig. 2.5, with $S_i = \{1, 4\}$, yielding $H(1, 4) = \{1, 2, 4, 5, 7, 8\}$.

TABLE 2.6. ALGORITHM 2.2 FOR $A3$ AND $S_i = \{1, 4\}$

k	$H_k(S_i) = H_1(H_{k-1}(S_i))$
0	1, 4
1	1, 2, 4, 5, 7
2	1, 2, 4, 5, 7, 8
3	1, 2, 4, 5, 7, 8

A machine or a submachine which contains two or more isolated submachines will be said to be *decomposable*. If S_i in the foregoing discussion contains a single state σ_i, $H(\sigma_i)$ constitutes the set of all states connected to σ_i via chains of branches of any length (in which branch direction is disregarded).   Hence, if $H(\sigma_i) \neq S$, $H(\sigma_i)$ constitutes a nondecomposable isolated submachine of M. If $H(\sigma_i) = S$, it can be concluded that M is not decomposable. We can now outline a procedure for the *maximal decomposition* of a machine, i.e., for decomposing a machine into the largest number of isolated submachines:

ALGORITHM 2.3.   To determine the maximal decomposition of a given machine M with the state set S: (1) Let $S_1 = S$.   Let $k = 1$. (2) Select any state in S_k, say σ_{i_k}, and determine $H(\sigma_{i_k})$. $H(\sigma_{i_k})$ is the state set of the kth isolated submachine of M. (3) (a) If $H(\sigma_{i_1}) \cup H(\sigma_{i_2}) \cup \cdots \cup H(\sigma_{i_k}) \neq S$, let S_{k+1} consist of the states of S not contained in $H(\sigma_{i_1}) \cup H(\sigma_{i_2}) \cup \cdots \cup H(\sigma_{i_k})$.   Increment k by 1 and return to (2). (b) If $H(\sigma_{i_1}) \cup H(\sigma_{i_2}) \cup \cdots \cup H(\sigma_{i_k}) = S$, the submachines represented by $H(\sigma_{i_1})$, $H(\sigma_{i_2})$, . . . , $H(\sigma_{i_k})$ constitute the maximal decomposition of machine M.   In particular, if $H(\sigma_{i_1}) = S$, M is not decomposable.

Algorithm 2.3, of course, is not necessary when the machine is specified in a diagrammatic form.   It is of use, however, when the maximal decomposition is to be carried out by nondiagrammatic means, such as a digital computer.

Two or more machines will be said to be *congruous* if they have identical input alphabets.   Let M_1, M_2, . . . , M_N be congruous machines,

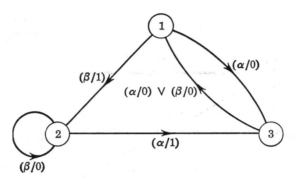

FIG. 2.6. Machine $A4$.

TABLE 2.7. MACHINE $A4$

s_ν \ x_ν	z_ν		$s_{\nu+1}$	
	α	β	α	β
1	0	1	3	2
2	1	0	3	2
3	0	0	1	1

representing N different systems, and let M be the machine of which M_1, M_2, . . . , M_N are the N isolated submachines. M is called the *disjunction machine* of M_1, M_2, . . . , M_N and is denoted by $\Delta(M_1, M_2, . . . , M_N)$.   Given the transition tables of M_1, M_2, . . . , M_N, the transition table of $\Delta(M_1, M_2, . . . , M_N)$ can be constructed as follows: (1) Relabel the states of the M_i, if necessary, so that no two states in the same machine or in two different machines will bear the same label.   (2) Write the rows of all N tables consecutively in a common table; this table is the transition table of $\Delta(M_1, M_2, . . . , M_N)$.   If the M_i are specified diagrammatically, the transition diagram of $\Delta(M_1, M_2, . . . , M_N)$ is simply the union of all the individual diagrams, with possible state relabeling, as instructed above.

Conceptually, the disjunction machine $\Delta(M_1, M_2, \ldots, M_N)$, and hence every machine containing a number of submachines identified as $M_1, M_2, \ldots, M_N$, may be regarded as a "system" which is M_1, or $M_2, \ldots,$ or M_N. This interpretation is justified by the fact that if $\Delta(M_1, M_2, \ldots, M_N)$ is in a state σ_u belonging to submachine M_i, it can never pass into a state of submachine M_j, where $j \neq i$, since M_i and M_j

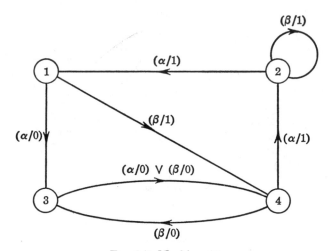

FIG. 2.7. Machine $A5$.

TABLE 2.8. MACHINE $A5$

s_ν \ x_ν	z_ν		$s_{\nu+1}$	
	α	β	α	β
1	0	1	3	4
2	1	1	1	2
3	0	0	4	4
4	1	0	2	3

are two isolated submachines. The behavior of $\Delta(M_1, M_2, \ldots, M_N)$ with the initial state σ_u is, therefore, identical to that of M_i with the initial state σ_u. Hence, $\Delta(M_1, M_2, \ldots, M_N)$ can represent M_1, or M_2, $\ldots,$ or M_N, depending on its initial state.

As an example, Fig. 2.6 and Table 2.7 represent machine $A4$, and Fig. 2.7 and Table 2.8 represent machine $A5$. The disjunction machine of $A4$ and $A5$, $\Delta(A4, A5)$, is represented by Fig. 2.8 and Table 2.9.

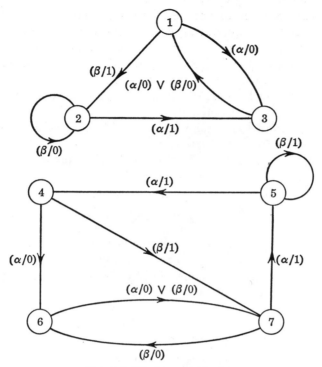

FIG. 2.8. Machine $\Delta(A4, A5)$.

TABLE 2.9. MACHINE $\Delta(A4, A5)$

s_ν \ x_ν	z_ν		$s_{\nu+1}$	
	α	β	α	β
1	0	1	3	2
2	1	0	3	2
3	0	0	1	1
4	0	1	6	7
5	1	1	4	5
6	0	0	7	7
7	1	0	5	6

2.8. The Transition Matrix[1]

The transition matrix is the mathematical counterpart of the transition diagram; it enables one to carry out mechanically a number of operations

---

[1] The material on transition matrices is based in part on the work of F. E. Hohn, S. Seshu, and D. D. Aufenkamp (The Theory of Nets, *IRE Trans.*, vol. EC-6, pp. 154–161, 1957).

which, in the transition diagram, can be carried out visually. The transition matrix is, therefore, advantageous wherever the operations cannot be carried out by a human investigator, and hence cannot be carried out visually, or wherever the transition diagram is complex to the extent that visual approach is futile.

For an n-state machine M, the transition matrix is composed of n rows and n columns and is denoted by $[M]$. Let $\{\sigma_1, \sigma_2, \ldots, \sigma_n\}$ be the state set of M, and let b_{ij} denote the branch which, in the transition diagram of M, points from state σ_i to state σ_j. The (i, j) entry (i.e., the entry common to the ith row and jth column) of $[M]$ is denoted by e_{ij} and is defined by

$$e_{ij} = \begin{cases} \text{label of } b_{ij} \text{ if } b_{ij} \text{ exists} \\ 0 \text{ if } b_{ij} \text{ does not exist} \end{cases} \tag{2.11}$$

For clarity, it is customary to attach the label of the kth state σ_k to the kth row and column and refer to the row and column as "row σ_k" and "column σ_k," respectively. Equation (2.12) shows the transition matrix of machine $A1$, specified diagrammatically by Fig. 2.2.

$$[A1] = \begin{array}{c} \\ 1 \\ 2 \\ 3 \\ 4 \\ 5 \end{array} \begin{bmatrix} (\pi/0) & (d/0) \vee (n/0) \vee (\lambda/0) & (u/0) & 0 & 0 \\ (\pi/0) & (d/0) \vee (n/0) \vee (u/0) \vee (\lambda/0) & 0 & 0 & 0 \\ (\pi/0) & (d/0) \vee (u/0) \vee (\lambda/0) & 0 & (n/0) & 0 \\ (\pi/0) & 0 & 0 & (n/0) \vee (u/0) \vee (\lambda/0) & (d/0) \\ (\pi/1) & 0 & 0 & (n/0) \vee (u/0) \vee (\lambda/0) & (d/0) \end{bmatrix} \tag{2.12}$$

If p is the size of the input alphabet of M, every row in $[M]$ must contain exactly p input-output pairs, each pair exhibiting a different input symbol. A converging branch of state σ_k is represented by an off-diagonal entry[1] in column σ_k; a diverging branch of state σ_k is represented by an off-diagonal entry in row σ_k; a reflecting branch of state σ_k is represented by a diagonal entry in row or column σ_k. Consequently, if σ_k is transient, all off-diagonal entries in column σ_k (but not in row σ_k) are zero; if σ_k is persistent, all off-diagonal entries in row σ_k (but not in column σ_k) are zero; if σ_k is isolated, all off-diagonal entries in row and column σ_k are zero.

If $S_i = \{\sigma_{i_1}, \sigma_{i_2}, \ldots, \sigma_{i_r}\}$, the set $G_1(S_i)$, as defined in Sec. 2.6, is given by the union of S_i and the labels of the columns in which rows σ_{i_1}, $\sigma_{i_2}, \ldots, \sigma_{i_r}$ are nonzero. The set $H_1(S_i)$, as defined in Sec. 2.7, is given by the union of S_i, the labels of the columns in which rows $\sigma_{i_1}, \sigma_{i_2} \ldots$, σ_{i_r} are nonzero, and the labels of the rows in which columns σ_{i_1}, $\sigma_{i_2}, \ldots, \sigma_{i_r}$ are nonzero. For example, $[A1]$ readily reveals that for machine $A1$, $G_1(1, 2) = \{1, 2, 3\}$ and $H_1(4, 5) = \{1, 3, 4, 5\}$. Thus,

---

[1] A *diagonal* entry in a matrix is an (i, j) entry where $i = j$; an *off-diagonal* entry is an (i, j) entry where $i \neq j$.

the transition matrix is seen to be a convenient tool for carrying out Algorithms 2.1, 2.2, and 2.3.

To determine whether $S_i = \{\sigma_{i_1}, \sigma_{i_2}, \ldots, \sigma_{i_r}\}$ constitutes a transient, persistent, or isolated submachine of M, one can permute the rows and columns of $[M]$, so that rows and columns $\sigma_{i_1}, \sigma_{i_2}, \ldots, \sigma_{i_r}$ would appear in adjacent positions, starting at the first row and column, respectively. As indicated by (2.13), this permutation divides $[M]$ into four submatrices—$[M_{11}]$, $[M_{12}]$, $[M_{21}]$, and $[M_{22}]$—where the rows and columns of $[M_{11}]$ are $\sigma_{i_1}, \sigma_{i_2}, \ldots, \sigma_{i_r}$. Denoting a matrix in which all entries are zero by $[0]$, it can be concluded that S_i constitutes a transient submachine if $[M_{21}] = [0]$ and $[M_{12}] \neq [0]$, a persistent submachine if $[M_{12}] = [0]$ and $[M_{21}] \neq [0]$, and an isolated submachine if $[M_{12}] = [M_{21}] = [0]$. Equation (2.14) is the transition matrix of machine $A3$ specified by Fig. 2.5, with the rows and columns permuted to place in evidence the persistent submachine $\{1, 4, 7\}$, the transient submachine $\{2, 5, 8\}$, and the isolated submachine $\{3, 6, 9\}$.

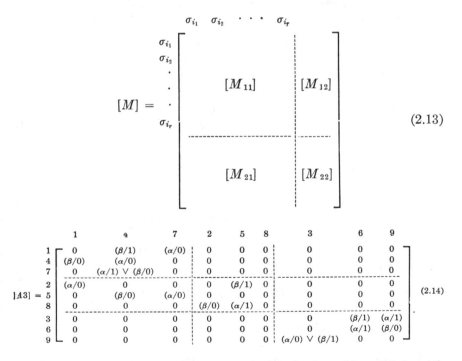

$$[M] = \begin{array}{c} \\ \sigma_{i_1} \\ \sigma_{i_2} \\ \cdot \\ \cdot \\ \cdot \\ \sigma_{i_r} \end{array} \left[\begin{array}{cc:cc} & & & \\ & [M_{11}] & & [M_{12}] \\ & & & \\ \hdashline & & & \\ & [M_{21}] & & [M_{22}] \\ & & & \end{array} \right] \qquad (2.13)$$

$[A3] =$

	1	4	7	2	5	8	3	6	9
1	0	$(\beta/1)$	$(\alpha/0)$	0	0	0	0	0	0
4	$(\beta/0)$	$(\alpha/0)$	0	0	0	0	0	0	0
7	0	$(\alpha/1) \lor (\beta/0)$	0	0	0	0	0	0	0
2	$(\alpha/0)$	0	0	0	$(\beta/1)$	0	0	0	0
5	0	$(\beta/0)$	$(\alpha/0)$	0	0	0	0	0	0
8	0	0	0	$(\beta/0)$	$(\alpha/1)$	0	0	0	0
3	0	0	0	0	0	0	0	$(\beta/1)$	$(\alpha/1)$
6	0	0	0	0	0	0	0	$(\alpha/1)$	$(\beta/0)$
9	0	0	0	0	0	0	$(\alpha/0) \lor (\beta/1)$	0	0

(2.14)

When S_i constitutes a persistent or an isolated submachine, $[M_{12}] = [0]$, and hence every row in $[M_{11}]$ contains all p input-output pairs, where p is the size of the input alphabet. Removing $[M_{12}]$, $[M_{21}]$, and $[M_{22}]$ from $[M]$, then, results in an $r \times r$ matrix $[M_{11}]$, which can be regarded as the matrix representation of an independent r-state machine M_{11} having the same input alphabet as M. One can thus reach the same conclusion arrived at in Sec. 2.6: if a machine is in a state belonging to a persistent or an isolated submachine, all the states which do not belong to this submachine, and all the branches originating from these states, may be eliminated.

2.9. Higher-order Transition Matrices

A sequence of k branches which lead from one state in the transition diagram to another is called a *path*; k is referred to as the *length* of the path. $P_{ij}^{(k)}$ denotes the set of all paths of length k which lead from state σ_i to state σ_j. $P_{ij}^{(1)}$, which constitutes the single branch leading from σ_i to σ_j, is written as π_{ij}. If π_{ij} is empty (i.e., if no single branch points from σ_i to σ_j), it is assigned the numerical value 0.

FIG. 2.9. The path $\pi_{il_1}\pi_{l_1l_2} \cdots \pi_{l_{k-1}j}$.

A path of length k composed of branch π_{il_1}, followed by branch $\pi_{l_1l_2}$, . . . , followed by branch $\pi_{l_{k-1}j}$, such as shown in Fig. 2.9, is symbolized by the ordered product $\pi_{il_1}\pi_{l_1l_2} \cdots \pi_{l_{k-1}j}$. Since a nonexisting branch constitutes, by agreement, a zero factor, then if any of the branches in the path symbolized by the above product does not exist, the entire product becomes zero. A set of paths is written as an unordered sum of products, each product representing a member of the set. Thus:

$$P_{ij}^{(k)} = \sum_{l_1=1}^{n} \sum_{l_2=1}^{n} \cdots \sum_{l_{k-1}=1}^{n} \pi_{il_1}\pi_{l_1l_2} \cdots \pi_{l_{k-1}j} \tag{2.15}$$

where zero components are interpreted as nonexisting paths.

LEMMA 2.2

$$P_{ij}^{(k+1)} = \sum_{u=1}^{n} \pi_{iu}P_{uj}^{(k)} \tag{2.16}$$

Proof. Using (2.15):

$$\sum_{u=1}^{n} \pi_{iu}P_{uj}^{(k)} = \sum_{u=1}^{n} \pi_{iu}\left\{ \sum_{l_1=1}^{n} \sum_{l_2=1}^{n} \cdots \sum_{l_{k-1}=1}^{n} \pi_{ul_1}\pi_{l_1l_2} \cdots \pi_{l_{k-1}j}\right\}$$

$$= \sum_{u=1}^{n} \sum_{l_1=1}^{n} \sum_{l_2=1}^{n} \cdots \sum_{l_{k-1}=1}^{n} \pi_{iu}\pi_{ul_1}\pi_{l_1l_2} \cdots \pi_{l_{k-1}j} \tag{2.17}$$

Replacing the running index u with l_1, and the running indices l_h, $h = 1, 2, \ldots, k - 1$, with l_{h+1}, we obtain

$$\sum_{u=1}^{n} \pi_{iu} P_{uj}^{(k)} = \sum_{l_1=1}^{n} \sum_{l_2=1}^{n} \cdots \sum_{l_k=1}^{n} \pi_{il_1} \pi_{l_1 l_2} \cdots \pi_{l_k j} = P_{ij}^{(k+1)} \quad (2.18)$$

For an n-state machine, the *kth-order transition matrix*, denoted by $[\bar{M}]^{(k)}$, is composed of n rows and n columns, labeled as in $[M]$. The (i, j) entry in $[\bar{M}]^{(k)}$ is denoted by $e_{ij}^{(k)}$ and defined by

$$e_{ij}^{(k)} = P_{ij}^{(k)} \quad (2.19)$$

For $k = 1$, we have

$$e_{ij}^{(1)} = P_{ij}^{(1)} = \pi_{ij} \quad (2.20)$$

$[\bar{M}]^{(1)}$ is written as $[\bar{M}]$ and can be obtained from $[M]$ by replacing every nonzero (i, j) entry in $[M]$ by π_{ij}.

Multiplication of higher-order transition matrices is defined as follows: If $[\bar{A}]$ has the (i, j) entry a_{ij}, $[\bar{B}]$ the (i, j) entry b_{ij}, and $[\bar{C}] = [\bar{A}][\bar{B}]$ the (i, j) entry c_{ij}, and if each of these matrices is an $n \times n$ higher-order transition matrix, then

$$c_{ij} = \sum_{u=1}^{n} a_{iu} b_{uj} \quad (2.21)$$

Multiplication of the entries a_{iu} and b_{uj} (each of which is, in general, a sum of products) is associative and distributive with respect to addition, but not commutative. Thus, multiplication of higher-order transition matrices is the same as the multiplication of ordinary matrices, except that the order of factors in each product $a_{iu} b_{uj}$ must be preserved: $a_{iu} b_{uj}$ is not equivalent to $b_{uj} a_{iu}$.

LEMMA 2.3

$$[\bar{M}]^{(k+1)} = [\bar{M}][\bar{M}]^{(k)} \quad (2.22)$$

Proof. From (2.19), (2.20), and (2.21), the (i, j) entry of the product matrix $[\bar{M}][\bar{M}]^{(k)}$ is $\sum_{u=1}^{n} \pi_{iu} P_{uj}^{(k)}$. However, from (2.16) and (2.19), this entry is $e_{ij}^{(k+1)}$, which proves the lemma.

THEOREM 2.3. The (i, j) entry of $[\bar{M}]^k$, $k = 1, 2, \ldots$, is the set of all paths of length k leading from state σ_i to state σ_j in machine M.

Proof. The theorem is equivalent to stating that $[\bar{M}]^{(k)} = [\bar{M}]^k$. For $k = 1$, this equality is valid by construction. If the equality is valid for $k = h$, then, by (2.22),

$$[\bar{M}]^{(h+1)} = [\bar{M}][\bar{M}]^{(h)} = [\bar{M}][\bar{M}]^h = [\bar{M}]^{h+1} \qquad (2.23)$$

which proves, by induction, that the equality is valid for every $k \geq 1$.

Theorem 2.3 shows that the set of all paths of length k leading from one state to another can be constructed systematically by raising $[\bar{M}]$ to the kth power. The subscripts associated with each path, as represented in the matrix, identify the branches of which the path is composed. By referring to the transition diagram or matrix, the labels of these branches, and hence the input and output sequences associated with the path, can be identified.

As an example, (2.24) is the first-order transition matrix, and (2.25) the second-order transition matrix, for machine $A1$ specified by the transition matrix (2.12). From (2.25) it is apparent, for example, that there are two paths of length 2 leading from state 3 to state 2, namely, $\pi_{31}\pi_{12}$ and $\pi_{32}\pi_{22}$, and that there is no path of length 2 leading from state 2 to state 4 or 5. Also, from (2.25) and (2.12) one can deduce that state 2 can be reached from state 5 by applying the input sequence πd, or πn, or $\pi\lambda$.

$$[\overline{A1}] = \begin{array}{c} \\ 1 \\ 2 \\ 3 \\ 4 \\ 5 \end{array} \begin{array}{ccccc} 1 & 2 & 3 & 4 & 5 \\ \left[\begin{array}{ccccc} \pi_{11} & \pi_{12} & \pi_{13} & 0 & 0 \\ \pi_{21} & \pi_{22} & 0 & 0 & 0 \\ \pi_{31} & \pi_{32} & 0 & \pi_{34} & 0 \\ \pi_{41} & 0 & 0 & \pi_{44} & \pi_{45} \\ \pi_{51} & 0 & 0 & \pi_{54} & \pi_{55} \end{array}\right] \end{array} \qquad (2.24)$$

$[\overline{A1}]^2 =$

	1	2	3	4	5
1	$\pi_{11}\pi_{11} + \pi_{12}\pi_{21} + \pi_{13}\pi_{31}$	$\pi_{11}\pi_{12} + \pi_{12}\pi_{22} + \pi_{13}\pi_{32}$	$\pi_{11}\pi_{13}$	$\pi_{13}\pi_{34}$	0
2	$\pi_{21}\pi_{11} + \pi_{22}\pi_{21}$	$\pi_{21}\pi_{12} + \pi_{22}\pi_{22}$	$\pi_{21}\pi_{13}$	0	0
3	$\pi_{31}\pi_{11} + \pi_{32}\pi_{21} + \pi_{34}\pi_{41}$	$\pi_{31}\pi_{12} + \pi_{32}\pi_{22}$	$\pi_{31}\pi_{13}$	$\pi_{34}\pi_{44}$	$\pi_{34}\pi_{45}$
4	$\pi_{41}\pi_{11} + \pi_{44}\pi_{41} + \pi_{45}\pi_{51}$	$\pi_{41}\pi_{12}$	$\pi_{41}\pi_{13}$	$\pi_{44}\pi_{44} + \pi_{45}\pi_{54}$	$\pi_{44}\pi_{45} + \pi_{45}\pi_{55}$
5	$\pi_{51}\pi_{11} + \pi_{54}\pi_{41} + \pi_{55}\pi_{51}$	$\pi_{51}\pi_{12}$	$\pi_{51}\pi_{13}$	$\pi_{54}\pi_{44} + \pi_{55}\pi_{54}$	$\pi_{54}\pi_{45} + \pi_{55}\pi_{55}$

$$(2.25)$$

2.10. Proper Paths

The path $\pi_{il_1}\pi_{l_1l_2} \cdots \pi_{l_{k-1}j}$, leading from state σ_i to state σ_j, is called a *proper path* (of length k), if the subscripts $i, l_1, l_2, \ldots, l_{k-1}, j$ are distinct. It is called a *proper cycle* (of length k), if the subscripts $i, l_1, l_2, \ldots, l_{k-1}$ are distinct, and if $i = j$. Thus, a proper path and a proper cycle are an open path and a closed path, respectively, which do not touch any state more than once. We thus have:

LEMMA 2.4. In an n-state machine, the length of a proper path cannot exceed $n - 1$, and the length of a proper cycle cannot exceed n.

A path which is not a proper path is said to be *redundant*. In the following section we shall introduce some problems in which only proper paths are of interest. When this is the case, all terms $\pi_{il_1}\pi_{l_1l_2} \cdots \pi_{l_{k-1}j}$ such that i, l_1, l_2, ... , l_{k-1}, j are not distinct can be eliminated from the kth-order transition matrix $[\bar{M}]^k$, to result in a modified matrix denoted by $[\bar{M}']^{(k)}$. The (i, j) entry of $[\bar{M}']^{(k)}$, then, is the set of all proper paths of length k leading from state σ_i to state σ_j in machine M. $[\bar{M}']^{(1)}$, written as $[\bar{M}']$, is $[\bar{M}]$ with all diagonal entries eliminated (i.e., with all diagonal entries replaced by zeros).

LEMMA 2.5. $[\bar{M}'][\bar{M}']^{(k)}$ contains all the proper paths contained in $[\bar{M}]^{k+1}$.

Proof. The process of multiplying $[\bar{M}]$ by $[\bar{M}]^k$ is, by (2.21), equivalent to extending the length of every path represented in $[\bar{M}]^k$ from k to $k + 1$ by attaching to its "tail end" single branches represented in $[\bar{M}]$. If either the k-branch path or the attached branch is redundant, the resulting $(k + 1)$-branch path must also be redundant. Hence $[\bar{M}'][\bar{M}']^{(k)}$, where $[\bar{M}']$ is formed by deleting from $[\bar{M}]$ all redundant paths of length 1, and where $[\bar{M}']^{(k)}$ is formed by deleting from $[\bar{M}]^k$ all redundant paths of length k, must contain all proper paths contained in $[\bar{M}][\bar{M}]^k$. Since $[\bar{M}][\bar{M}]^k = [\bar{M}]^{k+1}$, the lemma follows.

Lemma 2.5 implies that in the process of constructing $[\bar{M}]^{k+1}$ from $[\bar{M}]$, all redundant paths may be eliminated as soon as they appear in any of the intermediate matrices, without affecting the enumeration of proper paths. This result suggests a simplified procedure for constructing $[\bar{M}']^{(k)}$, which is considerably less laborious than the process of first constructing $[\bar{M}]^k$ and then eliminating from $[\bar{M}]^k$ all redundant paths:

ALGORITHM 2.4. Given $[\bar{M}]$, to construct $[\bar{M}']^{(l)}$ for $l > 1$: (1) Construct $[\bar{M}']$ by replacing all the diagonal entries of $[\bar{M}]$ by zeros. Let $k = 1$. (2) Construct $[\bar{M}'][\bar{M}']^{(k)}$. In the product matrix, replace every term representing a redundant path by zero. Let the resulting matrix be $[\bar{M}']^{(k+1)}$. (3) (a) If $k + 1 < l$, increment k by 1 and return to (2). (b) If $k + 1 = l$, then $[\bar{M}']^{(k+1)} = [\bar{M}']^{(l)}$.

Matrices (2.26) to (2.29) illustrate how Algorithm 2.4 can be employed for the construction of $[\overline{A1}']$, $[\overline{A1}']^{(2)}$, $[\overline{A1}']^{(3)}$, and $[\overline{A1}']^{(4)}$ from the matrix $[\overline{A1}]$ given by (2.24).

$$[\overline{A1}'] = \begin{array}{c} \\ 1 \\ 2 \\ 3 \\ 4 \\ 5 \end{array} \begin{array}{ccccc} 1 & 2 & 3 & 4 & 5 \\ \left[\begin{array}{ccccc} 0 & \pi_{12} & \pi_{13} & 0 & 0 \\ \pi_{21} & 0 & 0 & 0 & 0 \\ \pi_{31} & \pi_{32} & 0 & \pi_{34} & 0 \\ \pi_{41} & 0 & 0 & 0 & \pi_{45} \\ \pi_{51} & 0 & 0 & \pi_{54} & 0 \end{array} \right] \end{array} \qquad (2.26)$$

$$[\overline{A1'}]^{(2)} = \begin{array}{c} \\ 1 \\ 2 \\ 3 \\ 4 \\ 5 \end{array} \begin{array}{ccccc} 1 & 2 & 3 & 4 & 5 \\ \left[\begin{array}{ccccc} 0 & \pi_{13}\pi_{32} & 0 & \pi_{13}\pi_{34} & 0 \\ 0 & 0 & \pi_{21}\pi_{13} & 0 & 0 \\ \pi_{32}\pi_{21} + \pi_{34}\pi_{41} & \pi_{31}\pi_{12} & 0 & 0 & \pi_{34}\pi_{45} \\ \pi_{45}\pi_{51} & \pi_{41}\pi_{12} & \pi_{41}\pi_{13} & 0 & 0 \\ \pi_{54}\pi_{41} & \pi_{51}\pi_{12} & \pi_{51}\pi_{13} & 0 & 0 \end{array}\right] \end{array} \quad (2.27)$$

$$[\overline{A1'}]^{(3)} = \begin{array}{c} \\ 1 \\ 2 \\ 3 \\ 4 \\ 5 \end{array} \begin{array}{ccccc} 1 & 2 & 3 & 4 & 5 \\ \left[\begin{array}{ccccc} 0 & 0 & 0 & 0 & \pi_{13}\pi_{34}\pi_{45} \\ 0 & 0 & 0 & \pi_{21}\pi_{13}\pi_{34} & 0 \\ \pi_{34}\pi_{45}\pi_{51} & \pi_{34}\pi_{41}\pi_{12} & 0 & 0 & 0 \\ 0 & \pi_{41}\pi_{13}\pi_{32} + \pi_{45}\pi_{51}\pi_{12} & \pi_{45}\pi_{51}\pi_{13} & 0 & 0 \\ 0 & \pi_{51}\pi_{13}\pi_{32} + \pi_{54}\pi_{41}\pi_{12} & \pi_{54}\pi_{41}\pi_{13} & \pi_{51}\pi_{13}\pi_{34} & 0 \end{array}\right] \end{array} \quad (2.28)$$

$$[\overline{A1'}]^{(4)} = \begin{array}{c} \\ 1 \\ 2 \\ 3 \\ 4 \\ 5 \end{array} \begin{array}{ccccc} 1 & 2 & 3 \quad 4 & 5 \\ \left[\begin{array}{ccccc} 0 & 0 & 0 \quad 0 & 0 \\ 0 & 0 & 0 \quad 0 & \pi_{21}\pi_{13}\pi_{34}\pi_{45} \\ 0 & \pi_{34}\pi_{45}\pi_{51}\pi_{12} & 0 \quad 0 & 0 \\ 0 & \pi_{45}\pi_{51}\pi_{13}\pi_{32} & 0 \quad 0 & 0 \\ 0 & \pi_{54}\pi_{41}\pi_{13}\pi_{32} & 0 \quad 0 & 0 \end{array}\right] \end{array} \quad (2.29)$$

It is seen that while the number of nonzero terms in $[\bar{M}]^k$ tends to grow exponentially with k, the number of terms in $[\bar{M}']^{(k)}$ tends to remain constant up to a certain value of k and to diminish for larger values of k. In fact, from Lemma 2.4 it can be concluded that if M is an n-state machine, then $[\bar{M}']^{(k)}$, for all $k \geq n$, consists entirely of zero terms.

2.11. Determination of Minimal Paths and Complete Cycles

In many problems of practical interest, a fixed cost is associated with the generation of each input symbol, so that passing the machine from one state to another incurs an expenditure which is proportional to the number of branches traversed in the passage. In order to minimize the total cost in this case, it is desirable to determine the shortest path, or *minimal path*, between the two states.

LEMMA 2.6. The minimal path leading from state σ_i to state σ_j, if it exists, must be a proper path.

Proof. Let the minimal path be $\pi_{il_1}\pi_{l_1l_2} \cdots \pi_{l_{k-1}j}$ of length k. If this path is redundant, two of the subscripts $i, l_1, l_2, \ldots, l_{k-1}, j$ must be identical. Suppose $l_g = l_h$, where $h > g$. Then the minimal path can be represented by the product

$$\pi_{il_1}\pi_{l_1l_2} \cdots \pi_{l_{g-1}l_g}\pi_{l_gl_{g+1}} \cdots \pi_{l_{h-1}l_h}\pi_{l_hl_{h+1}} \cdots \pi_{l_{k-1}j}$$
$$= \pi_{il_1}\pi_{l_1l_2} \cdots \pi_{l_{g-1}l_g}\pi_{l_gl_{g+1}} \cdots \pi_{l_{h-1}l_g}\pi_{l_gl_{h+1}} \cdots \pi_{l_{k-1}j}$$

If this path exists, no factor in the above product is zero. Consequently, no factor in $\pi_{il_1}\pi_{l_1l_2} \cdots \pi_{l_{g-1}l_g}\pi_{l_gl_{h+1}} \cdots \pi_{l_{k-1}j}$ is zero, which implies that this path also exists. Since the latter path is shorter than the former and, like the former, leads from σ_i to σ_j, the former cannot be minimal. By contradiction, therefore, the minimal path cannot be redundant.

Lemmas 2.4 and 2.6 can now be combined in the following theorem:

THEOREM 2.4. If a path exists which leads from state σ_i to state σ_j in the n-state machine M, then the shortest such path is represented by an (i, j) entry in one of the matrices $[\bar{M}']^{(k)}$, where $1 \leq k \leq n - 1$.

Theorem 2.4 suggests the following procedure for determining minimal paths:

ALGORITHM 2.5. To determine the minimal path leading from state σ_i to state σ_j in an n-state machine M: (1) Let $k = 1$. (2) Construct $[\bar{M}']^{(k)}$. (3) (a) If the (i, j) entry is zero and $k < n - 1$, increment k by 1 and return to (2). (b) If the (i, j) entry is zero and $k = n - 1$, the path does not exist. (c) If the (i, j) entry is nonzero, it represents the desired path (or paths).

As an example, to find the minimal path leading from state 1 to state 5 in machine $A1$, $[\bar{A1}']^{(k)}$ is constructed for $k = 1, 2, \ldots,$ until, for the first time, the entry common to row 1 and column 5 becomes nonzero, or until $k = 5$ (in which case the path does not exist). Matrices (2.26) to (2.29) show that the first nonzero entry common to row 1 and column 5 occurs in $[\bar{A1}']^{(3)}$, where this entry is given by $\pi_{13}\pi_{34}\pi_{45}$. Reference to the transition diagram of Fig. 2.2, or the transition matrix (2.12), reveals that this minimal path can be traversed by applying the input sequence *und*.

In an n-state machine, a *complete cycle* is any proper cycle of length n. A complete cycle, then, is a closed path which touches every state in the machine exactly once. The problem of determining proper cycles arises when each input symbol has a fixed cost and it is desirable to pass the machine, in the least expensive manner, from the initial state through all other states and back to the initial state (for testing purposes, say).

LEMMA 2.7. The principal diagonal of $[\bar{M}'][\bar{M}']^{(n-1)}$ contains all complete cycles for machine M.

Proof. Since a complete cycle is a proper cycle, any $n - 1$ consecutive branches in a complete cycle of length n constitute a proper path. The set of all paths constructed by attaching proper paths of length 1 to the "tail end" of proper paths of length $n - 1$ contains, therefore, all complete cycles of length n. Since $[\bar{M}'][\bar{M}']^{(n-1)}$ contains this set, and since complete cycles are paths leading from a state back to the same state, the lemma follows.

Clearly, any state of M may be regarded as the initial state in a complete cycle. Hence, if one diagonal entry in $[\bar{M}'][\bar{M}']^{(n-1)}$ is zero, which is the case whenever a complete cycle does not exist in M, then all diagonal entries in this matrix must be zero. Any nonzero diagonal entry (i, i) in $[\bar{M}'][\bar{M}']^{(n-1)}$ represents the set of all possible complete cycles in M; the diagonal entry $(j, j), j \neq i$, contains cyclic permutations of the terms contained in the (i, i) entry.

For example, constructing $[\overline{A1'}][\overline{A1'}]^{(4)}$ results in a matrix in which all entries are zero, which implies that $A1$ contains no complete cycles. Figure 2.6 and matrix (2.30) represent machine $A4$, in which a complete cycle does exist. Matrices (2.31) to (2.33) illustrate the procedure for determining this cycle. Since the number of states in $A4$ is 3, $[\overline{A4'}][\overline{A4'}]^{(2)}$, shown in (2.33), must contain all complete cycles on its principal diagonal. The desired complete cycle, then, is $\pi_{12}\pi_{23}\pi_{31}$, or any cyclic permutation thereof. Reference to Fig. 2.6 or matrix (2.30) reveals that, if the initial state of $A4$ is 1, the complete cycle can be traversed by applying either $\beta\alpha\alpha$ or $\beta\alpha\beta$.

$$[A4] = \begin{array}{c} 1 \\ 2 \\ 3 \end{array} \begin{bmatrix} 0 & (\beta/1) & (\alpha/0) \\ 0 & (\beta/0) & (\alpha/1) \\ (\alpha/0) \vee (\beta/0) & 0 & 0 \end{bmatrix} \quad\quad (2.30)$$

$$[\overline{A4'}] = \begin{array}{c} 1 \\ 2 \\ 3 \end{array} \begin{bmatrix} 0 & \pi_{12} & \pi_{13} \\ 0 & 0 & \pi_{23} \\ \pi_{31} & 0 & 0 \end{bmatrix} \quad\quad (2.31)$$

$$[\overline{A4'}]^{(2)} = \begin{array}{c} 1 \\ 2 \\ 3 \end{array} \begin{bmatrix} 0 & 0 & \pi_{12}\pi_{23} \\ \pi_{23}\pi_{31} & 0 & 0 \\ 0 & \pi_{31}\pi_{12} & 0 \end{bmatrix} \quad\quad (2.32)$$

$$[\overline{A4'}][\overline{A4'}]^{(2)} = \begin{array}{c} 1 \\ 2 \\ 3 \end{array} \begin{bmatrix} \pi_{12}\pi_{23}\pi_{31} & \pi_{13}\pi_{31}\pi_{12} & 0 \\ 0 & \pi_{23}\pi_{31}\pi_{12} & 0 \\ 0 & 0 & \pi_{31}\pi_{12}\pi_{23} \end{bmatrix} \quad\quad (2.33)$$

2.12. The Skeleton Matrix

In many problems, the detailed entries of the higher-order transition matrices are not essential, and solutions can be obtained by considering powers of the so-called *skeleton matrix*, which feature much simpler entries. For an n-state machine M, the skeleton matrix is composed of n rows and n columns, labeled as in $[M]$ and denoted by $[\tilde{M}]$. The (i, j) entry in

$[\tilde{M}]$ is denoted by $\tilde{e}_{ij}$. If b_{ij} denotes the branch pointing from state σ_i to state σ_j in M, $\tilde{e}_{ij}$ is defined by

$$\tilde{e}_{ij} = \begin{cases} 1 \text{ if } b_{ij} \text{ exists} \\ 0 \text{ if } b_{ij} \text{ does not exist} \end{cases} \tag{2.34}$$

$[\tilde{M}]$, then, can be constructed from $[M]$ or $[\bar{M}]$ by replacing every nonzero entry in these matrices by 1.

THEOREM 2.5. The (i, j) entry of $[\tilde{M}]^k$, $k = 1, 2, \ldots$, equals the number of paths of length k leading from state σ_i to state σ_j in machine M.

Proof. For $k = 1$ the theorem is true by construction. Suppose the theorem is true for k; then the (u, j) entry of $[\tilde{M}]^k$, denoted by $\tilde{e}_{uj}^{(k)}$, is the number of paths of length k leading from σ_u to σ_j. The (i, j) entry of $[\tilde{M}][\tilde{M}]^k = [\tilde{M}]^{k+1}$ is given by

$$\tilde{e}_{ij}^{(k+1)} = \sum_{u=1}^{n} \tilde{e}_{iu}\tilde{e}_{uj}^{(k)} \tag{2.35}$$

In (2.35), $\tilde{e}_{uj}^{(k)}$ is multiplied by 1 if σ_u is reachable from σ_i via a single branch, and by 0 otherwise. Hence, $\tilde{e}_{ij}^{(k+1)}$ equals the number of paths of length $k + 1$ leading from σ_i to σ_j. By induction, then, the theorem is true for all $k > 0$.

The concise numerical form of the skeleton matrix can be exploited in problems where the *existence* or the *number* of paths between specified states is in question, and where the branches contained in each path are of no interest. One can determine the number of minimal paths leading from state σ_i to state σ_j by constructing $[\tilde{M}]^k$ for successive values of $k \leq n - 1$; if the (i, j) entry is zero in $[\tilde{M}]^{k-1}$ but nonzero in $[\tilde{M}]^k$, this entry is the number of minimal paths (and k is their length); if the (i, j) entry is zero in $[\tilde{M}]^{n-1}$, the path does not exist.

Matrices (2.36) to (2.38) illustrate the construction of the skeleton matrix for machine $A1$ of Fig. 2.2 and the construction of the second and third powers of this matrix. $[\widetilde{A1}]^3$ reveals, for example, that state 5 is not reachable from state 2 by any path whose length is less than 4 and that state 1 is reachable from state 4 by 9 distinct paths of length 4.

$$[\widetilde{A1}] = \begin{array}{c} \\ 1 \\ 2 \\ 3 \\ 4 \\ 5 \end{array} \begin{array}{c} \begin{array}{ccccc} 1 & 2 & 3 & 4 & 5 \end{array} \\ \begin{bmatrix} 1 & 1 & 1 & 0 & 0 \\ 1 & 1 & 0 & 0 & 0 \\ 1 & 1 & 0 & 1 & 0 \\ 1 & 0 & 0 & 1 & 1 \\ 1 & 0 & 0 & 1 & 1 \end{bmatrix} \end{array} \tag{2.36}$$

$$[\widetilde{A1}]^2 = \begin{array}{c} \\ 1 \\ 2 \\ 3 \\ 4 \\ 5 \end{array} \begin{array}{ccccc} 1 & 2 & 3 & 4 & 5 \\ \left[\begin{array}{ccccc} 3 & 3 & 1 & 1 & 0 \\ 2 & 2 & 1 & 0 & 0 \\ 3 & 2 & 1 & 1 & 1 \\ 3 & 1 & 1 & 2 & 2 \\ 3 & 1 & 1 & 2 & 2 \end{array}\right] \end{array} \tag{2.37}$$

$$[\widetilde{A1}]^3 = \begin{array}{c} \\ 1 \\ 2 \\ 3 \\ 4 \\ 5 \end{array} \begin{array}{ccccc} 1 & 2 & 3 & 4 & 5 \\ \left[\begin{array}{ccccc} 8 & 7 & 3 & 2 & 1 \\ 5 & 5 & 2 & 1 & 0 \\ 8 & 6 & 3 & 3 & 2 \\ 9 & 5 & 3 & 5 & 4 \\ 9 & 5 & 3 & 5 & 4 \end{array}\right] \end{array} \tag{2.38}$$

It may be noticed that, since a branch may correspond to more than one input-output pair, a nonzero (i, j) entry in $[\tilde{M}]^k$ is not necessarily the number of all input sequences of length k which pass M from state σ_i to state σ_j. If the number of input sequences, rather than the number of paths, is of interest, a *modified skeleton matrix*, denoted by $[\tilde{M}']$, can be defined, where the (i, j) entry $\tilde{e}'_{ij}$ is given by

$$\tilde{e}'_{ij} = \begin{cases} \text{number of input-output pairs labeling } b_{ij} \\ 0 \text{ if } b_{ij} \text{ does not exist} \end{cases} \tag{2.39}$$

$[\tilde{M}']$, then, can be constructed from $[M]$ by replacing every nonzero entry in $[M]$ by the number of input-output pairs contained in this entry. $[\tilde{M}']$ may be regarded as the skeleton matrix of M, where every branch labeled with h input-output pairs is "split" into h parallel branches, each labeled with a single input-output pair. Since this "splitting" operation forces the number of branches contained in any path to equal the number of input-output pairs labeling the path, the (i, j) entry of $[\tilde{M}']^k$ must coincide with the total number of input sequences of length k which pass M from σ_i to σ_j.

Matrices (2.40) and (2.41) illustrate the construction of the modified skeleton matrix for machine $A1$ of Fig. 2.2 and the construction of the second power of this matrix. $[\widetilde{A1'}]^2$ reveals, for example, that there are 3 shortest input sequences which pass $A1$ from state 4 to state 2 and that there are 12 input sequences of length 2 which pass $A1$ from state 5 to state 4.

$$[\widetilde{A1'}] = \begin{array}{c} \\ 1 \\ 2 \\ 3 \\ 4 \\ 5 \end{array} \begin{array}{ccccc} 1 & 2 & 3 & 4 & 5 \\ \left[\begin{array}{ccccc} 1 & 3 & 1 & 0 & 0 \\ 1 & 4 & 0 & 0 & 0 \\ 1 & 3 & 0 & 1 & 0 \\ 1 & 0 & 0 & 3 & 1 \\ 1 & 0 & 0 & 3 & 1 \end{array}\right] \end{array} \tag{2.40}$$

$$[\widetilde{A1'}]^2 = \begin{array}{c} \\ 1 \\ 2 \\ 3 \\ 4 \\ 5 \end{array} \begin{array}{ccccc} 1 & 2 & 3 & 4 & 5 \\ \left[\begin{array}{ccccc} 5 & 18 & 1 & 1 & 0 \\ 5 & 19 & 1 & 0 & 0 \\ 5 & 15 & 1 & 3 & 1 \\ 5 & 3 & 1 & 12 & 4 \\ 5 & 3 & 1 & 12 & 4 \end{array}\right] \end{array} \tag{2.41}$$

2.13. Partial Construction of Matrices

The matrices discussed in the preceding sections are characterized by the fact that they are square. Consequently, they provide information concerning the paths not only between a *specified* pair of states but also between *any* pair of states. This feature is often desirable, but is obtained at the cost of laborious matrix manipulations, whose complexity rises roughly as the square of the number of states in the machine. In cases where only those paths originating at some specified initial state are of interest, some of the encumbrance involved in these manipulations can be avoided through partial construction of matrices, as will be shown below.

LEMMA 2.8. Let $[\bar{M}]_i^k$ denote the row matrix constructed from the ith row of $[\bar{M}]^k$. Then

$$[\bar{M}]_i^{k+1} = [\bar{M}]_i^k[\bar{M}] \tag{2.42}$$

Proof. From the definitions of $P_{ij}^{(k)}$ and π_{ij}, and a development analogous to that shown in (2.17), we have

$$P_{ij}^{(k+1)} = \sum_{u=1}^{n} \pi_{iu} P_{uj}^{(k)} = \sum_{u=1}^{n} P_{iu}^{(k)} \pi_{uj} \tag{2.43}$$

For a fixed i, the sets $P_{ij}^{(k+1)}$ constitute the entries of the ith row of $[\bar{M}]^{k+1}$. Also, for a fixed i, the sets $\sum_{u=1}^{n} P_{iu}^{(k)} \pi_{uj}$ constitute the entries of the row matrix obtained by multiplying $[\bar{M}]_i^k$ by $[\bar{M}]$. Equation (2.42), therefore, follows.

Lemma 2.8 implies that $[\bar{M}]_i^k$ can be constructed by successive multiplication of $[\bar{M}]$ by a row matrix, rather than by a square matrix. When only paths originating at σ_i are of interest, this partial matrix construction is sufficient, since $[\bar{M}]_i^k$ conveys the same information on such paths as conveyed by the complete matrix $[\bar{M}]^k$. As a result, the construction manipulations are simplified by a factor which is roughly proportional to the number of rows in $[\bar{M}]$. The partial construction scheme is seen to be directly applicable to the construction of the $[\bar{M}']^{(k)}$ matrices, as outlined in Algorithm 2.4.

Matrices (2.44) to (2.47) illustrate the partial construction scheme in determining all proper paths of lengths 1, 2, 3, and 4, originating in state 1 of machine $A1$. $[\overline{A1}']_i^{(k)}$ denotes the ith row of the matrix $[\overline{A1}']^{(k)}$.

$$
\begin{array}{ccccc}
1 & 2 & 3 & 4 & 5
\end{array}
$$
$$[\overline{A1}']_1 = [0 \quad \pi_{12} \quad \pi_{13} \quad 0 \quad 0] \tag{2.44}$$

$$
\begin{array}{ccccc}
1 & 2 & 3 & 4 & 5
\end{array}
$$
$$[\overline{A1}']_1^{(2)} = [0 \quad \pi_{13}\pi_{32} \quad 0 \quad \pi_{13}\pi_{34} \quad 0] \tag{2.45}$$

$$
\begin{array}{ccccc}
1 & 2 & 3 & 4 & 5
\end{array}
$$
$$[\overline{A1}']_1^{(3)} = [0 \quad 0 \quad 0 \quad 0 \quad \pi_{13}\pi_{34}\pi_{45}] \tag{2.46}$$

$$
\begin{array}{ccccc}
1 & 2 & 3 & 4 & 5
\end{array}
$$
$$[\overline{A1}']_1^{(4)} = [0 \quad 0 \quad 0 \quad 0 \quad 0] \tag{2.47}$$

Lemma 2.8 can be readily shown to be valid with $[\bar{M}]$ replaced by $[\tilde{M}]$ or $[\tilde{M}']$. Partial construction, therefore, can be applied to the determination of selected rows in powers of skeleton matrices and modified skeleton matrices.

PROBLEMS

2.1. Construct the transition table, transition diagram, and transition matrix for each of the cases described in Probs. 1.2 to 1.9. In each case, consider a number of possible initial states and input sequences, and verify that the machine representations yield the output sequences expected from the corresponding verbal descriptions.

2.2. A finite-state machine is known to have the input alphabet $\{\alpha, \beta\}$, the output alphabet $\{0, 1\}$, and the state set $\{1, 2, 3\}$. Draw a transition diagram which satisfies the above specifications.

2.3. Compute the number of distinct machines satisfying each of the following sets of specifications: (a) (n, p, q) machine in which the present response depends only on the present state, and not on the present excitation. (b) (n, p, q) machine in which $n = p$, and in which every state can be passed into any of the n states by the application of a single input symbol. (c) (n, p, q) machine in which there are no isolated states. (d) (n, p, q) machine in which every symbol of the q output symbols appears at least once in the transition table (a recurrence formula for computing this number is sufficient).

2.4. Construct a machine isomorphic to that shown in Table P 2.1 by replacing the state labels 1, 2, 3, 4, 5, and 6 by the labels 2, 3, 4, 5, 6, and 1, respectively.   Without constructing the entire permutation family of the machine, show that this family is of size 6!.

TABLE P 2.1

s_ν \ x_ν	z_ν		$s_{\nu+1}$	
	α	β	α	β
1	0	0	1	1
2	0	0	2	1
3	0	1	3	2
4	0	1	4	2
5	1	0	5	3
6	1	0	6	3

2.5. Show that if b denotes the number of branches in a transition diagram representing an (n, p, q) machine, then $n \leq b \leq np$.

2.6. (a) Construct the transition table and transition matrix of the machine shown in Fig. P 2.1.   (b) Identify the transient, persistent, and isolated states in the machine.   (c) Determine $G(1), G(2), \ldots , G(8)$ of the machine.

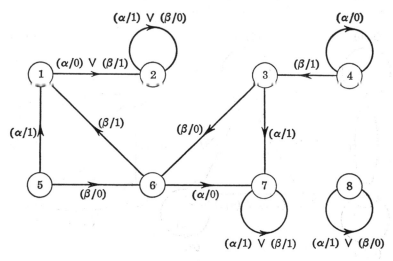

FIG. P 2.1

2.7. Let σ_i be a state in the state set S of machine M.   Let $G(\sigma_i)$ be the σ_i-reachable set, and let $G'(\sigma_i)$ consist of the elements of S not contained in $G(\sigma_i)$.   Show that: (a) If $G'(\sigma_i) \neq 0$ and $G(\sigma_i) \cap G(G'(\sigma_i)) = 0$,† then $G(\sigma_i)$ and $G'(\sigma_i)$ are two

† The set $R_1 \cap R_2$, called the *intersection* of the sets R_1 and R_2, consists of all the elements included in both R_1 and R_2. 0 denotes an empty set.

isolated submachines of M.   (b) If $G'(\sigma_i) \neq 0$ and $G(\sigma_i) \cap G(G'(\sigma_i)) \neq 0$, then $G(\sigma_i)$ and $G'(\sigma_i)$ are persistent and transient submachines, respectively.   (c) If $G'(\sigma_i) = 0$, then M contains no isolated submachines.

2.8. Table P 2.2 represents machine A.   (a) Find $G(5, 9)$ of A.   (b) Using the results of Prob. 2.7, show that $G(6)$ is an isolated submachine and that $G(2)$ is a persistent submachine.   (c) Find the maximal decomposition of A.

TABLE P 2.2

s_ν \ x_ν	z_ν		$s_{\nu+1}$	
	α	β	α	β
1	0	1	3	2
2	0	0	2	1
3	1	0	2	2
4	0	1	1	5
5	0	0	3	2
6	1	0	5	4
7	1	1	9	8
8	1	0	8	9
9	0	1	7	7

2.9. Construct the transition table for the disjunction machine composed of machines A, B, and C, shown in Fig. P 2.2.

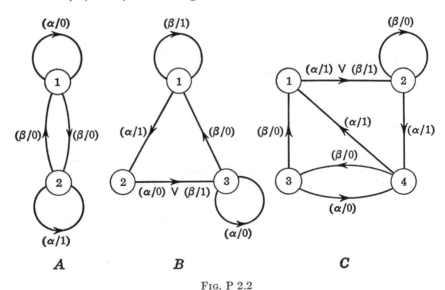

FIG. P 2.2

2.10. Let $F_k(S_i)$ be the set of all states of machine M from which any of the states in the set S_i is reachable by the application of input sequences of length k or less. (a) Formulate an algorithm for determining $F(S_i)$, the set of states from which S_i

is reachable by an input sequence of *any* length. (*b*) Apply the algorithm to machine A of Prob. 2.8, and $S_i = \{3\}$. (*c*) Show that $G(S_i) \cup F(S_i) = H(S_i)$.

2.11. Machine A is specified by the transition matrix $[A]$. (*a*) Identify the transient, persistent, and isolated states of A. (*b*) Determine $G_1(5, 7)$ and $H_1(2, 3)$. (*c*) By reordering rows and columns in $[A]$, determine whether the sets of states $\{1, 2, 4, 7\}$ and $\{3, 5, 6, 8\}$ constitute a pair of transient and persistent submachines, a pair of isolated submachines, or a pair of machines of neither type.

	1	2	3	4	5	6	7	8
1	$(\alpha/1) \vee (\beta/0)$	0	0	0	0	0	0	0
2	0	$(\alpha/0)$	0	$(\beta/1)$	0	0	0	0
3	0	0	$(\alpha/1) \vee (\beta/1)$	0	0	0	0	0
4	0	0	$(\alpha/1)$	0	$(\beta/0)$	0	0	0
5	0	0	$(\alpha/0)$	0	0	0	0	$(\beta/1)$
6	0	0	0	0	0	$(\alpha/1) \vee (\beta/0)$	0	0
7	0	0	0	0	$(\beta/0)$	0	0	$(\alpha/1)$
8	0	0	0	0	0	$(\alpha/0) \vee (\beta/1)$	0	0

$[A] = $

2.12. (*a*) Show that if $e_{ii}^{(1)}$ is the only nonzero entry in the ith row of $[\bar{M}]$, then $e_{ii}^{(k)}$ is the only nonzero entry in the ith row of $[\bar{M}]^k$ (for any integer $k \geq 1$). (*b*) Show that if $e_{jj}^{(1)}$ is the only nonzero entry in the jth column of $[\bar{M}]$, then $e_{jj}^{(k)}$ is the only nonzero entry in the jth column of $[\bar{M}]^k$ (for any integer $k \geq 1$).

2.13. Show that $[\bar{M}]^{l-k}[\bar{M}]^k = [M]^l$ for all $k < l$.

2.14. For machine A of Prob. 2.11: (*a*) Construct $[\bar{A}]$, $[\bar{A}]^2$, $[\bar{A}]^3$. (*b*) Construct $[\bar{A}']$, $[\bar{A}']^{(2)}$, . . . , $[\bar{A}']^{(7)}$. (*c*) Construct $[\bar{A}]$, $[\bar{A}]^2$, $[\bar{A}]^3$. (*d*) Construct $[\bar{A}']$, $[\bar{A}']^2$, $[\bar{A}']^3$. (*e*) Verify that A has no complete cycles.

2.15. Show that a necessary condition for a complete cycle to exist in machine M is that every row and every column in $[M]$ shall contain at least one off-diagonal nonzero entry. Prove, by example, that this condition is not sufficient.

2.16. Compute the number of different skeleton matrices and different modified skeleton matrices which describe (n, p, q) machines.

2.17. It is desired to determine whether a path exists in machine M which leads from state σ_i to state σ_k via state σ_l, and, if so, the length of the minimal path which accomplishes it. Formulate an algorithm for solving this problem.

2.18. It is desired to apply an input sequence to an n-state machine M such that, starting in state σ_1, state σ_k will be reached after $(k - 1)h$ excitations ($2 \leq k \leq n$) and state σ_n after nh excitations. Letting the (i, j) entry of $[\bar{M}']^r$ be $d_{ij}^{(r)}$, find the number of possible sequences which meet the above requirements.

2.19. The transition diagram for machine M has n states, labeled $\sigma_1, \sigma_2, \ldots, \sigma_n$, and m branches, designated by $\beta_1, \beta_2, \ldots, \beta_m$. The $n \times m$ matrix $[M_a]$, with the (i, j) entry a_{ij}, is defined by

$$a_{ij} = \begin{cases} 1 & \text{if } \beta_j \text{ is a diverging or reflecting branch of } \sigma_i \\ 0 & \text{otherwise} \end{cases}$$

The $n \times m$ matrix $[M_b]$, with the (i, j) entry b_{ij}, is defined by

$$b_{ij} = \begin{cases} 1 & \text{if } \beta_j \text{ is a converging or reflecting branch of } \sigma_i \\ 0 & \text{otherwise} \end{cases}$$

Show that $[\tilde{M}] = [M_a][M_b]_t$, where $[M_b]_t$ is the transpose of $[M_b]$.

2.20. Using the partial construction scheme described in Sec. 2.13, answer the following questions referring to the machine of Table P 2.3: (*a*) What are the shortest input sequences passing state 3 into state 1?   (b) What are the input sequences of length 4 or less which pass state 3 back to itself?   (c) Does the machine have a complete cycle?   If so, produce an input sequence which corresponds to a complete cycle starting at state 3.

TABLE P 2.3

x_ν \ s_ν	z_ν		$s_{\nu+1}$	
	α	β	α	β
1	1	0	2	3
2	1	1	4	1
3	0	1	3	2
4	0	0	1	3

EQUIVALENCE AND MACHINE MINIMIZATION

3.1. Introduction

In the preceding chapters it was emphasized that the states of a finite-state machine need not be observable or even physical quantities, and that their only function is to assist in the formulation of the input-output relationships of the machine. Consequently, any state set which fulfills this function is a satisfactory set, regardless of whether the states convey any intuitive meaning or not. This freedom inherent in the choice of a state set is quite advantageous, since it permits the replacement of one set with another set which may be considered more convenient for various purposes. More specifically, it permits one to carry out operations aiming at producing a state set which is "optimal" or "minimal" in one sense or another. In all these considerations the concept of "equivalence" plays a major role. As will become apparent in this and later chapters, this concept not only paves the way for more precise and more concise formulation of finite-state machines, but sheds new light on the entire problem of machine analysis (as well as synthesis).[1]

3.2. State Equivalence

In what follows, the notation $M|\sigma$ will be used as an abbreviation for the phrase "machine M in state σ."

DEFINITION 3.1. State σ_i of machine M_1 and state σ_j of machine M_2 are said to be *equivalent*, if $M_1|\sigma_i$ and $M_2|\sigma_j$, when excited by any input sequence, yield identical output sequences. If σ_i and σ_j are not equivalent, they are said to be *distinguishable*. M_1 and M_2 may refer to the same machine.

Thus, σ_i and σ_j are equivalent if and only if there is no way of distinguishing, by observing the external terminals, between machine M_1 at

---

[1] The material in this chapter is based in part on the work of D. A. Huffman (The Synthesis of Sequential Switching Networks, *J. Franklin Inst.*, vol. 257, pp. 161–190, 275–303, 1954), E. F. Moore (Gedanken-Experiments on Sequential Machines, "Automata Studies," pp. 129–153, Princeton University Press, Princeton, N.J., 1956), G. H. Mealy (Method for Synthesizing Sequential Circuits, *Bell System Tech. J.*, vol. 34, pp. 1054–1079, 1955), and D. D. Aufenkamp and F. E. Hohn (Analysis of Sequential Machines, *IRE Trans.*, vol. EC-6, pp. 276–285, 1957).

the initial state σ_i and machine M_2 at the initial state σ_j.† σ_i and σ_j are distinguishable if and only if there is at least one input sequence which, when applied to both $M_1|\sigma_i$ and $M_2|\sigma_j$, yields different output sequences.

Equivalence between σ_i and σ_j is indicated by $\sigma_i = \sigma_j$, and distinguishability between σ_i and σ_j is indicated by $\sigma_i \neq \sigma_j$. From Definition 3.1 it can be readily verified that state equivalence obeys the reflexive law ($\sigma_i = \sigma_i$), the symmetric law (if $\sigma_i = \sigma_j$, then $\sigma_j = \sigma_i$), and the transitive law (if $\sigma_i = \sigma_j$ and $\sigma_j = \sigma_k$, then $\sigma_i = \sigma_k$). Consequently, state equivalence can be treated as an ordinary equivalence relation and applied directly to sets of states of any size. State distinguishability, on the other hand, does not obey the reflexive and transitive laws and, hence, can be applied only to pairs of states.

In some cases equivalence or distinguishability of a pair of states belonging to the same machine can be established by inspection of the transition table of this machine. Some of these cases are described by means of the following three lemmas.

LEMMA 3.1. Let σ_i and σ_j be states of machine M. If rows σ_i and σ_j in the z_ν subtable of M are distinct, then $\sigma_i \neq \sigma_j$.

Proof. There must be at least one input symbol which, when applied to $M|\sigma_i$ and $M|\sigma_j$, yields distinct output symbols. By Definition 3.1, then, $\sigma_i \neq \sigma_j$.

LEMMA 3.2. Let σ_i and σ_j be states of machine M. If rows σ_i and σ_j, spanning the entire transition table of M, are identical, then $\sigma_i = \sigma_j$.

Proof. When any input symbol is applied to $M|\sigma_i$ and $M|\sigma_j$, the output symbols and next states are identical in the two alternatives. Once $M|\sigma_i$ and $M|\sigma_j$ pass into the same state, their responses to all subsequent excitations must coincide. By Definition 3.1, then, $\sigma_i = \sigma_j$.

LEMMA 3.3. Let σ_i and σ_j be states of machine M. If rows σ_i and σ_j, spanning the entire transition table of M, become identical when every σ_i is replaced by σ_j (or every σ_j is replaced by σ_i), then $\sigma_i = \sigma_j$.

Proof. When any input symbol is applied to $M|\sigma_i$ and $M|\sigma_j$, the output symbols are identical in the two alternatives. $M|\sigma_i$ and $M|\sigma_j$ either pass into the same state or into states σ_i and σ_j (not necessarily respectively). If the next state is the same, their responses to all subsequent excitations must coincide. If the next states are σ_i and σ_j, the original situation is restored and the above argument can be repeated to show that the next output symbols are identical in the two alternatives. By induction, then, the responses of σ_i and σ_j to any input sequence are identical, which implies that $\sigma_i = \sigma_j$.

---

† The phrases "distinguishing between $M_1|\sigma_i$ and $M_2|\sigma_j$" and "distinguishing between σ_i and σ_j" will be used interchangeably when M_1 and M_2 are understood from the context. Similarly, "the response of $M|\sigma$" and "the response of σ" will be used interchangeably when M is understood from the context.

Pairs of rows which exhibit the property cited in Lemma 3.1 are said to be *simply distinguishable*, and the states in the stub of these rows are called simply distinguishable states. Pairs of rows which exhibit the properties cited in Lemma 3.2 or 3.3 are said to be *simply equivalent*, and the states in the stub of these rows are called simply equivalent states. We thus have:

THEOREM 3.1. If σ_i and σ_j are simply distinguishable, then $\sigma_i \neq \sigma_j$. If σ_i and σ_j are simply equivalent, then $\sigma_i = \sigma_j$.

It should be pointed out that the converse of Theorem 3.1 is not true: not every distinguishable pair of states is simply distinguishable, and not

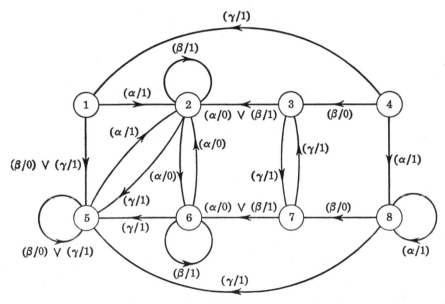

FIG. 3.1. Machine $A6$.

every equivalent pair of states is simply equivalent. Using the class definitions introduced in Sec. 2.3, it can be concluded that in a simply minimal machine all pairs of states are distinguishable and in a simply reducible machine at least one pair of states is equivalent.

To illustrate Lemmas 3.1 to 3.3, consider machine $A6$, specified by Fig. 3.1 and Table 3.1. It can be noted that rows 1 and 5 in the transition table are identical and that rows 2 and 6 become identical when every "2" is replaced by "6" (or every "6" is replaced by "2"). Consequently, each of the state pairs $\{1, 5\}$ and $\{2, 6\}$ is equivalent. A glance at the z_ν subtable of $A6$ reveals that no state in the set $\{1, 4, 5, 8\}$ can be equivalent to any state in the set $\{2, 3, 6, 7\}$.

TABLE 3.1. MACHINE $A6$

s_ν \ x_ν	z_ν			$s_{\nu+1}$		
	α	β	γ	α	β	γ
1	1	0	1	2	5	5
2	0	1	1	6	2	5
3	0	1	1	2	2	7
4	1	0	1	8	3	1
5	1	0	1	2	5	5
6	0	1	1	2	6	5
7	0	1	1	6	6	3
8	1	0	1	8	7	5

3.3. k-equivalence

A notion which will be found useful in further discussions is that of "k-equivalence":

DEFINITION 3.2.   State σ_i of machine M_1 and state σ_j of machine M_2 are said to be k-*equivalent*, if $M_1|\sigma_i$ and $M_2|\sigma_j$, when excited by an input sequence of length k, yield identical output sequences.   If σ_i and σ_j are not k-equivalent, they are said to be k-*distinguishable*. M_1 and M_2 may refer to the same machine.

Thus, σ_i and σ_j are k-equivalent if and only if there is no way of distinguishing, by using input sequences of length k and by observing the external terminals, between machine M_1 at state σ_i and machine M_2 at state σ_j. σ_i and σ_j are k-distinguishable if and only if there is at least one input sequence of length k which, when applied to both $M_1|\sigma_i$ and $M_2|\sigma_j$, yields different output sequences.   Two states which are 1-distinguishable are seen to be simply distinguishable, as defined in Sec. 3.2.

From Definition 3.2 it can be readily verified that k-equivalence obeys the reflexive, symmetric, and transitive laws.   Consequently, k-equivalence can be treated as ordinary equivalence relation and applied directly to sets of states of any size. k-distinguishability, on the other hand, does not obey the reflexive and transitive laws, and hence can be applied only to pairs of states.

LEMMA 3.4.   (a) If two states are k-equivalent, then they are l-equivalent for every $l \leq k$.   (b) If two states are k-distinguishable, then they are l-distinguishable for every $l \geq k$.

Proof.   (a) Suppose σ_i and σ_j are k-equivalent but distinguishable by some input sequence, say $\mathcal{E}_l$, of length $l \leq k$.   Then σ_i and σ_j must be distinguishable by the input sequence $\mathcal{E}_l\mathcal{E}_{k-l}$, where $\mathcal{E}_{k-l}$ is any input sequence of length $k - l$.   Hence, σ_i and σ_j are k-distinguishable, which

is a contradiction.   (*b*) Suppose σ_i and σ_j are k-distinguishable but
l-equivalent for some $l \geq k$.   By part *a*, however, if σ_i and σ_j are l-equiva-
lent, they must be k-equivalent for every $k \leq l$.   By contradiction, then,
part *b* follows.

The state into which state σ_i passes when an input sequence of length
k is applied is called the *kth successor* of σ_i with respect to this sequence.
The zeroth successor of a state is the state itself.

THEOREM 3.2.   If states σ_i and σ_j are k-equivalent, and if their kth
successors with respect to any input sequence of length k are equivalent,
then $\sigma_i = \sigma_j$.

Proof.   If σ_i and σ_j are k-equivalent, then, by Lemma 3.4, they yield
identical responses to all input sequences of length k or less.   If their kth

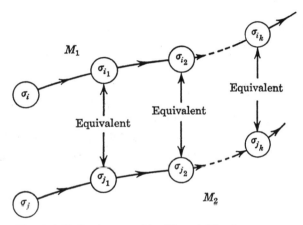

FIG. 3.2. Paths traversed in M_1 and M_2 when $\sigma_i = \sigma_j$.

successors, with respect to any input sequence of length k, are equivalent,
then they yield identical responses to all input sequences which follow the
first k symbols.   Hence, σ_i and σ_j yield identical responses to input
sequences of *any* length, which implies that $\sigma_i = \sigma_j$.

THEOREM 3.3.   If states σ_i and σ_j are equivalent, then their kth successors, with respect to any input sequence of length k and for any k, are
equivalent.

Proof.   Let σ_i' and σ_j' denote the kth successors of σ_i and σ_j, respectively,
with respect to an arbitrary input sequence $\mathcal{E}_k$.   If $\sigma_i' \neq \sigma_j'$, then there is a
sequence, say $\mathcal{E}_l$, for which σ_i' and σ_j' yield different responses.   Hence, the
responses of σ_i and σ_j to $\mathcal{E}_k\mathcal{E}_l$ must be different, which contradicts the
assumption that $\sigma_i = \sigma_j$.

An input sequence applied to both $M_1|\sigma_i$ and $M_2|\sigma_j$ may be associated
with a pair of paths originating in states σ_i and σ_j in the transition dia-

grams of M_1 and M_2, respectively. Theorem 3.3 implies that if the pair of initial states in these paths is equivalent, then every pair of corresponding states in the paths (i.e., states reached from the initial states after the traversal of the same number of branches) is also equivalent. This situation is illustrated in Fig. 3.2, where the shown paths are the paths traversed in M_1 and M_2 when a certain input sequence is applied to $M_1|\sigma_i$ and $M_2|\sigma_j$. If σ_i and σ_j are equivalent, then the kth successors σ_{i_k} and σ_{j_k} must be equivalent for all k.

The preceding results can be used, in many cases, to establish equivalence of states when the equivalence of other states is already established. Suppose, for example, that the pairs of states $\{1, 5\}$ and $\{3, 7\}$ in machine $A6$ of Fig. 3.1 are known to be equivalent. Consequently, the pair $\{4, 8\}$ must also be equivalent, since 4 and 8 are 1-equivalent, with the pairs $\{1, 5\}$ and $\{3, 7\}$ being their first successors. If the pair $\{4, 8\}$ is known to be equivalent, then the pairs $\{1, 5\}$, $\{2, 6\}$, and $\{3, 7\}$ must also be equivalent, since they constitute pairs of corresponding states in paths originating in states 4 and 8.

3.4. k-equivalence Partitions

For purposes which will become apparent in later sections, it is of interest to divide, or "partition," the states of a machine into classes according to the following criteria: (1) All states which belong to the same class must be k-equivalent. (2) All states which belong to different classes must be k-distinguishable. This partition is called the *k-equivalence partition* of the machine and is denoted by P_k. The classes of P_k are called *k-equivalence classes* and are denoted by Σ_{k1}, Σ_{k2}, Σ_{k3}, etc. States belonging to the same class are called *adjoint states;* states belonging to different classes are called *disjoint states.*

Figure 3.3 and Table 3.2 represent machine $A7$. For this machine, the 2-equivalence partition is given by

$$P_2: \quad \begin{aligned} \Sigma_{21} &= \{1, 3, 5, 7, 8\} \\ \Sigma_{22} &= \{2, 4, 6\} \\ \Sigma_{23} &= \{9\} \end{aligned} \qquad (3.1)$$

As can be readily verified through the transition diagram of $A7$, adjoint states in P_2, as given by (3.1), are 2-equivalent, and disjoint states are 2-distinguishable. No state in $A7$ is 2-equivalent to state 9 (except state 9 itself), and hence 9 constitutes a single-state class, or a *singleton.*

Clearly, no state can belong to two different k-equivalence classes simultaneously, since this would imply that the state is k-distinguishable with respect to itself. Hence, the total number of states in P_k equals the total number of states in the machine.

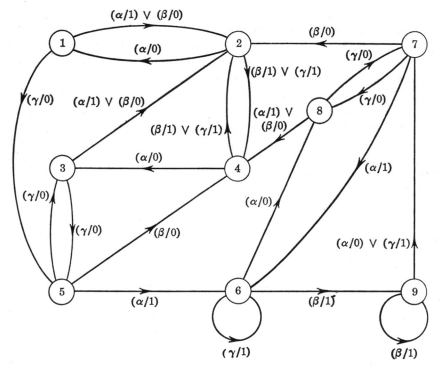

FIG. 3.3. Machine $A7$.

TABLE 3.2. MACHINE $A7$

s_ν \ x_ν	z_ν			$s_{\nu+1}$		
	α	β	γ	α	β	γ
1	1	0	0	2	2	5
2	0	1	1	1	4	4
3	1	0	0	2	2	5
4	0	1	1	3	2	2
5	1	0	0	6	4	3
6	0	1	1	8	9	6
7	1	0	0	6	2	8
8	1	0	0	4	4	7
9	0	1	1	7	9	7

LEMMA 3.5.   The k-equivalence partition of a machine is unique.

Proof.   Suppose P_k, consisting of $\Sigma_{k1}, \Sigma_{k2}, \ldots, \Sigma_{ku}$, is not unique. Then, there must be another k-equivalence partition, say P'_k, consisting of $\Sigma'_{k1}, \Sigma'_{k2}, \ldots, \Sigma'_{kv}$, for the same machine.   Let $\Sigma_{kr} = \{\sigma_{r_1}, \sigma_{r_2}, \ldots, \sigma_{r_d}\}$. Since the states of Σ_{kr} are k-equivalent, and since there is no state outside Σ_{kr} which is equivalent to any state in Σ_{kr}, there must be a class in P'_k, say Σ'_{ks}, which consists of the states $\sigma_{r_1}, \sigma_{r_2}, \ldots, \sigma_{r_d}$ and no other states. Applying this argument to $r = 1, 2, \ldots, u$, it follows that to every class in P_k there corresponds an identical class in P'_k.   Since the total number of states in P'_k must be the same as that in P_k, P_k and P'_k must be identical, and hence P_k is unique.

LEMMA 3.6.   States which are disjoint in P_k must also be disjoint in P_{k+1}.

Proof.   From Lemma 3.4, if two states are k-distinguishable, they must also be $(k + 1)$-distinguishable.   The present lemma, then, follows immediately from the definition of P_k and P_{k+1}.

As an example, P_3 of machine $A7$ cannot contain classes such as $\{1, 3, 6\}$ or $\{2, 5, 9\}$, since these classes, as can be deduced from (3.1), contain states which are disjoint in P_2.

LEMMA 3.7.   If machine M contains two distinguishable states which are k-equivalent, then it must also contain two states which are k-equivalent but $(k + 1)$-distinguishable.

Proof.   Let σ_i and σ_j be the distinguishable states of M which are k-equivalent, and let the input sequence $\xi_{h_1}\xi_{h_2} \cdots \xi_{h_l}$ be the shortest input sequence which distinguishes between σ_i and σ_j. σ_i and σ_j, then, yield distinct output symbols when ξ_{h_l} is applied, but not before.   Since σ_i and σ_j are k-equivalent, we must have $l > k$.   Let the $(l$-k-$1)$st successors of σ_i and σ_j with respect to $\xi_{h_1}\xi_{h_2} \cdots \xi_{h_{l-k-1}}$ be σ'_i and σ'_j, respectively; since $l > k$, l-k-$1 \geq 0$ and these successors always exist. σ'_i and σ'_j, then, can be distinguished by the input sequence $\xi_{h_{l-k}}\xi_{h_{l-k+1}} \cdots \xi_{h_l}$ whose length is l-$(l$-k-$1) = k + 1$.   They cannot be distinguished by any shorter sequence, since this would contradict the assumption that σ_i and σ_j are k-equivalent.   Hence, σ'_i and σ'_j are k-equivalent but $(k + 1)$-distinguishable, which proves the theorem.   The above situation is illustrated in Fig. 3.4.

Suppose now that the adjoint states in each equivalence class of P_k are equivalent.   Then, clearly, P_{k+u} is identical with P_k for all nonnegative integers u.   If two adjoint states in P_k are distinguishable, then they constitute two distinguishable states which are k-equivalent.   In this case, by Lemma 3.7, the machine must contain two states which are k-equivalent but $(k + 1)$-distinguishable.   Hence, P_k must contain two adjoint states which become disjoint in P_{k+1}.   Thus, if the adjoint states in any class of P_k are distinguishable, P_{k+1} must differ from P_k.   By

Lemma 3.6, if P_{k+1} differs from P_k, it must be a "proper refinement" of P_k, that is, it must be obtainable by splitting one or more classes of P_k into two or more subclasses.   In conclusion, the following can be stated:

THEOREM 3.4. P_{k+1} must be a proper refinement of P_k, unless the adjoint states in every class of P_k are equivalent, in which case P_k and P_{k+1} are identical.

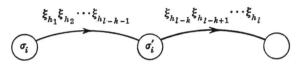

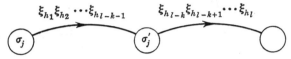

FIG. 3.4. Illustration for Lemma 3.7.

For machine $A7$, for example, we have

$$P_3: \quad \begin{aligned} \Sigma_{31} &= \{1, 3, 5, 7, 8\} \\ \Sigma_{32} &= \{2, 4\} \\ \Sigma_{33} &= \{6\} \\ \Sigma_{34} &= \{9\} \end{aligned} \qquad (3.2)$$

which is a proper refinement of P_2, and

$$P_4: \quad \begin{aligned} \Sigma_{41} &= \{1, 3, 8\} \\ \Sigma_{42} &= \{2, 4\} \\ \Sigma_{43} &= \{5, 7\} \\ \Sigma_{44} &= \{6\} \\ \Sigma_{45} &= \{9\} \end{aligned} \qquad (3.3)$$

which is a proper refinement of P_3.   However,

$$P_5: \quad \begin{aligned} \Sigma_{51} &= \{1, 3, 8\} \\ \Sigma_{52} &= \{2, 4\} \\ \Sigma_{53} &= \{5, 7\} \\ \Sigma_{54} &= \{6\} \\ \Sigma_{55} &= \{9\} \end{aligned} \qquad (3.4)$$

is seen to be identical to P_4, and hence the adjoint states in every class of P_4 are equivalent.

3.5. Equivalence Partitions

A k-equivalence partition for machine M is called an *equivalence partition* of M, and denoted by $\hat{P}$, if the adjoint states in every class of this partition are equivalent. Under these conditions, each class in the partition is called an *equivalence class*. From the discussion in Sec. 3.4 it follows that $\hat{P}$ is the most refined P_k partition. By Theorem 3.4, $\hat{P}$ can be obtained by constructing P_k for $k = 1, 2, 3, \ldots$, until, for the first time, a partition is produced which is identical to the one previously produced; this partition is $\hat{P}$. Let $P_i = P_j$ signify the fact that P_i and P_j are identical partitions, and let $|P_i|$ denote the number of classes in P_i. Using this notation, the preceding results can be summarized as follows:

$$|P_k| \leq |P_{k+1}| \tag{3.5}$$

If $|P_k| = |P_{k+1}|$, then

$$P_k = P_{k+u} = \hat{P} \qquad u = 0, 1, 2, \ldots \tag{3.6}$$

If all the states in a given n-state machine are 1-equivalent, P_1 consists of a single class containing n states. Clearly, if all n states are 1-equivalent, their first successors, with respect to any input sequence, are also 1-equivalent. Consequently, all n states must be 2-equivalent, and hence $P_1 = P_2$. By (3.6), then, $P_1 = \hat{P}$, and all n states are equivalent. For a machine of this type, $f_z(x_\nu, s_\nu)$ is the same for all s_ν, and hence $f_z(x_\nu, s_\nu) = f_z(x_\nu)$. From the definition introduced in Sec. 1.6, then, it can be stated that a machine in which all states are equivalent is a trivial machine. Unless otherwise specified, further discussion will be confined to nontrivial machines only, i.e., to machines in which there is at least one distinguishable pair of states, or in whose 1-equivalence partition there are at least two classes.

LEMMA 3.8. If $P_k \neq P_{k-1}$, then

$$|P_k| \geq k + 1 \tag{3.7}$$

Proof. If $P_k \neq P_{k-1}$, then, by (3.5) and (3.6), $|P_r| > |P_{r-1}|$ for $r = 1, 2, \ldots, k$. Since $|P_1| \geq 2$, (3.7) follows by induction.

LEMMA 3.9. If for an n-state machine $P_k \neq P_{k-1}$, then the number of states in each class of P_k is at most $n - k$.

Proof. By Lemma 3.8, the number of classes in P_k is at least $k + 1$. Suppose one class contains more than $n - k$, say $n - k + 1$ states. Then, since every other class in P_k must contain at least one state, the total number of states in P_k is at least $k + (n - k + 1) = n + 1$. Since the total number of states cannot exceed n, the lemma follows by contradiction.

LEMMA 3.10. In an n-state machine, $P_n = P_{n-1}$.

Proof. If $P_n \neq P_{n-1}$, then, by Lemma 3.8, $|P_n| \geq n + 1$. Since the number of classes in a k-equivalence partition of an n-state machine cannot exceed n, the lemma follows by contradiction.

From Lemma 3.10 and Eq. (3.6), the following can be concluded:

THEOREM 3.5. In an n-state machine,

$$P_{n-1} = \hat{P} \tag{3.8}$$

Thus, in the process of determining $\hat{P}$ for an n-state machine, by successively constructing P_k for $k = 1, 2, 3, \ldots$, at most $n - 1$ such constructions are needed. An alternative formulation of Theorem 3.5 is the following:

COROLLARY 3.1. Two states in an n-state machine are equivalent if they are $(n - 1)$-equivalent and distinguishable if they are $(n - 1)$-distinguishable.

Determination of P_1. P_1 can be determined through the following rule: States are adjoint in P_1 if and only if, for every input symbol, they yield identical output symbols.

Determination of P_{k+1} *from* $P_k(k \geq 1)$. A pair of adjoint states in P_k which, for every input symbol, pass into adjoint states in P_k represent k-equivalent states whose first successors, with respect to every input symbol, are k-equivalent. Such adjoint states, then, are $(k + 1)$-equivalent and must be adjoint in P_{k+1}. A pair of adjoint states in P_k which, for some input symbol, pass into disjoint states in P_k represent k-equivalent states whose first successors, with respect to some input symbol, are k-distinguishable. Such adjoint states, then, are $(k + 1)$-distinguishable and must be disjoint in P_{k+1}. A pair of disjoint states in P_k must be disjoint in P_{k+1}. Thus, P_{k+1} can be determined from P_k by dividing the states of every class in P_k into subclasses, such that two states are in the same subclass if and only if their first successors, with respect to every input symbol, are adjoint states in P_k. The resulting subclasses are the classes of P_{k+1}. Since singletons cannot be divided into subclasses, singletons which appear in P_k can be automatically assigned as singletons to P_{k+1}.

Consider, for example, P_3 of machine $A7$, as given in (3.2). The first successors of states 1, 3, and 8 are adjoint in Σ_{32} when α or β is applied and in Σ_{31} when γ is applied. The first successors of states 5 and 7 are adjoint in Σ_{33} when α is applied, in Σ_{32} when β is applied, and in Σ_{31} when γ is applied. Consequently, $\{1, 3, 8\}$ and $\{5, 7\}$ are classes of P_4. The first successors of states 2 and 4, with respect to every input symbol, are adjoint states in P_3; $\{2, 4\}$, therefore, is a class in P_4. The singletons $\{6\}$ and $\{9\}$ appear as singletons in P_4. The resulting partition P_4, then, is as shown in (3.3).

We have thus outlined the criteria for the successive construction of P_k, for $k = 1, 2, 3, \ldots$. When, for every input symbol, every pair of adjoint states in P_k passes into adjoint states in P_k, no further refinement of P_k is possible, and hence $P_k = \hat{P}$. The outlined criteria, then, lead to the determination of the equivalence partition of the given machine.

3.6. Partitioning by P_k Tables

In any but the simplest cases, the process of determining the equivalence partition of a given machine by inspection of the transition table, diagram, or matrix is virtually impossible. In this section we shall describe a method by which the partitioning can be carried out systematically, by constructing a series of so-called P_k *tables*.

TABLE 3.3. P_1 TABLE FOR $A7$

Σ	$\begin{array}{c}x_\nu\\ s_\nu\end{array}$	α	β	γ
			$s_{\nu+1}$	
a	1	2_b	2_b	5_a
	3	2_b	2_b	5_a
	5	6_b	4_b	3_a
	7	6_b	2_b	8_a
	8	4_b	4_b	7_a
b	2	1_a	4_b	4_b
	4	3_a	2_b	2_b
	6	8_a	9_b	6_b
	9	7_a	9_b	7_a

TABLE 3.4. P_2 TABLE FOR $A7$

Σ	$\begin{array}{c}x_\nu\\ s_\nu\end{array}$	α	β	γ
			$s_{\nu+1}$	
a	1	2_b	2_b	5_a
	3	2_b	2_b	5_a
	5	6_b	4_b	3_a
	7	6_b	2_b	8_a
	8	4_b	4_b	7_a
b	2	1_a	4_b	4_b
	4	3_a	2_b	2_b
	6	8_a	9_c	6_b
c	9	7_a	9_c	7_a

The P_k table of a given machine is essentially the same as the $s_{\nu+1}$ subtable for that machine, with the following modifications: (1) If $\{\sigma_{i_1}, \sigma_{i_2}, \ldots, \sigma_{i_r}\}$ is a class in P_k, rows $\sigma_{i_1}, \sigma_{i_2}, \ldots, \sigma_{i_r}$ are grouped together, each group separated from the adjacent ones by a rule. The order of the groups in the table and the order of the rows within each group are arbitrary. Rows which belong to the same group, and hence represent a k-equivalence class, will be called *adjoint rows;* rows which belong to different groups will be called *disjoint* rows. (2) A "Σ" column is added, which labels each group of rows in the P_k table. The labels are arbitrary and may be chosen independently in each new P_k table. (3) A subscript is attached to every $s_{\nu+1}$ entry, which identifies the group in the P_k table to which the entry belongs. Thus, if row σ_i is in the group labeled "a," then every $s_{\nu+1}$ entry "σ_i" is assigned the subscript "a."

Tables 3.3 to 3.6 are the P_1, P_2, P_3, and P_4 tables for machine $A7$ of Fig. 3.3.

Construction of the P_1 Table. Reorder the rows of the transition table so that rows which are identical in the z_ν subtable become adjacent. Each group of such rows corresponds to a 1-equivalence class, and hence to a group of adjoint rows in the P_1 table. The P_1 table can now be constructed by deleting the z_ν subtable, separating the row groups by rules, adding a "Σ" column, and subscripting the $s_{\nu+1}$ entries as described above. For an illustration, refer to Tables 3.2 and 3.3.

TABLE 3.5. P_3 TABLE FOR A7

| Σ | x_ν / s_ν | $s_{\nu+1}$ | | |
		α	β	γ
a	1	2_b	2_b	5_a
	3	2_b	2_b	5_a
	5	6_c	4_b	3_a
	7	6_c	2_b	8_a
	8	4_b	4_b	7_a
b	2	1_a	4_b	4_b
	4	3_a	2_b	2_b
c	6	8_a	9_d	6_c
d	9	7_a	9_d	7_a

TABLE 3.6. P_4 TABLE FOR A7

| Σ | x_ν / s_ν | $s_{\nu+1}$ | | |
		α	β	γ
a	1	2_b	2_b	5_c
	3	2_b	2_b	5_c
	8	4_b	4_b	7_c
b	2	1_a	4_b	4_b
	4	3_a	2_b	2_b
c	5	6_d	4_b	3_a
	7	6_d	2_b	8_a
d	6	8_a	9_e	6_d
e	9	7_c	9_e	7_c

Construction of the P_{k+1} Table from the P_k Table ($k \geq 1$). A pair of adjoint rows in the P_k table which, in every column, exhibit identical subscripts are adjoint rows in the P_{k+1} table. A pair of adjoint rows in the P_k table which, in some column, exhibit different subscripts are disjoint rows in the P_{k+1} table. Disjoint rows in the P_k table are also disjoint in the P_{k+1} table. A group in the P_k table consisting of a single row remains a single-row group in the P_{k+1} table. Thus, the groups of the P_{k+1} table can be established by inspection of the subscripts in the P_k table. Once the groups are established, the table itself can be constructed according to the format stipulated above. The justification for the foregoing rules follows directly from the manner in which the subscripts are assigned and from the criteria for determining P_{k+1} from P_k, as outlined in Sec. 3.5.

As an example, consider the P_3 table for $A7$, shown in Table 3.5. In group "a," rows 1, 3, and 8 have identical subscripts in every column, and so do rows 5 and 7 (whose subscripts differ from those of 1, 3, and 8).

Consequently, rows 1, 3, and 8 and rows 5 and 7 constitute two groups of rows in the P_4 table. In group "b" all rows exhibit identical subscripts in every column, and hence the group remains intact in the P_4 table. Groups "c" and "d," consisting of one row each, can be transferred intact to the P_4 table.

Given a procedure for constructing the P_1 table, and the P_{k+1} table from the P_k table ($k \geq 1$), one can construct the P_k table for successive values of k, until a table is obtained in which all adjoint rows exhibit identical subscripts in every column. The stub entries of these adjoint rows represent equivalent states, and hence the groups of stub entries in this table represent the desired equivalence classes. By Theorem 3.5, this condition must occur for some value of $k \leq n - 1$. For machine $A7$ the condition is exhibited by the P_4 table in Table 3.6. The equivalence partition for $A7$ is, therefore, given by

$$P: \quad \{1, 3, 8\}, \{2, 4\}, \{5, 7\}, \{6\}, \{9\} \qquad (3.9)$$

3.7. Partitioning by Pairs Table

Another way of determining the equivalence partition of a machine is via the so-called *pairs table*. The partitioning is carried out by successive modifications of this table, resulting in a series of tables, the kth table of which is called the *kth version* of the pairs table. In the original table, or the first version of the pairs table, the stub, called the *pairs column*, consists of all unordered pairs of 1-equivalent states $\{\sigma_i, \sigma_j\}$, where $i \neq j$. In addition, the table contains a column for every symbol ξ_h in the input alphabet. The entry common to row $\{\sigma_i, \sigma_j\}$ and column ξ_h comprises the first successors of σ_i and σ_j with respect to ξ_h. The order of pairs in the pairs column and the order in which the states are written in any table entry are arbitrary. The pairs table can be constructed directly from the transition table, where 1-equivalent states are states which exhibit identical rows in the z_ν subtable. Table 3.7 shows the first version of the pairs table for machine $A7$ of Fig. 3.3.

In what follows, a *distinct pair* will refer to an entry in which the two states are not identical and a *circled row* to a row whose stub entry is circled.

Construction of the $(k + 1)$st Version of the Pairs Table from the kth Version ($k \geq 1$). Scan every uncircled row in the kth version, and circle a row if it contains a distinct pair which either is absent from the pairs column or is circled in the pairs column. The table obtained after the last uncircled row is scanned is the $(k + 1)$st version of the pairs table.

LEMMA 3.11. The uncircled stub entries in the kth version of the pairs table for machine M constitute all k-equivalent pairs of states in M.

Proof. For $k = 1$, the lemma is true by construction. Suppose it is true for k. Then an uncircled stub entry is a pair of k-equivalent states. These states are $(k + 1)$-distinguishable only if their first successors, with respect to at least one input symbol, are k-distinguishable. Since such successors are either circled stub entries or distinct pairs missing from the stub (such pairs are 1-distinguishable and hence k-distinguishable), pairs of states circled in the process of constructing the $(k + 1)$st version from the kth version must be $(k + 1)$-distinguishable; stub entries which remain uncircled must be $(k + 1)$-equivalent. Since the uncircled stub entries in the kth version constitute all the k-equivalent pairs of states in M, the uncircled stub entries in the $(k + 1)$st version must constitute all the $(k + 1)$-equivalent pairs in M. By induction, then, the lemma is valid for all $k \geq 1$.

If the kth version is the last version of the pairs table (i.e., the version in which all stub entries are circled, or in which no additional circling can be carried out), the uncircled stub entries in the kth version constitute all k-equivalent pairs, where k can be made arbitrarily large. These entries, therefore constitute all equivalent pairs of states in the given machine. By Theorem 3.5, this must occur for some value of $k \leq n - 1$. The equivalence classes can be compiled from the equivalent pairs by exploiting the fact that if $\{\sigma_{i_1}, \sigma_{i_2}, \ldots, \sigma_{i_r}\}$ is an equivalence class, then $\{\sigma_{i_1}, \sigma_{i_2}\}, \{\sigma_{i_2}, \sigma_{i_3}\}, \ldots, \{\sigma_{i_{r-1}}, \sigma_{i_r}\}$ are equivalent pairs. Specifically, the compilation can be organized as follows:

ALGORITHM 3.1. Given the set of all equivalent pairs of states of machine M, $\{\sigma_{i_1}, \sigma_{j_1}\}, \{\sigma_{i_2}, \sigma_{j_2}\}, \ldots, \{\sigma_{i_l}, \sigma_{j_l}\}$, to find the equivalence partition of M: (1) Let $k = 1$ and $d = 1$. (2) Initiate the dth equivalence class by assigning the pair $\{\sigma_{i_k}, \sigma_{j_k}\}$ to it. (3) (a) If $k < l$, increment k by 1 and proceed to (4). (b) If $k = l$, the d equivalence classes and the singletons comprising the states not included in any of the d classes constitute the equivalence partition of M. (4) (a) If both states in $\{\sigma_{i_k}, \sigma_{j_k}\}$ are included in any previously initiated class, return to (3). (b) If exactly one of the states $\{\sigma_{i_k}, \sigma_{j_k}\}$ is included in any previously initiated class, add the remaining state to this class and return to (3). (c) If no state in $\{\sigma_{i_k}, \sigma_{j_k}\}$ is included in any previously initiated class, increment d by 1 and return to (2).

Tables 3.7 to 3.10 illustrate the construction of the first to fourth versions of the pairs table for machine $A7$. The entire construction, of course, can be carried out on the original table, and the tables are repeated here only to illustrate the successive steps involved in the procedure. Table 3.10 shows the pairs table in its final form, with the equivalence pairs $\{1, 3\}$, $\{1, 8\}$, $\{2, 4\}$, $\{3, 8\}$, and $\{5, 7\}$ exhibited by the uncircled stub entries. Employing Algorithm 3.1 yields the equivalence partition $\{1, 3, 8\}$, $\{2, 4\}$, $\{5, 7\}$, $\{6\}$, and $\{9\}$, as given in (3.9).

The pairs-table method of partitioning, as compared with the P_k table

TABLE 3.7. PAIRS TABLE FOR $A7$
(FIRST VERSION)

Pairs	α	β	γ
1, 3	2, 2	2, 2	5, 5
1, 5	2, 6	2, 4	3, 5
1, 7	2, 6	2, 2	5, 8
1, 8	2, 4	2, 4	5, 7
2, 4	1, 3	2, 4	2, 4
2, 6	1, 8	4, 9	4, 6
2, 9	1, 7	4, 9	4, 7
3, 5	2, 6	2, 4	3, 5
3, 7	2, 6	2, 2	5, 8
3, 8	2, 4	2, 4	5, 7
4, 6	3, 8	2, 9	2, 6
4, 9	3, 7	2, 9	2, 7
5, 7	6, 6	2, 4	3, 8
5, 8	4, 6	4, 4	3, 7
6, 9	7, 8	9, 9	6, 7
7, 8	4, 6	2, 4	7, 8

TABLE 3.8. PAIRS TABLE FOR $A7$
(SECOND VERSION)

Pairs	α	β	γ
1, 3	2, 2	2, 2	5, 5
1, 5	2, 6	2, 4	3, 5
1, 7	2, 6	2, 2	5, 8
1, 8	2, 4	2, 4	5, 7
2, 4	1, 3	2, 4	2, 4
2, 6	1, 8	4, 9	4, 6
(2, 9)	1, 7	4, 9	4, 7
3, 5	2, 6	2, 4	3, 5
3, 7	2, 6	2, 2	5, 8
3, 8	2, 4	2, 4	5, 7
4, 6	3, 8	2, 9	2, 6
(4, 9)	3, 7	2, 9	2, 7
5, 7	6, 6	2, 4	3, 8
5, 8	4, 6	4, 4	3, 7
(6, 9)	7, 8	9, 9	6, 7
7, 8	4, 6	2, 4	7, 8

TABLE 3.9. PAIRS TABLE FOR $A7$
(THIRD VERSION)

Pairs	α	β	γ
1, 3	2, 2	2, 2	5, 5
1, 5	2, 6	2, 4	3, 5
1, 7	2, 6	2, 2	5, 8
1, 8	2, 4	2, 4	5, 7
2, 4	1, 3	2, 4	2, 4
(2, 6)	1, 8	4, 9	4, 6
(2, 9)	1, 7	4, 9	4, 7
3, 5	2, 6	2, 4	3, 5
3, 7	2, 6	2, 2	5, 8
3, 8	2, 4	2, 4	5, 7
(4, 6)	3, 8	2, 9	2, 6
(4, 9)	3, 7	2, 9	2, 7
5, 7	6, 6	2, 4	3, 8
5, 8	4, 6	4, 4	3, 7
(6, 9)	7, 8	9, 9	6, 7
7, 8	4, 6	2, 4	7, 8

TABLE 3.10. PAIRS TABLE FOR $A7$
(FOURTH VERSION)

Pairs	α	β	γ
1, 3	2, 2	2, 2	5, 5
(1, 5)	2, 6	2, 4	3, 5
(1, 7)	2, 6	2, 2	5, 8
1, 8	2, 4	2, 4	5, 7
2, 4	1, 3	2, 4	2, 4
(2, 6)	1, 8	4, 9	4, 6
(2, 9)	1, 7	4, 9	4, 7
(3, 5)	2, 6	2, 4	3, 5
(3, 7)	2, 6	2, 2	5, 8
3, 8	2, 4	2, 4	5, 7
(4, 6)	3, 8	2, 9	2, 6
(4, 9)	3, 7	2, 9	2, 7
5, 7	6, 6	2, 4	3, 8
(5, 8)	4, 6	4, 4	3, 7
(6, 9)	7, 8	9, 9	6, 7
(7, 8)	4, 6	2, 4	7, 8

method described in Sec. 3.6, has the advantage that only one table needs to be constructed; for an n-state machine, the P_k-table method may require as many as $n - 1$ different tables. On the other hand, each P_k table is often much smaller than the corresponding pairs table and has the additional advantage of displaying the k-equivalence partitions for every k, which is useful in many problems.

3.8. Matrix Method of Partitioning

The partitioning method to be presented in this section is essentially the same as the one described in Sec. 3.6, except that the operations are conducted on the transition matrix instead of the s_{r+1} subtable. Although the matrix-partitioning method has no advantages over methods previously described, it offers a new and useful interpretation to the notion of equivalence classes.

A *symmetrical permutation* of a matrix refers to the process of reordering both the rows and columns of the matrix according to the same rule. Thus, if the labels attached to the rows and columns of $[M]$ are symmetrical about the principal diagonal, so are the labels attached to any symmetrical permutation of $[M]$. A *symmetrical partitioning* of $[M]$ is a process of separating groups of rows and columns by dashed lines, such that if there is a dashed line separating rows σ_i and σ_j, there is also a dashed line separating columns σ_i and σ_j, and conversely.

Matrix $[M]^{(k)}$ for machine M is the matrix $[M]$ where symmetrical permutation and symmetrical partitioning have been carried out to yield the following properties: Rows (and columns) which correspond to adjoint states in P_k are grouped together, each group separated from the adjacent ones by dashed lines. The order of the groups in the matrix and the order of the rows (and columns) in each group are arbitrary. If P_k contains r_k classes, the symmetrical partitioning produces r_k rows of submatrices, with r_k submatrices per row.

Construction of $[M]^{(1)}$. Group the rows of $[M]$ such that two rows belong to the same group if and only if they exhibit identical sets of input-output pairs. Each such group represents a 1-equivalence class. Performing symmetrical permutation and symmetrical partitioning on $[M]$ according to the format stipulated above results in $[M]^{(1)}$. As an example, (3.10) is the transition matrix of machine $A7$ of Fig. 3.3. Rows 1, 3, 5, 7, and 8 in $[A7]$ exhibit the input-output pairs $(\alpha/1)$, $(\beta/0)$, and $(\gamma/0)$; rows 2, 4, 6, and 9 exhibit the input-output pairs $(\alpha/0)$, $(\beta/1)$, and $(\gamma/1)$. $[A7]^{(1)}$, then, is constructed by grouping rows (and columns) 1, 3, 5, 7, and 8 together, and rows (and columns) 2, 4, 6, and 9 together, and separating the groups by a dashed line. The resulting matrix $[A7]^{(1)}$ is shown in (3.11).

Construction of $[M]^{(k+1)}$ *from* $[M]^{(k)}$ $(k \geq 1)$. Let σ_i and σ_j be two rows in the same group of rows of $[M]^{(k)}$. If in each of the r_k submatrices intersected by rows σ_i and σ_j, rows σ_i and σ_j have identical sets of input-output pairs, σ_i and σ_j represent k-equivalent states whose first successors, with respect to any input symbol, are k-equivalent; σ_i and σ_j, therefore, are $(k + 1)$-equivalent. If this condition does not hold, σ_i and σ_j are $(k + 1)$-distinguishable. Thus, $[M]^{(k+1)}$ can be constructed from $[M]^{(k)}$ by dividing each group of rows in $[M]^{(k)}$ into subgroups, such that two rows belong to the same subgroup if and only if they have identical sets of input-output pairs in each of the r_k submatrices they intersect. Each such group represents a $(k + 1)$-equivalence class. Performing symmetrical permutation and symmetrical partitioning on $[M]^{(k)}$ to yield the required format results in $[M]^{(k+1)}$. As an example, rows 1, 3, 5, 7, and 8 in $[A7]^{(1)}$ have identical sets of input-output pairs in every submatrix they intersect. On the other hand, rows 2, 4, and 6 exhibit sets of input-output pairs in the intersected submatrices, which differ from the set of input-output pairs exhibited by row 9. Consequently, rows 2, 4, and 6 and row 9 become two separate groups in $[A7]^{(2)}$, as shown in (3.12).

$[M]^{(k)}$ exhibits the equivalence partition when no further partitioning can be performed (i.e., when every submatrix is 1×1, or when the rows within every submatrix exhibit identical sets of input-output pairs). Under these conditions the separate groups of rows (or columns) represent the k-equivalence classes, where k can be made arbitrarily large; these groups, then, represent the equivalence classes of M. By Theorem 3.5, this must occur for some value of $k \leq n - 1$.

$[A7]$

	1	2	3	4	5	6	7	8	9
1	0	$(\alpha/1) \vee (\beta/0)$	0	0	$(\gamma/0)$	0	0	0	0
2	$(\alpha/0)$	0	0	$(\beta/1) \vee (\gamma/1)$	0	0	0	0	0
3	0	$(\alpha/1) \vee (\beta/0)$	0	0	$(\gamma/0)$	0	0	0	0
4	0	$(\beta/1) \vee (\gamma/1)$	$(\alpha/0)$	0	0	0	0	0	0
= 5	0	0	$(\gamma/0)$	$(\beta/0)$	0	$(\alpha/1)$	0	0	0
6	0	0	0	0	0	$(\gamma/1)$	0	$(\alpha/0)$	$(\beta/1)$
7	0	$(\beta/0)$	0	0	0	$(\alpha/1)$	0	$(\gamma/0)$	0
8	0	0	0	$(\alpha/1) \vee (\beta/0)$	0	0	$(\gamma/0)$	0	0
9	0	0	0	0	0	0	$(\alpha/0) \vee (\gamma/1)$	0	$(\beta/1)$

$$(3.10)$$

$[A7]^{(1)}$

	1	3	5	7	8	2	4	6	9
1	0	0	$(\gamma/0)$	0	0	$(\alpha/1) \vee (\beta/0)$	0	0	0
3	0	0	$(\gamma/0)$	0	0	$(\alpha/1) \vee (\beta/0)$	0	0	0
5	0	$(\gamma/0)$	0	0	0	0	$(\beta/0)$	$(\alpha/1)$	0
7	0	0	0	0	$(\gamma/0)$	$(\beta/0)$	0	$(\alpha/1)$	0
= 8	0	0	0	$(\gamma/0)$	0	0	$(\alpha/1) \vee (\beta/0)$	0	0
2	$(\alpha/0)$	0	0	0	0	0	$(\beta/1) \vee (\gamma/1)$	0	0
4	0	$(\alpha/0)$	0	0	0	$(\beta/1) \vee (\gamma/1)$	0	0	0
6	0	0	0	0	$(\alpha/0)$	0	0	$(\gamma/1)$	$(\beta/1)$
9	0	0	0	$(\alpha/0) \vee (\gamma/1)$	0	0	0	0	$(\beta/1)$

$$(3.11)$$

$[A7]^{(2)}$

	1	3	5	7	8	2	4	6	9
1	0	0	$(\gamma/0)$	0	0	$(\alpha/1) \vee (\beta/0)$	0	0	0
3	0	0	$(\gamma/0)$	0	0	$(\alpha/1) \vee (\beta/0)$	0	0	0
5	0	$(\gamma/0)$	0	0	0	0	$(\beta/0)$	$(\alpha/1)$	0
7	0	0	0	0	$(\gamma/0)$	$(\beta/0)$	0	$(\alpha/1)$	0
= 8	0	0	0	$(\gamma/0)$	0	0	$(\alpha/1) \vee (\beta/0)$	0	0
2	$(\alpha/0)$	0	0	0	0	0	$(\beta/1) \vee (\gamma/1)$	0	0
4	0	$(\alpha/0)$	0	0	0	$(\beta/1) \vee (\gamma/1)$	0	0	0
6	0	0	0	0	$(\alpha/0)$	0	0	$(\gamma/1)$	$(\beta/1)$
9	0	0	0	$(\alpha/0) \vee (\gamma/1)$	0	0	0	0	$(\beta/1)$

$$(3.12)$$

$[A7]^{(3)}$

	1	3	5	7	8	2	4	6	9
1	0	0	$(\gamma/0)$	0	0	$(\alpha/1) \vee (\beta/0)$	0	0	0
3	0	0	$(\gamma/0)$	0	0	$(\alpha/1) \vee (\beta/0)$	0	0	0
5	0	$(\gamma/0)$	0	0	0	0	$(\beta/0)$	$(\alpha/1)$	0
7	0	0	0	0	$(\gamma/0)$	$(\beta/0)$	0	$(\alpha/1)$	0
= 8	0	0	0	$(\gamma/0)$	0	0	$(\alpha/1) \vee (\beta/0)$	0	0
2	$(\alpha/0)$	0	0	0	0	0	$(\beta/1) \vee (\gamma/1)$	0	0
4	0	$(\alpha/0)$	0	0	0	$(\beta/1) \vee (\gamma/1)$	0	0	0
6	0	0	0	0	$(\alpha/0)$	0	0	$(\gamma/1)$	$(\beta/1)$
9	0	0	0	$(\alpha/0) \vee (\gamma/1)$	0	0	0	0	$(\beta/1)$

$$(3.13)$$

$[A7]^{(4)}$

	1	3	8	2	4	5	7	6	9
1	0	0	0	$(\alpha/1) \vee (\beta/0)$	0	$(\gamma/0)$	0	0	0
3	0	0	0	$(\alpha/1) \vee (\beta/0)$	0	$(\gamma/0)$	0	0	0
8	0	0	0	0	$(\alpha/1) \vee (\beta/0)$	0	$(\gamma/0)$	0	0
2	$(\alpha/0)$	0	0	0	$(\beta/1) \vee (\gamma/1)$	0	0	0	0
= 4	0	$(\alpha/0)$	0	$(\beta/1) \vee (\gamma/1)$	0	0	0	0	0
5	0	$(\gamma/0)$	0	0	$(\beta/0)$	0	0	$(\alpha/1)$	0
7	0	0	$(\gamma/0)$	$(\beta/0)$	0	0	0	$(\alpha/1)$	0
6	0	0	$(\alpha/0)$	0	0	0	0	$(\gamma/1)$	$(\beta/1)$
9	0	0	0	0	0	0	$(\alpha/0) \vee (\gamma/1)$	0	$(\beta/1)$

$$(3.14)$$

Matrices (3.10) to (3.14) illustrate the described method for the equivalence partitioning of machine $A7$. Matrix $[A7]^{(4)}$, which cannot be partitioned any further, places in evidence the equivalence partition $\{1, 3, 8\}$, $\{2, 4\}$, $\{5, 7\}$, $\{6\}$, and $\{9\}$, as given by (3.9).

3.9. Machine Equivalence

The concept of equivalence can be extended to entire machines, through the following definition:

DEFINITION 3.3. Machine M_1 and machine M_2 are said to be *equivalent* if to each state σ_i of M_1 there corresponds at least one state of M_2 which is equivalent to σ_i and to each state σ_j of M_2 there corresponds at least one state of M_1 which is equivalent to σ_j. If M_1 and M_2 are not equivalent, they are said to be *distinguishable*.

Thus, M_1 and M_2 are equivalent if and only if there is no way of distinguishing, by observing the external terminals, between machine M_1

at any of its states and machine M_2 and between machine M_2 at any of its states and machine M_1. M_1 and M_2 are distinguishable if and only if there is at least one state in M_1 which is not equivalent to any state in M_2, or at least one state in M_2 which is not equivalent to any state in M_1.

Equivalence between M_1 and M_2 is indicated by $M_1 = M_2$, and distinguishability between M_1 and M_2 is indicated by $M_1 \neq M_2$. From Definition 3.3 it can be readily verified that machine equivalence obeys

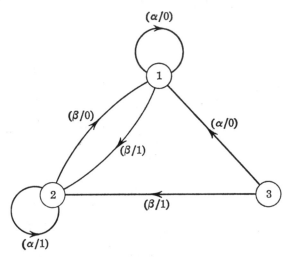

Fig. 3.5. Machine $A8$.

the reflexive law $(M_i = M_i)$, the symmetric law (if $M_i = M_j$, then $M_j = M_i$), and the transitive law (if $M_i = M_j$ and $M_j = M_k$, then $M_i = M_k$). Consequently, machine equivalence can be treated as an ordinary equivalence relation and applied directly to sets of machines of any size. Machine distinguishability, on the other hand, does not obey the reflexive and transitive laws, and hence can be applied only to pairs of machines.

The definition of machine equivalence implies that two machines which exhibit identical transition tables (or diagrams, or matrices) must be equivalent. Moreover, since the equivalence or distinguishability of a pair of states is independent of the state labels, two isomorphic machines must also be equivalent.

Machines $A8$ and $A9$ of Figs. 3.5 and 3.6, respectively, represent two equivalent machines. This can be verified by noticing that $A9$ becomes identical to $A8$ when state 3 of $A8$ is ignored; consequently, states 1 and 2 of $A8$ are equivalent to states 1 and 2, respectively, of $A9$. Also, states 1 and 3 of $A8$ are simply equivalent, and hence equivalent; consequently, state 3 of $A8$ is equivalent to state 1 of $A9$. Thus, for every state of $A8$ we find an equivalent state in $A9$, and for every state of $A9$ we find an equivalent state in $A8$, which implies that $A8$ and $A9$ are equivalent. Comparing machine $A9$ with machine $A10$ of Fig. 3.7, it can be seen that $A9$ becomes identical to $A10$ when state 3 of $A10$ is ignored; consequently, for every state of $A9$ we find an equivalent state in $A10$. However, since the state pairs $\{1, 3\}$ and $\{2, 3\}$ are simply

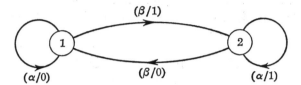

FIG. 3.6. Machine $A9$.

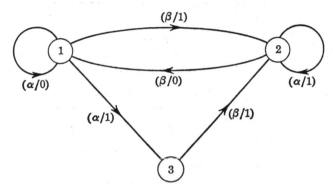

Fig. 3.7. Machine $A10$.

distinguishable, and hence distinguishable, the converse of the last statement is not true. $A9$ and $A10$, therefore, are not equivalent.

3.10. Equivalence Partitioning of Sets of Machines

The *machine equivalence partition* of a set $\mathfrak{M} = \{M_1, M_2, \ldots, M_N\}$ of machines is a partition of $\mathfrak{M}$ into classes such that two machines belong to the same class if and only if they are equivalent. Each class of machines in this partition is called a *machine equivalence class*. Clearly, machines cannot be equivalent if they are not congruous. Consequently, to partition $\mathfrak{M}$ into machine equivalence classes, $\mathfrak{M}$ may first be partitioned into subsets such that two machines belong to the same subset if and only if they are congruous. Subsequently, each subset can be individually subjected to further partitioning. Since partitioning a set of machines according to their input alphabets is a trivial task, there will be little loss in generality if we assume that all the machines in $\mathfrak{M}$ are congruous.

Once the above assumption is made, the disjunction machine $\Delta(M_1,$ $M_2, \ldots, M_N)$ can be constructed as described in Sec. 2.7. Partitioning the machine $\Delta(M_1, M_2, \ldots, M_N)$ into ordinary equivalence classes by any of the techniques described in Secs. 3.6 to 3.8 reveals whether or not any two machines M_i and M_j in $\mathfrak{M}$ are equivalent: By Definition 3.3, M_i and M_j are equivalent if every equivalence class which contains a state of M_i also contains a state of M_j and if every equivalence class which contains a state of M_j also contains a state of M_i; otherwise, M_i and M_j are distinguishable. Once all pairs of equivalent machines in $\mathfrak{M}$ are determined, the machine equivalence partition of $\mathfrak{M}$ can be constructed by an algorithm which is analogous to Algorithm 3.1 (with machines playing the role originally played by states).

In cases where the number of machines N is large, the determination of machine equivalence classes is facilitated by constructing the so-called *equivalence table* for the disjunction machine $\Delta(M_1, M_2, \ldots, M_N)$. This table contains a row for every equivalence class of the machine $\Delta(M_1, M_2, \ldots, M_N)$ and a column for every machine M_i in $\mathfrak{M}$. The general format of the table is shown in Table 3.11. The entries of the

TABLE 3.11. EQUIVALENCE TABLE FOR $\Delta(M_1, M_2, \ldots, M_N)$

Class \ Machine	M_1	M_2	$\cdots$	M_N
$\sigma_{11}, \sigma_{12}, \ldots, \sigma_{1r_1}$ $\sigma_{21}, \sigma_{22}, \ldots, \sigma_{2r_2}$ $\cdots \cdots \cdots$ $\sigma_{l1}, \sigma_{l2}, \ldots, \sigma_{lr_l}$		Entries: 0 or 1		

equivalence table are completed according to the following rule: The entry common to row $\{\sigma_{h1}, \sigma_{h2}, \ldots, \sigma_{hr_h}\}$ and column M_i is 1 if any state in the equivalence class $\{\sigma_{h1}, \sigma_{h2}, \ldots, \sigma_{hr_h}\}$ belongs to M_i, and is 0 otherwise. Thus, M_i and M_j are equivalent if and only if columns M_i and M_j in the equivalence table are identical in all rows. The machine equivalence partitioning, therefore, reduces to partitioning the columns of the equivalence table into subsets, such that two columns belong to the same subset if and only if they are identical in all rows. Column partitioning can be carried out by inspection even for large values of N, readily yielding the machine equivalence partition without the need for listing all pairs of equivalent machines.

To illustrate, Fig. 3.8 shows machines $A11$, $A12$, $A13$, and $A14$ combined as a single disjunction machine $\Delta(A11, A12, A13, A14)$. The transition table for this disjunction machine is shown in Table 3.12. Application of any of the equivalence partitioning techniques described in Secs. 3.6 to 3.8 reveals the equivalence classes of $\Delta(A11, A12, A13, A14)$ to be $\{1, 4, 5, 7, 9, 12\}$, $\{2, 3, 6, 10, 11\}$, and $\{8\}$. Table 3.13 shows the equivalence table for $\Delta(A11, A12, A13, A14)$, which demonstrates that the machine equivalence partition for the set of machines $\{A11, A12, A13, A14\}$ is $\{A11, A12, A14\}$ and $\{A13\}$.

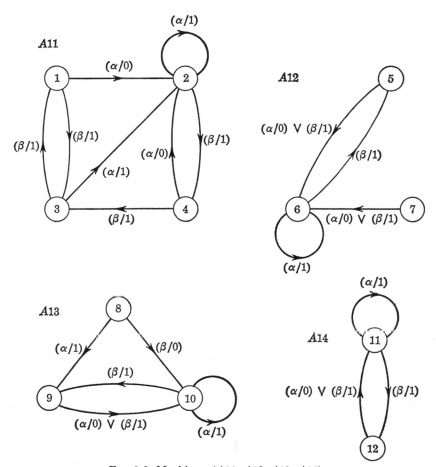

FIG. 3.8. Machine $\Delta(A11, A12, A13, A14)$.

Notice that a by-product of the machine equivalence partitioning process is the ordinary equivalence partitioning of each machine in the given set. For example, the equivalence partition of $\Delta(A11, A12, A13, A14)$, as displayed in Table 3.13, reveals that the equivalence partition of $A11$ is $\{1, 4\}$ and $\{2, 3\}$, the equivalence partition of $A12$ is $\{5, 7\}$ and $\{6\}$, the equivalence partition of $A13$ is $\{8\}$, $\{9\}$, and $\{10\}$, and the equivalence partition of $A14$ is $\{11\}$ and $\{12\}$.

TABLE 3.12. MACHINE $\Delta(A11, A12, A13, A14)$

s_ν \ x_ν	z_ν		$s_{\nu+1}$	
	α	β	α	β
1	0	1	2	3
2	1	1	2	4
3	1	1	2	1
4	0	1	2	3
5	0	1	6	6
6	1	1	6	5
7	0	1	6	6
8	1	0	9	10
9	0	1	10	10
10	1	1	10	9
11	1	1	11	12
12	0	1	11	11

TABLE 3.13. EQUIVALENCE TABLE FOR $\Delta(A11, A12, A13, A14)$

Class \ Machine	$A11$	$A12$	$A13$	$A14$
1, 4, 5, 7, 9, 12	1	1	1	1
2, 3, 6, 10, 11	1	1	1	1
8	0	0	1	0

3.11. The Minimal Form

Let M be a machine with $\check{n}$ equivalence classes, labeled $\Sigma_1, \Sigma_2, \ldots,$ $\Sigma_{\check{n}}$, and let $\sigma^{(l)}$ represent any state in Σ_l. The *minimal form* of M, denoted by $\check{M}$, is an $\check{n}$-state machine with the state set $\{\sigma'_1, \sigma'_2, \ldots, \sigma'_{\check{n}}\}$ constructed from M according to the following criterion: Denoting the characterizing functions of M by f_z and f_s and those of $\check{M}$ by $\check{f}_z$ and $\check{f}_s$,

If
$$f_z(\xi_i, \sigma^{(u)}) = \zeta_j \quad \text{and} \quad f_s(\xi_i, \sigma^{(u)}) = \sigma^{(v)}$$
then
$$\check{f}_z(\xi_i, \sigma'_u) = \zeta_j \quad \text{and} \quad \check{f}_s(\xi_i, \sigma'_u) = \sigma'_v \tag{3.15}$$

Notice that if ξ_i, when applied to M at a specified state which belongs to Σ_u, yields the output symbol ζ_j, then ξ_i, when applied to *any* state belonging to Σ_u, yields the output symbol ζ_j. Similarly, if ξ_i, when applied to M at a specified state which belongs to Σ_u, passes M into a state belonging to Σ_v, then ξ_i, when applied to *any* state belonging to Σ_u, passes M into a state belonging to Σ_v. Thus, in constructing $\check{M}$ through the criterion (3.15), no ambiguity results from the fact that $\sigma^{(u)}$ is an arbitrary state belonging to the class Σ_u and that $\sigma^{(v)}$ is an arbitrary state belonging to the class Σ_v.

The process of finding the minimal form of a machine is called *machine minimization*. The minimization of machine M, then, consists of determining the equivalence partition of M, and then applying (3.15) to construct $\check{M}$. Since in the process of applying (3.15) all states of M belonging to the same equivalence class play identical roles, the individual identity of each state becomes immaterial; what is significant for purposes of minimization is the identity of the class to which each state belongs. There is no risk, then, in assigning a common label, say σ'_l, to all the states of M which belong to the equivalence class Σ_l. When this is done, (3.15) may be interpreted as stating that machine $\check{M}$ is obtainable from M by "merging" all identically labeled states into a single representative state. The manner in which this merging is effected depends on whether the machine is specified in a tabular, diagrammatic, or matrix form, and will be described in the procedures given below. Although the understanding of these procedures is facilitated through the foregoing intuitive interpretation of the criterion (3.15), their validity is independent of this interpretation and stems directly from the criterion itself.

The Transition Table of $\check{M}$. Given the transition table of M and the equivalence partition $\Sigma_1, \Sigma_2, \ldots, \Sigma_{\hat{n}}$ of M, the transition table of $\check{M}$ can be constructed as follows: (1) Replace every state label which appears in the transition table of M by a label identifying the class to which the state belongs. (2) From any group of rows exhibiting identical stub entries (all such rows are identical in both the z_ν and $s_{\nu+1}$ subtables), delete all but one row. The resulting table is the transition table of $\check{M}$.

As an example, for machine $A7$ of Table 3.2 we have the equivalence

TABLE 3.14. STEP 1 IN CONSTRUCTING THE TRANSITION TABLE
FOR MACHINE $\check{A}7$

s_ν \\ x_ν	z_ν			$s_{\nu+1}$		
	α	β	γ	α	β	γ
1	1	0	0	2	2	3
2	0	1	1	1	2	2
1	1	0	0	2	2	3
2	0	1	1	1	2	2
3	1	0	0	4	2	1
4	0	1	1	1	5	4
3	1	0	0	4	2	1
1	1	0	0	2	2	3
5	0	1	1	3	5	3

classes $\{1, 3, 8\}$, $\{2, 4\}$, $\{5, 7\}$, $\{6\}$, and $\{9\}$, which may be labeled (arbitrarily) as 1, 2, 3, 4, and 5, respectively. Performing step 1 of the procedure, every "1," "3," and "8" in the stub and $s_{\nu+1}$ subtable of Table 3.2 is replaced by "1," every "2" and "4" is replaced by "2," every "5" and "7" is replaced by "3," every "6" is replaced by "4," and every "9" is replaced by "5." The resulting transition table is shown in Table 3.14. Deleting all duplicate rows yields the transition table for $\breve{A}7$, shown in Table 3.15.

TABLE 3.15. MACHINE $\breve{A}7$

x_ν \ s_ν	z_ν			$s_{\nu+1}$		
	α	β	γ	α	β	γ
1	1	0	0	2	2	3
2	0	1	1	1	2	2
3	1	0	0	4	2	1
4	0	1	1	1	5	4
5	0	1	1	3	5	3

The Transition Diagram of $\breve{M}$. Given the transition diagram of M and the equivalence partition $\Sigma_1, \Sigma_2, \ldots, \Sigma_{\hat{n}}$ of M, the transition diagram of $\breve{M}$ can be constructed as follows: (1) Replace every state label which appears in the transition diagram of M by a label identifying the class to which it belongs. (2) Superpose all identically labeled states (regarding branches as "flexible wires"), and represent superposed states by a single state bearing the common label. (3) From any group of branches having a common starting state and a common terminating state (all such branches are identically labeled), delete all but one branch. The resulting diagram is the transition diagram of $\breve{M}$.

As an example, Fig. 3.9 shows the transition diagram of machine $\breve{A}7$, obtained by carrying out the above procedure on the transition diagram of Fig. 3.3. The labels used for the equivalence classes of $A7$ are the same as those used in the construction of the transition table.

The Transition Matrix of $\breve{M}$. Given the transition matrix of M and the equivalence partition $\Sigma_1, \Sigma_2, \ldots, \Sigma_{\hat{n}}$ of M, the transition matrix of $\breve{M}$ can be constructed as follows: (1) Perform a symmetrical permutation and a symmetrical partitioning on $[M]$, such that the row (and column) groups correspond to the equivalence classes of M (the result is the same as the final $[M]^{(k)}$ matrix obtained in the matrix method of equivalence partitioning). (2) Replace all labels attached to any given group of rows (and columns) which represents an equivalence class by a single label which identifies the class. (3) Replace every submatrix in the partitioned matrix by a single entry, consisting of all the input-output pairs which appear in any row of this submatrix (all rows in any given submatrix contain the same set of input-output pairs). The resulting matrix is the transition matrix of $\breve{M}$.

As an example, (3.16) is the transition matrix of machine $\breve{A}7$, constructed from $[A7]^{(4)}$, shown in (3.14). The labels used for the equiva-

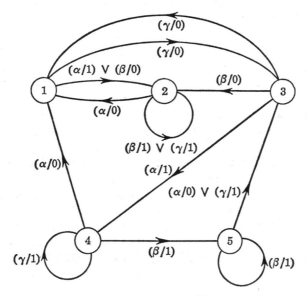

FIG. 3.9. Machine $\breve{A}7$.

lence classes of $A7$ are the same as those used in the construction of the transition table.

$$
[\breve{A}7] = \begin{array}{c} \\ 1 \\ 2 \\ 3 \\ 4 \\ 5 \end{array}
\begin{array}{c}
\begin{array}{ccccc} 1 & 2 & 3 & 4 & 5 \end{array} \\
\left[\begin{array}{ccccc}
0 & (\alpha/1) \vee (\beta/0) & (\gamma/0) & 0 & 0 \\
(\alpha/0) & (\beta/1) \vee (\gamma/1) & 0 & 0 & 0 \\
(\gamma/0) & (\beta/0) & 0 & (\alpha/1) & 0 \\
(\alpha/0) & 0 & 0 & (\gamma/1) & (\beta/1) \\
0 & 0 & (\alpha/0) \vee (\gamma/1) & 0 & (\beta/1)
\end{array} \right]
\end{array}
$$
$$(3.16)$$

3.12. Properties of the Minimal Form

In what follows, machine M_1 will be said to be *smaller* than or *larger* than machine M_2, depending on whether M_1 has a smaller or a larger number of states, respectively, than M_2.

THEOREM 3.6. If $\check{M}$ is the minimal form of M, then (a) $\check{M}$ is unique up to isomorphism[1]; (b) $\check{M} = M$; (c) no two states in $\check{M}$ are equivalent; (d) no machine equivalent to M is smaller than $\check{M}$.

Proof. (a) From Lemma 3.5, P_k is unique for any $k \geq 1$, and hence $P_{n-1} = \hat{P}$ is unique. Since the construction of $\check{M}$ from M, when $\hat{P}$ is specified, is unique except for state labeling, $\check{M}$ is unique up to isomorphism. (b) Consider any input sequence $\xi_{i_1}\xi_{i_2} \cdots \xi_{i_l}$ applied to $M|\sigma^{(u)}$. Let the resulting sequence of states be $\sigma^{(u_1)}, \sigma^{(u_2)}, \ldots, \sigma^{(u_l)}$ and the resulting output sequence be $\zeta_{j_1}\zeta_{j_2} \cdots \zeta_{j_l}$. Now, let the same input sequence be applied to $\check{M}|\sigma'_u$. By criterion (3.15), on which the construction of $\check{M}$ from M is based, the resulting sequence of states must be $\sigma'_{u_1}, \sigma'_{u_2}, \ldots, \sigma'_{u_l}$, and the resulting output sequence must be $\zeta_{j_1}\zeta_{j_2} \cdots \zeta_{j_l}$. Since l and u in the above argument are arbitrary, it follows that any state of M which belongs to any equivalence class Σ_u is equivalent to state σ'_u of $\check{M}$. Thus, for every state in M we find an equivalent state in $\check{M}$, and for every state in $\check{M}$ we find an equivalent state in M, which implies that $\check{M} = M$. (c) Let σ'_u and σ'_v be any two states of $\check{M}(u \neq v)$. From the proof to part b, σ'_u is equivalent to the states of M which belong to the equivalence class Σ_u, and σ'_v is equivalent to the states of M which belong to the equivalence class Σ_v. Since no state in class Σ_u can be equivalent to any state in class Σ_v, states σ'_u and σ'_v of machine $\check{M}$ must be distinguishable. (d) Suppose there is a machine M' which is equivalent to M and smaller than $\check{M}$. Since $\check{M} = M$ and $M' = M$, it follows that $\check{M} = M'$ and that every state of $\check{M}$ is equivalent to some state of M'. Since $\check{M}$ is larger than M', there are at least two states in $\check{M}$ which are equivalent to the same state in M', and hence are equivalent to each other. However, by part c of the theorem, this is impossible, which proves, by contradiction, that no machine equivalent to M can be smaller than $\check{M}$.

A machine which is the minimal form of itself, and thus has no smaller equivalent, is called a *minimal machine*. Every n-state machine which has n equivalence classes, and hence in which every pair of states is distinguishable, is a minimal machine. Theorem 3.6 shows that, given any machine M, we can find a minimal machine $\check{M}$ which is equivalent to M and which is unique up to isomorphism. This result is extremely significant, inasmuch as it tells us that every machine has some "canonic" representation, which is independent of the manner in which the machine is originally specified. Since, in general, there is a variety of ways in which a machine can be described (especially when this is done verbally), it is gratifying to learn that all this variety can be finally reduced to the same standard representation. Moreover, the result shows that the standard representation is the most compact one, in terms of the number

---

[1] That is, $\check{M}$ is unique except for state labeling.

of states employed. Thus, if lack of experience or ingenuity causes the investigator to produce an initial representation which is full of redundancies, there is always a straightforward method by which this representation can be reduced to its bare essentials.

To illustrate the foregoing remarks, consider the following game: A coin is tossed repeatedly, and a point is scored at the νth toss if the coin

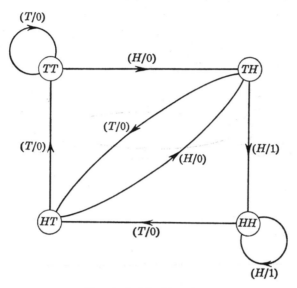

Fig. 3.10. Machine $A15$.

faces obtained at the $(\nu\text{-}2)$d, $(\nu\text{-}1)$st, and νth tosses are tail, head, and head, respectively, or head, head, and head, respectively; no point is scored otherwise. Denoting "head" by H, "tail" by T, "point" by 1, and "no point" by 0, we may choose the following input alphabet, output alphabet, and state set:

$$X = \{H, T\}$$
$$Z = \{0, 1\}$$
$$S = \{TT, TH, HT, HH\}$$

where the four states are identified with all possible face combinations at the $(\nu\text{-}2)$d and $(\nu\text{-}1)$st tosses. The resulting transition diagram for the game, denoted by $A15$, is shown in Fig. 3.10. Now, a more compact representation results when it is recognized that the score at the νth toss is, in fact, independent of the coin face at the $(\nu\text{-}2)$d toss (although this fact may be obscured by the verbal description of the game). Accordingly, we may choose the following input alphabet, output alphabet, and state set:

$$X = \{H, T\}$$
$$Z = \{0, 1\}$$
$$S = \{H, T\}$$

where the two states are identified with all possible face combinations at the $(\nu\text{-}1)$st toss. The resulting transition diagram, denoted by $A16$, is shown in Fig. 3.11. As can be readily verified by the method described in Sec. 3.10, $A16 = A\breve{1}5$. Thus, if we fail to detect the redundancy in the verbal description of the game, $A16$ can still be obtained (within

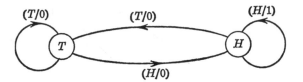

FIG. 3.11. Machine $A16$.

isomorphism) by subjecting $A15$ to any of the standard machine minimization techniques.

In passing, it will be remarked that the role played by the minimal form in the theory of finite-state machines is analogous to the role played by the "Thévenin equivalent circuit" in the theory of linear networks. Both representations serve to describe the behavior of the system, as exhibited by the accessible terminals, in the most compact manner possible.

3.13. Machine Reduction by Successive Merging

Let M be a machine in which two states, say σ_i and σ_j, are known to be equivalent. Another machine, M_1, can be constructed by merging σ_i and σ_j in the same manner that equivalent states are merged in the minimization procedures outlined in Sec. 3.11: σ_i and σ_j are replaced by a single state, say σ_{ij}, which passes into the same state as σ_i (or σ_j) and yields the same output symbol as σ_i (or σ_j), when subjected to the same input symbol as σ_i (or σ_j). σ_{ij}, then, is equivalent to σ_i and σ_j, and hence $M_1 = M$. Now, if two states in M_1 are known to be equivalent, the merging operation can be repeated to produce $M_2 = M_1$. This procedure can be continued until $M_k = M_{k-1}$ is produced in which no states are known to be equivalent. Letting M_0 stand for the original machine M, it can be stated that M_k $(k \geq 1)$, as produced by the above procedure, is always smaller than M_{k-1}, and hence constitutes a *reduced form* of M.

Reduction of a machine by successive merging is especially convenient when the machine at hand contains simply equivalent states, which can be spotted by inspection of the transition table. Since, by Theorem 3.1, simply equivalent states are equivalent, they can be merged as described in the preceding paragraph, to yield a reduction of the given machine. The merging of two simply equivalent states, say σ_i and σ_j, can be most conveniently performed via the transition table, by deleting row σ_j and replacing every "σ_j" in the $s_{\nu+1}$ subtable by "σ_i."

As an example, Tables 3.16 to 3.19 show the successive stages in the

TABLE 3.16. MACHINE $A6$

s_ν \ x_ν	z_ν			$s_{\nu+1}$		
	α	β	γ	α	β	γ
1	1	0	1	2	5	5
2	0	1	1	6	2	5
3	0	1	1	2	2	7
4	1	0	1	8	3	1
5	1	0	1	2	5	5
6	0	1	1	2	6	5
7	0	1	1	6	6	3
8	1	0	1	8	7	5

reduction of machine $A6$ of Fig. 3.1 and Table 3.1. For convenience, Table 3.1 is reproduced here as Table 3.16. In this table, the state pairs $\{1, 5\}$ and $\{2, 6\}$ are recognized as simply equivalent; deleting rows 5 and 6 and replacing every "5" by "1" and every "6" by "2" results in machine $A6_1 = A6$, represented by Table 3.17. In $A6_1$, the state pair $\{3, 7\}$ is recognized as simply equivalent; deleting row 7 and replacing every "7" by "3" results in machine $A6_2 = A6_1$, represented by Table 3.18. In $A6_2$, the state pair $\{4, 8\}$ is recognized as simply equivalent; deleting row

TABLE 3.17. MACHINE $A6_1$

s_ν \ x_ν	z_ν			$s_{\nu+1}$		
	α	β	γ	α	β	γ
1	1	0	1	2	1	1
2	0	1	1	2	2	1
3	0	1	1	2	2	7
4	1	0	1	8	3	1
7	0	1	1	2	2	3
8	1	0	1	8	7	1

8 and replacing every "8" by "4" results in machine $A6_3 = A6_2$, represented by Table 3.19. Since no simply equivalent states can be recognized in $A6_3$, the reduction by merging, as performed above, must terminate at this point. As it turns out, $A6_3$ is also the minimal form of $A6$. The transition diagram of $A6_3 = A6$ is shown in Fig. 3.12.

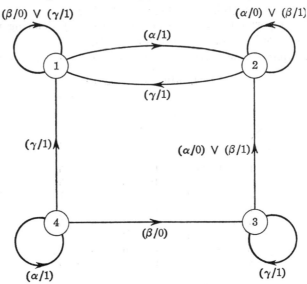

FIG. 3.12. Machine $\breve{A}6$.

TABLE 3.18. MACHINE $A6_2$

x_ν s_ν	z_ν			$s_{\nu+1}$		
	α	β	γ	α	β	γ
1	1	0	1	2	1	1
2	0	1	1	2	2	1
3	0	1	1	2	2	3
4	1	0	1	8	3	1
8	1	0	1	8	3	1

TABLE 3.19. MACHINE $A6_3$

x_ν s_ν	z_ν			$s_{\nu+1}$		
	α	β	γ	α	β	γ
1	1	0	1	2	1	1
2	0	1	1	2	2	1
3	0	1	1	2	2	3
4	1	0	1	4	3	1

It should be emphasized that, since not every equivalent pair of states is simply equivalent, the described reduction procedure does not always lead to a minimal machine. After the smallest machine achievable by successive merging is constructed, standard equivalence partitioning should be performed on it to reduce it further into the minimal form, or to ascertain its minimality when further reduction is impossible.

3.14. The Class of Minimal Machines

Using the definitions introduced in Sec. 2.3, as a consequence of Theorem 3.1 and the definition of machine equivalence, we have:

LEMMA 3.12.   A simply minimal (n, p, q) machine must be minimal. A simply reducible (n, p, q) machine cannot be minimal.

In addition, we shall now prove:

LEMMA 3.13.   The size of the permutation family of a minimal (n, p, q) machine is $n!$.

Proof.   Let M_1 be a minimal (n, p, q) machine and M_2 a machine obtained by permuting the state labels of M_1. Suppose that the permutation scheme through which M_2 is obtained from M_1 involves the relabeling of state σ_i of M_1 as "σ_j" $(j \neq i)$. If M_1 and M_2 have identical transition tables, then the responses of $M_1|\sigma_j$ and $M_2|\sigma_j$ to any input sequence must be identical, and hence the responses of $M_1|\sigma_j$ and $M_1|\sigma_i$ to any input sequence must be identical. This implies that states σ_i and σ_j in M_1 are equivalent, and hence that M_1 is not minimal. By contradiction, then, different permutation schemes must result in distinct transition tables. Since there are $n!$ different permutation schemes, the lemma follows

LEMMA 3.14.   The size $\check{N}_{n,p,q}$ of the class of minimal (n, p, q) machines, such that no two machines are isomorphic to each other, is given by

$$\check{N}_{n,p,q} \leq \frac{1}{n!} \prod_{r=0}^{n-1} [(qn)^p - r] \qquad (3.17)$$

Proof.   Let the number of (n, p, q) machines which are not simply reducible be $N''_{n,p,q}$, and let the number of minimal (n, p, q) machines (whether isomorphic to each other or not) be $\check{N}'_{n,p,q}$. Then, by Lemma 3.12,

$$\check{N}'_{n,p,q} \leq N''_{n,p,q} \qquad (3.18)$$

By Lemma 3.13,

$$\check{N}'_{n,p,q} = n!\check{N}_{n,p,q} \qquad (3.19)$$

or

$$\check{N}_{n,p,q} = \frac{1}{n!} \check{N}'_{n,p,q} \leq \frac{1}{n!} N''_{n,p,q} \qquad (3.20)$$

Using Eq. (2.3) for $N''_{n,p,q}$, the lemma follows.

Since two minimal machines which are not isomorphic to each other must be distinguishable, $\check{N}_{n,p,q}$ is also the number of minimal (n, p, q) machines, such that no two machines are equivalent. This number must contain the number $N_{n,p,q}^{(SM)}$ of simply minimal (n, p, q) machines, such that no two machines are isomorphic. Using Theorem 2.1 for $N_{n,p,q}^{(SM)}$, we thus have:

THEOREM 3.7. The class of minimal (n, p, q) machines, such that no two machines are equivalent, is of size $\check{N}_{n,p,q}$, where

$$\frac{1}{n!} n^{pn} \prod_{r=0}^{n-1} (q^p - r) \leq \check{N}_{n,p,q} \leq \frac{1}{n!} \prod_{r=0}^{n-1} [(qn)^p - r] \qquad (3.21)$$

For example, the total number of minimal $(2, 2, 2)$ machines, such that no two machines are equivalent, lies between 96 and 120.

PROBLEMS

3.1. Show that if $\sigma_i = \sigma_j$ and $\sigma_j \not\eqsim \sigma_k$, then $\sigma_i \not\eqsim \sigma_k$.

3.2. Exploiting the symmetry of the transition diagram shown in Fig. P 3.1, show that $\sigma_1 = \sigma_2, \sigma_3 = \sigma_4, \sigma_5 = \sigma_6$.

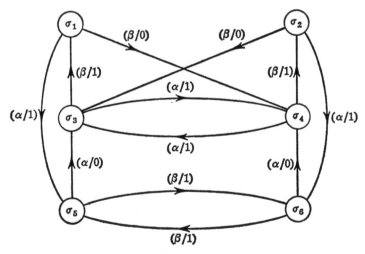

FIG. P 3.1

3.3. In the z_ν subtable of machine M all rows are identical. Show that M is a trivial machine.

3.4. Show that if the ith and jth rows of $[M]$ are identical, then states σ_i and σ_j of machine M are equivalent.

3.5. States σ_i and σ_j are k_1-equivalent, and their k_1th successors, with respect to every input sequence of length k_1, are k_2-equivalent. Show that if $k_1 + k_2 \geq n - 1$, then $\sigma_i = \sigma_j$.

3.6. States σ_i and σ_j are k_1-equivalent, and their k_1th successors, with respect to every input sequence of length k_1, are k_2-equivalent but $(k_2 + 1)$-distinguishable. Show that if $\sigma_i \not\equiv \sigma_j$, then $k_1 + k_2 \leq n + 2$.

3.7. Machine M has the 1-equivalence classes $\Sigma_{11}, \Sigma_{12}, \ldots, \Sigma_{1r}$, where Σ_{1i}, $i = 1, 2, \ldots, r$, contains n_i states. Compute the number of rows in the pairs table for M.

3.8. The partition P_1 of an n-state machine has r classes. (a) If $P_k \neq P_{k-1}$, what is the minimum number of classes that P_k contains? (b) If $P_k \neq P_{k-1}$, what is the maximum number of states that a class in P_k contains? (c) What is the smallest value of k for which P_k is guaranteed to be identical to P_{k+1}?

3.9. Table P 3.1 is a partially completed P_3 table of a 6-state machine. Determine the 2-equivalence partition of this machine.

3.10. Find the equivalence partition of the machine specified by Table P 3.2 (a) by constructing the P_k tables, (b) by processing the pairs table.

3.11. Find the equivalence partition of the machine specified by Fig. P 3.2 (a) by constructing the P_k tables, (b) by processing the pairs table, (c) by matrix partitioning.

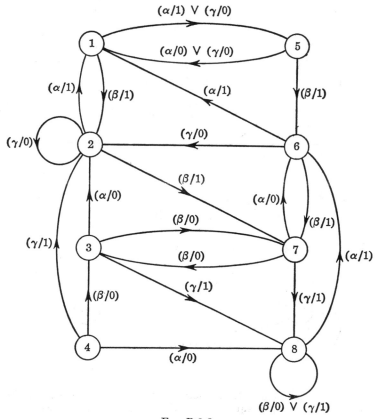

FIG. P 3.2

3.12. Show that if $M_1 = M_2$ and $M_2 \neq M_3$, then $M_1 \neq M_3$.

TABLE P 3.1

Σ	s_ν \ x_ν	$s_{\nu+1}$ α	$s_{\nu+1}$ β
a	1	4	?
	2	?	?
	3	6	?
b	4	?	?
c	5	?	?
d	6	?	?

TABLE P 3.2

s_ν \ x_ν	z_ν α	z_ν β	$s_{\nu+1}$ α	$s_{\nu+1}$ β
1	0	0	5	4
2	0	1	3	3
3	0	0	7	9
4	1	1	3	3
5	0	0	3	3
6	0	0	2	5
7	0	0	8	6
8	0	0	5	5
9	0	0	1	8

3.13. Figure P 3.3 shows the transition diagram of a 4-state machine. Construct the transition diagram of a 5-state machine which is equivalent to the machine shown.

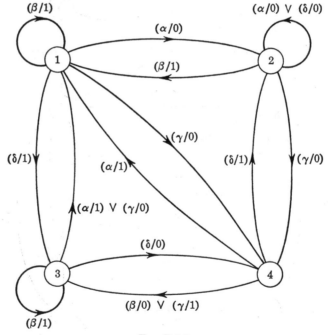

FIG. P 3.3

3.14. Every state of machine M_1 is equivalent to some state of machine M_2, but $M_1 \neq M_2$. Show that M_1 is equivalent to either an isolated or a persistent submachine of M_2.

3.15. Let σ_i, a state of machine M_1, be equivalent to σ_j, a state of machine M_2. It is found that there is a certain input sequence that passes $M_1|\sigma_i$ through all the states of M_1, and at the same time passes $M_2|\sigma_j$ through all the states of M_2. Show that $M_1 = M_2$.

3.16. Determine which pairs of the three machines shown in Fig. P 3.4 are equivalent, and which are distinguishable. Which of the machines are minimal?

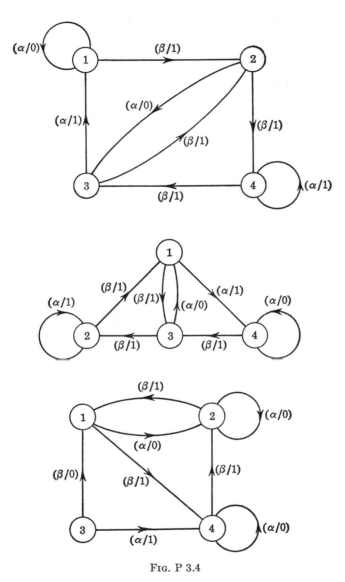

Fig. P 3.4

3.17. Show that if M' is a persistent or an isolated submachine of M, then $\breve{M}$ contains a submachine M'' which is the minimal form of M', and which is a persistent submachine of $\breve{M}$, an isolated submachine of $\breve{M}$, or the entire machine $\breve{M}$.

3.18. Show that if $M_1 = M_2 = \cdots = M_N$, then $\breve{M}_1$ is the minimal form of $\Delta(M_1, M_2, \ldots, M_N)$.

3.19. Show, by an example, that two nonminimal equivalent machines, having the same number of states, are not necessarily isomorphic.

3.20. Given two machines (not necessarily minimal), formulate an algorithm for determining whether or not the machines are isomorphic.

3.21. Determine the minimal forms of the machines specified in Probs. 1.2 to 1.9 of Chap. 1.

3.22. Construct the transition table, diagram, and matrix of the minimal form of the machine shown in Fig. P 3.2.

3.23. Formulate a rule for determining all simply equivalent pairs of states by inspection of the pairs table.

3.24. Obtain the minimal form of the machine shown in Fig. P 3.2 by the successive merging procedure described in Sec. 3.13.

CHAPTER 4

STATE IDENTIFICATION EXPERIMENTS

4.1. Introduction

As was pointed out in Chap. 1, the response of a nontrivial machine M to specified excitations is unpredictable if the state of M is unknown; this response, on the other hand, can always be predicted if the initial state is known. One of the basic tasks in the analysis of finite-state machines, therefore, is to identify the state of the machine under investigation. Once the state is identified, the behavior of the machine under all future conditions becomes determinable, and steps may be taken to force the machine into various modes of operation desirable to the investigator.

In this chapter we shall discuss two of the most important state identification problems—that of identifying the initial state of a machine (i.e., the state in which a machine exists when presented to the investigator) and that of identifying the final state of a machine (i.e., the state in which a machine exists when the probing operations conducted by the investigator are completed). The solution to either of these problems constitutes the solution to the basic problem of rendering the machine predictable to the investigator. As will be seen in a later chapter, this solution is also useful in other problems, where the number of unknown quantities of interest is considerably larger than that involved in the state identification problem.[1]

4.2. Classification of Experiments

The process of applying input sequences to the input terminals of a machine, observing the resulting output sequences, and drawing conclusions based on these observations will be called an *experiment*. In all our discussions, without exception, it will be assumed that a machine on

---

[1] The material in this chapter is based in part on the work of E. F. Moore (Gedanken-Experiments on Sequential Machines, "Automata Studies," pp. 129–153, Princeton University Press, Princeton, N.J., 1956), S. Ginsburg (On the Length of the Smallest Uniform Experiment Which Distinguishes the Terminal States of a Machine, *J. Assoc. Comput. Mach.*, vol. 5, pp. 266–280, 1958), and A. Gill (State Identification Experiments in Finite Automata, *Information and Control*, vol. 4, pp. 132–154, 1961).

which an experiment is conducted is a sealed "black box" with only the input and output terminals accessible. Conclusions may be based only on applied excitations, observed responses, and possibly, on transition tables (or diagrams, or matrices) which may be available for the task at hand.

We shall distinguish between two types of experiments:

1. *Preset experiments*, where the applied input sequence is completely determined in advance

2. *Adaptive experiments*, where the applied input sequence is composed of two or more subsequences, each subsequence (except the first) determined on the basis of responses resulting from preceding subsequences

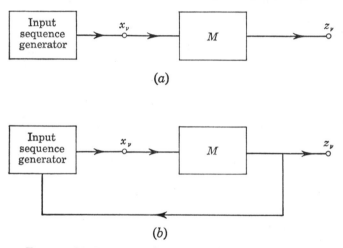

Fig. 4.1. (a) Preset experiment; (b) adaptive experiment.

A preset experiment, as a rule, is easier to implement than an adaptive one: whereas the latter requires a number of intermediate decisions before the final decision is made, the former requires no such intermediate decisions. Envisioning a human or a mechanical "input-sequence generator," whose function is to supply the machine with the required input sequences, it can be seen that in preset experiments the generator should be capable of supplying a single sequence only. In adaptive experiments, on the other hand, the generator should be capable of generating a number of sequences, each sequence based on information fed back from the output terminal of the machine. As we shall see, the advantage of some adaptive experiments is that they are relatively concise; also, in some cases, adaptive experiments are easier to design than preset ones. A schematic representation of the two types of experiments is shown in Fig. 4.1.

One machine is referred to as the *copy* of another machine, if both machines have identical transition tables, and if both are at the same state before the experiment commences. Experiments can be classified according to the number of copies which they require of the machine under investigation:

1. *Simple experiments*, where only one copy of the machine is required

2. *Multiple experiments*, where more than one copy of the machine is required

As most machines encountered in practice are available in one copy only, simple experiments are preferable to multiple ones.

The *length* of an experiment is taken as the total number of input symbols applied in the course of conducting the experiment. The *order* of an experiment is taken as the number of input subsequences (i.e., sequences separated by decision-making operations) of which the experiment is composed. The *multiplicity* of an experiment is the number of copies it requires of the machine under investigation. Thus, a preset experiment is an experiment of order 1, and an adaptive experiment is an experiment of order 2 or greater. A simple experiment is an experiment of multiplicity 1, and a multiple experiment is an experiment of multiplicity 2 or greater. The length, order, and multiplicity of an experiment may be regarded as rough measures of its execution cost.

4.3. Diagnosing and Homing Experiments

Our main concern in this chapter is to devise experiments for solving the following two problems:

1. *The diagnosing problem:* It is known that a given machine M, whose transition table is available, is in one of the states $\sigma_{i_1}, \sigma_{i_2}, \ldots, \sigma_{i_m}$. Find this state.

2. *The homing problem:* It is known that a given machine M, whose transition table is available, is in one of the states $\sigma_{i_1}, \sigma_{i_2}, \ldots, \sigma_{i_m}$. Pass M into a known state.

The diagnosing problem, then, is that of identifying the initial state of M, and the homing problem is that of identifying the final state of M. An experiment which solves the diagnosing problem is called a *diagnosing experiment;* an experiment which solves the homing problem is called a *homing experiment.* Clearly, every diagnosing experiment is also a homing experiment, since the knowledge of the initial state of M and the applied sequence implies the knowledge of the final state. The converse, however, is not necessarily true.

Unless otherwise specified, it will be assumed throughout this chapter that M is a minimal machine. If M, as originally specified by its transition table, is not minimal, it can always be minimized by methods introduced in Chap. 3. Since only the external behavior of M is of interest, there is no risk in replacing the original table by that of the minimal form, and, hence, there is no loss in generality in assuming that M is minimal.

The set of states $\{\sigma_{i_1}, \sigma_{i_2}, \ldots, \sigma_{i_m}\}$, one of which is, to the investigator's knowledge, the initial state of M, is called the *admissible set* of M and denoted by $A(M)$. The states in $A(M)$ are called *admissible states*. Both the diagnosing and homing problems are trivial when $A(M)$ is a singleton, i.e., when $m = 1$. Our attention, therefore, will concentrate on the cases where $m \geq 2$.

It can be noted that preset diagnosing or homing experiments are independent of the true initial state of M. On the other hand, adaptive diagnosing or homing experiments depend, in general, on the true initial state of M. This follows from the fact that the initial state determines the response of M to the first input subsequence; since the composition of the next input subsequence is based on the response of the currently applied subsequence, the initial state determines all input subsequences except the first.

4.4. Pairwise Diagnosing Experiments

The problem of identifying the initial state of machine M when $A(M)$ is of an arbitrary size m is inherently much more complex than that pertaining to the special case $m = 2$. To differentiate between the general and special problems, the former will be referred to as the *m-wise diagnosing problem*, while the latter will be referred to as the *pairwise diagnosing problem*.

In this section we shall tackle the pairwise diagnosing problem, assuming that the given machine M is an n-state machine, with $A(M) = \{\sigma_{i_0}, \sigma_{j_0}\}$. Since M is minimal, σ_{i_0} and σ_{j_0} must be distinguishable, and hence $(n - 1)$-distinguishable. Consequently, there exists an input sequence of length $n - 1$ or less which, when applied to $M|\sigma_{i_0}$ and $M|\sigma_{j_0}$, yields distinct output sequences. Such an input sequence is called a *diagnosing sequence* for $\{\sigma_{i_0}, \sigma_{j_0}\}$. The pairwise diagnosing experiment for M and

$$A(M) = \{\sigma_{i_0}, \sigma_{j_0}\}$$

consists, therefore, of applying the diagnosing sequence for $\{\sigma_{i_0}, \sigma_{j_0}\}$ to M and observing the response; on the basis of this response, the true initial state can be identified. In the remainder of this section we shall show how diagnosing sequences for specified pairs of states can be constructed.

Let σ_{i_0} and σ_{j_0} be l-distinguishable and $(l - 1)$-equivalent, for some $1 \leq l \leq n - 1$.† Then the length of the shortest diagnosing sequence for $\{\sigma_{i_0}, \sigma_{j_0}\}$ is l. Any diagnosing sequence for $\{\sigma_{i_0}, \sigma_{j_0}\}$ whose length is l, as specified above, will be called a *minimal diagnosing sequence* for $\{\sigma_{i_0}, \sigma_{j_0}\}$ and denoted by $\mathcal{E}(\sigma_{i_0}, \sigma_{j_0})$. If σ_{i_0} and σ_{j_0} are l-distinguishable and $(l - 1)$-

† Since 0-equivalence is undefined, states which are 1-distinguishable and 0-equivalent are to be considered simply as 1-distinguishable.

equivalent, σ_{i_0} and σ_{j_0} must be disjoint states in P_l and adjoint in P_{l-1}. l, therefore, can be determined by constructing the k-equivalence partitions for the given machine M and noting the lowest value of k such that P_k contains σ_{i_0} and σ_{j_0} in two separate classes; this value must equal l.

When $\mathcal{E}(\sigma_{i_0}, \sigma_{j_0})$ is applied to $M|\sigma_{i_0}$ and $M|\sigma_{j_0}$, the output sequences are identical except for the very last—the lth—symbol. Consequently, the kth successors of σ_{i_0} and σ_{j_0} with respect to $\mathcal{E}(\sigma_{i_0}, \sigma_{j_0})$ are $(l - k)$-distinguishable and $(l - k - 1)$-equivalent, for all $0 \le k \le l - 1$. This situation is depicted in Fig. 4.2, where $\mathcal{E}(\sigma_{i_0}, \sigma_{j_0})$ is taken as $\xi_{u_1}\xi_{u_2} \cdots \xi_{u_l}$.

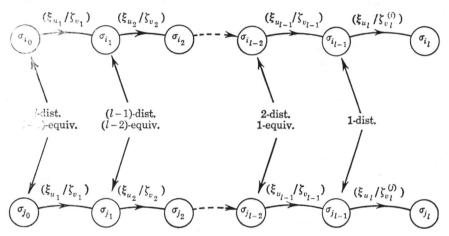

FIG. 4.2. Minimal diagnosing sequence for $\{\sigma_{i_0}, \sigma_{j_0}\}$.

The sequence of states traversed by $M|\sigma_{i_0}$ is $\sigma_{i_1}, \sigma_{i_2}, \ldots, \sigma_{i_l}$, the sequence of states traversed by $M|\sigma_{j_0}$ is $\sigma_{j_1}, \sigma_{j_2}, \ldots, \sigma_{j_l}$, the output sequence yielded by $M|\sigma_{i_0}$ is $\zeta_{v_1}\zeta_{v_2} \cdots \zeta_{v_l}^{(i)}$, and the output sequence yielded by $M|\sigma_{j_0}$ is $\zeta_{v_1}\zeta_{v_2} \cdots \zeta_{v_l}^{(j)}$, where $\zeta_{v_l}^{(j)} \ne \zeta_{v_l}^{(i)}$. Using the notation of Fig. 4.2, it can be stated that, if σ_{i_0} and σ_{j_0} are l-distinguishable and $(l - 1)$-equivalent, and if $\xi_{u_1}\xi_{u_2} \cdots \xi_{u_l}$ is a minimal diagnosing sequence for $\{\sigma_{i_0}, \sigma_{j_0}\}$, then: (1) For $1 \le k \le l - 1$, ξ_{u_k} is an input symbol which passes $\sigma_{i_{k-1}}$ and $\sigma_{j_{k-1}}$ into a pair of $(l - k)$-distinguishable and $(l - k - 1)$-equivalent states σ_{i_k} and σ_{j_k}. (2) ξ_{u_l} is an input symbol which yields distinct output symbols when applied to $M|\sigma_{i_{l-1}}$ and $M|\sigma_{j_{l-1}}$.

Determining $\xi_{u_k}, \sigma_{i_k}, and \sigma_{j_k} from \sigma_{i_{k-1}} and \sigma_{j_{k-1}} (1 \le k \le l - 1)$. The determination of ξ_{u_k}, σ_{i_k}, and σ_{j_k} when $\sigma_{i_{k-1}}$ and $\sigma_{j_{k-1}}$ are known can be most conveniently carried out with the aid of the P_k tables, whose construction for the equivalence partitioning of a given machine is described in Sec. 3.6. $\sigma_{i_{k-1}}$ and $\sigma_{j_{k-1}}$ are $(l - k + 1)$-distinguishable and $(l - k)$-equivalent states; consequently, they constitute adjoint rows in the P_{l-k} table and disjoint rows in the P_{l-k+1} table. Rows $\sigma_{i_{k-1}}$ and $\sigma_{j_{k-1}}$ in the P_{l-k} table must, therefore, exhibit two entries, say $\sigma'_{i_{k-1}}$ and $\sigma'_{j_{k-1}}$, respectively, which have different subscripts in at least one column, say $\xi'_{u_{k-1}}$. Now, $\sigma'_{i_{k-1}}$ and $\sigma'_{j_{k-1}}$ must be $(l - k - 1)$-equivalent, since they are first successors of the $(l - k)$-equivalent states $\sigma_{i_{k-1}}$ and $\sigma_{j_{k-1}}$, with respect to the input symbol $\xi'_{u_{k-1}}$; they also must be $(l - k)$-distinguishable, since "$\sigma'_{i_{k-1}}$" and "$\sigma'_{j_{k-1}}$" bear different subscripts in the P_{l-k} table. Consequently, $\sigma'_{i_{k-1}}$ and $\sigma'_{j_{k-1}}$ are the sought states σ_{i_k} and σ_{j_k}, respectively, and the input symbol $\xi'_{u_{k-1}}$ is the sought input symbol ξ_{u_k}. Thus, ξ_{u_k}, σ_{i_k}, and σ_{j_k} can be determined by inspection of the P_{l-k} table.

Determining ξ_{u_l} *from* $\sigma_{i_{l-1}}$ *and* $\sigma_{j_{l-1}}$. $\sigma_{i_{l-1}}$ and $\sigma_{j_{l-1}}$ are l-distinguishable; hence, there must exist at least one input symbol which yields distinct output symbols when applied to $M|\sigma_{i_{l-1}}$ and $M|\sigma_{j_{l-1}}$. This symbol, which is the sought ξ_{u_l}, can be readily determined by locating a column in the z_ν subtable, in which rows $\sigma_{i_{l-1}}$ and $\sigma_{j_{l-1}}$ have distinct entries.

The foregoing procedures can now be combined as follows:

ALGORITHM 4.1. σ_{i_0} and σ_{j_0} are two states in machine M. To determine the minimal diagnosing sequence for $\{\sigma_{i_0}, \sigma_{j_0}\}$: (1) Construct the P_k tables for M. Find l such that σ_{i_0} and σ_{j_0} are adjoint rows in the P_{l-1} table and disjoint rows in the P_l table. Let $k = 1$. (2) (a) If $l - k > 0$, proceed to step 3. (b) If $l - k = 0$, ξ_{u_k} is given by the heading of any column in the z_ν subtable of M, such that rows $\sigma_{i_{k-1}}$ and $\sigma_{j_{k-1}}$ in this column are distinct. $\xi_{u_1} \xi_{u_2} \cdots \xi_{u_k}$ is the minimal diagnosing sequence for $\{\sigma_{i_0}, \sigma_{j_0}\}$. (3) ξ_{u_k} is the heading of any column in the P_{l-k} table of M, such that rows $\sigma_{i_{k-1}}$ and $\sigma_{j_{k-1}}$ in this column have differently subscripted entries; these entries are σ_{i_k} and σ_{j_k}, respectively. Increment k by 1 and return to (2).

Machine $A17$ of Fig. 4.3 and Table 4.1 will be used for illustration. Tables 4.2 to 4.5 are the P_1, P_2, P_3, and P_4 tables of $A17$. For example, to find the minimal diagnosing sequence for $\{1, 2\}$, namely, $\mathcal{E}(1, 2)$, we start from the P_3 table, which is the "last" table in which rows 1 and 2 are adjoint. Rows 1 and 2 in the P_3 table have distinct subscripts in entries "4_c" and "5_d," which appear in column β. β, then, is the first symbol in $\mathcal{E}(1, 2)$. In the P_2 table, rows 4 and 5 have distinct subscripts in entries "3_b" and "2_a," which appear in column α. α, then, is the second symbol in $\mathcal{E}(1, 2)$. In the P_1 table, rows 3 and 2 have distinct subscripts in entries "5_b" and "1_a," which appear in column α. α, then, is the third symbol in $\mathcal{E}(1, 2)$. Alternatively, β could be chosen as the third symbol, since rows 3 and 2 have distinct subscripts in entries "1_a" and "5_b," which appear in column β. In the z_ν subtable, rows 1 and 5 have distinct entries (0 and 1) in column α. α, then, is the fourth and last symbol in $\mathcal{E}(1, 2)$. Thus, $(1, 2)$ is either $\beta\alpha\alpha\alpha$ or $\beta\alpha\beta\alpha$. From Table 4.1 or Fig. 4.3 it can be readily verified that when $\beta\alpha\alpha\alpha$ is applied to $A17$ at state 1 and state 2, the last output symbol is 1 and 0, respectively. Consequently, if {1, 2} is the admissible set of $A17$, the diagnosing experiment may be conducted by applying $\beta\alpha\alpha$ and observing the last input symbol: if this symbol is 1, the initial state is 1, and if this symbol is 0, the initial state is 2. Table 4.6 lists the minimal diagnosing sequences for all pairs of states $\{\sigma_{i_0}, \sigma_{j_0}\}$ in $A17$; the last two columns in this table indicate the last output symbols $\zeta_{vl}^{(i)}$ and $\zeta_{vl}^{(j)}$ observed when the minimal diagnosing sequence is applied to σ_{i_0} and σ_{j_0}, respectively. Where two or more mini-

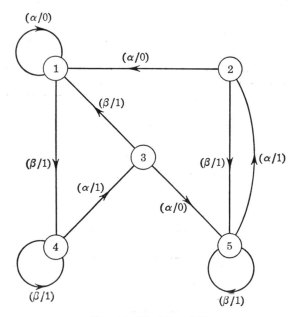

FIG. 4.3. Machine $A17$.

mal diagnosing sequences can be constructed for a given state pair, only one such sequence is listed in the table.

TABLE 4.1. MACHINE $A17$

	z_v		s_{v+1}	
x_v / s_v	α	β	α	β
1	0	1	1	4
2	0	1	1	5
3	0	1	5	1
4	1	1	3	4
5	1	1	2	5

TABLE 4.2. P_1 TABLE FOR $A17$

		s_{v+1}	
Σ	x_v / s_v	α	β
a	1	1_a	4_b
	2	1_a	5_b
	3	5_b	1_a
b	4	3_a	4_b
	5	2_a	5_b

TABLE 4.3. P_2 TABLE FOR $A17$

Σ	$\begin{smallmatrix}x_\nu\\s_\nu\end{smallmatrix}$	$s_{\nu+1}$	
		α	β
a	1	1_a	4_c
	2	1_a	5_c
b	3	5_c	1_a
c	4	3_b	4_c
	5	2_a	5_c

TABLE 4.4. P_3 TABLE FOR $A17$

Σ	$\begin{smallmatrix}x_\nu\\s_\nu\end{smallmatrix}$	$s_{\nu+1}$	
		α	β
a	1	1_a	4_c
	2	1_a	5_d
b	3	5_d	1_a
c	4	3_b	4_c
d	5	2_a	5_d

TABLE 4.5. P_4 TABLE FOR $A17$

Σ	$\begin{smallmatrix}x_\nu\\s_\nu\end{smallmatrix}$	$s_{\nu+1}$	
		α	β
a	1	1_a	4_d
b	2	1_a	5_e
c	3	5_e	1_a
d	4	3_c	4_d
e	5	2_b	5_e

TABLE 4.6. MINIMAL DIAGNOSING SEQUENCES FOR STATE PAIRS IN $A17$

σ_{i_0}	σ_{j_0}	$\mathcal{E}(\sigma_{i_0}, \sigma_{j_0})$	$\zeta_{v_l}^{(i)}$	$\zeta_{v_l}^{(j)}$
1	2	$\beta\alpha\alpha$	1	0
1	3	$\alpha\alpha$	0	1
1	4	α	0	1
1	5	α	0	1
2	3	$\alpha\alpha$	0	1
2	4	α	0	1
2	5	α	0	1
3	4	α	0	1
3	5	α	0	1
4	5	$\alpha\alpha\alpha$	1	0

4.5. Ramifications of the Pairwise Diagnosing Problem

The discussion in the preceding section can be summarized in the following theorem:

THEOREM 4.1. The diagnosing problem for an n-state machine with two admissible states can always be solved by a simple preset experiment of length l, where

$$l \leq n - 1 \tag{4.1}$$

The bound in Eq. (4.1) can be achieved with equality for any n, as demonstrated by machine $A18$ of Fig. 4.4. Clearly no two states in $A18$ can yield distinct output symbols before state n is reached from one of these states and α is applied; consequently, the diagnosing experiment

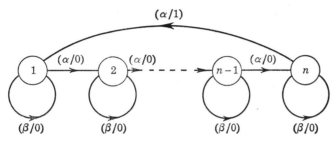

FIG. 4.4. Machine $A18$.

for $A18$ and the admissible set $\{1, 2\}$ cannot be shorter than $n - 1$. The minimal diagnosing sequence for $\{1, 2\}$ consists of $n - 1$ successive α's; the output sequence terminates with 0 if the initial state is 1 and with 1 if the initial state is 2.

The pairwise diagnosing problem is directly related to the following problem: It is known that a given machine M is either machine M_1 in state σ_i or machine M_2 in state σ_j, where the transition tables of M_1 and M_2 are available and where M_1 and M_2 are congruous. It is desired to identify the machine and its initial state. Through the simple artifice of regarding M as the disjunction machine of M_1 and M_2, namely, $\Delta(M_1, M_2)$, the above problem can be rephrased as follows: It is known that a given machine $\Delta(M_1, M_2)$, whose transition table is available, is in one of the states σ_i, σ_j; find this state. The latter problem is precisely the pairwise diagnosing problem for machine $\Delta(M_1, M_2)$ and the admissible set $\{\sigma_i, \sigma_j\}$. When $\sigma_i \neq \sigma_j$, this problem can be solved by the method described in Sec. 4.4. By Theorem 4.1, then, we have:

COROLLARY 4.1. A given machine is known to be either M_1 in state σ_i or M_2 in state σ_j, where $\sigma_i \neq \sigma_j$, where M_1 and M_2 are congruous, and where the transition tables of M_1 and M_2 are available. If M_1 is an n_1-state machine and M_2 an n_2-state machine, the given machine and its initial state can always be identified by a simple preset experiment of length l, where

$$l \le n_1 + n_2 - 1 \tag{4.2}$$

The bound in Eq. (4.2) can be achieved with equality for any n_1 and n_2, as demonstrated by machines $A19$ and $A20$ of Fig. 4.5, where it is assumed

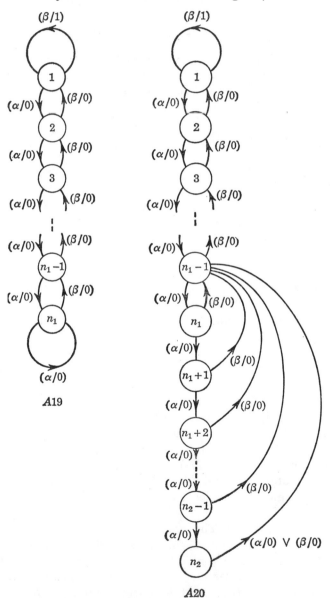

FIG. 4.5. Machines $A19$ and $A20$.

that $n_2 \geq n_1$ [when $n_1 = n_2$, state n_1 of $A20$ has a single diverging branch, labeled $(\alpha/0) \vee (\beta/0)$, which points to state $n_1 - 1$]. First notice that no two states i of $A19$ and j of $A20$ can yield distinct output symbols before state 1 is reached from i or j and β is applied. Next, observe the effect on $A20$ of deleting the input-output pair $(\alpha/0)$ from the diverging branch labeled $(\alpha/0) \vee (\beta/0)$ of state n_2 and adding the reflecting branch $(\alpha/0)$ to n_2. When this is done, states n_2 and $n_2 - 1$ become simply equivalent and can be replaced by a single state, say $n_2 - 1$; states $n_2 - 1$ and $n_2 - 2$ are now simply equivalent and can be replaced by a single state, say $n_2 - 2$; . . . ; states $n_1 + 1$ and n_1 are now simply equivalent and can be replaced by a single state, say n_1. In its reduced form, $A20$ is now identical to $A19$, and hence state i of $A19$ is equivalent to state i of $A20$, for all $1 \leq i \leq n_1$. It can, therefore, be concluded that the shortest input sequence which is to yield distinct output sequences in $A19$ and $A20$, when both machines are at the initial state 1, must pass $A20$ from state 1 into state n_2 and then into state $n_1 - 1$ with the input symbol α. Since state 1 must be recovered in either $A19$ or $A20$ before distinct output symbols can be observed, the same sequence must pass $A20$ from state n_2 to state 1 and then terminate with the input symbol β. The shortest experiment distinguishing between $A19$ at state 1 and $A20$ at state 1 consists, therefore, of applying n_2 α's followed by $n_1 - 1$ β's, with the total length of $n_1 + n_2 - 1$. The last output symbol observed in this experiment is 0 if the state is 1 of $A19$ and is 1 if the state is 1 of $A20$.

It should be noted that the only requirement imposed on M_1 and M_2 in Corollary 4.1 is that $\sigma_i \neq \sigma_j$. This requirement is independent of the distinguishability or equivalence of M_1 and M_2 (σ_i and σ_j may be distinguishable states in two equivalent machines). Consequently, the assumption that the individual machines M_1 and M_2 are minimal need not be extended to the disjunction machine $\Delta(M_1, M_2)$.

4.6. The Successor Tree

In what follows, a σ *set* of machine M will be any finite set of states of M; the elements of a σ set need not be distinct.[1] A σ set containing only one element is said to be *simple;* a σ set containing two or more identical elements is said to be *multiple;* a σ set in which all the elements are identical is said to be *homogeneous* (a simple σ set being a special case).

For a machine whose admissible set is of size m, an *A group* is a set of σ sets, with m being the total number of elements in all the included σ sets. The number of σ sets in an A group is referred to as the *resolution* of the group. The resolution of an A group cannot exceed m. An

---

[1] Although a σ set is not a "set" in the formal sense (since it contains duplicate elements), it will be indicated by braces, as was adopted for ordinary sets.

A group in which all the σ sets are simple is said to be *simple;* an A group in which all the σ sets are homogeneous is said to be *homogeneous.*

Let G be an A group consisting of the σ sets $g_1, g_2, \ldots, g_r$. The $\xi_{i_1}\xi_{i_2} \cdots \xi_{i_l}$ *successor* of G is another A group, constructed according to the following rules: (1) Partition every set g_i into subsets, such that two states of g_i are included in the same subset if and only if they yield identical responses to the input sequence $\xi_{i_1}\xi_{i_2} \cdots \xi_{i_l}$. Regard each subset as a σ set and the set of all such σ sets as an A group, denoted by G'. (2) In the σ sets of G', replace every state by its successor with respect to the input sequence $\xi_{i_1}\xi_{i_2} \cdots \xi_{i_l}$. The resulting A group is the $\xi_{i_1}\xi_{i_2} \cdots \xi_{i_l}$ successor of G.

The *successor tree* is a structure defined for a given machine M and a specified admissible set $A(M)$. The structure is composed of branches arranged in successive *levels*, the highest level being the "zeroth" level, the next to highest being the "first" level, and so forth. The zeroth tree level consists of a single branch, called the *initial branch.* In a successor tree constructed for a machine whose input alphabet is $\{\xi_1, \xi_2, \ldots, \xi_p\}$, each branch in the kth level ($k \geq 0$) splits into p branches, representing $\xi_1, \xi_2, \ldots, \xi_p$, respectively, which constitute branches of the $(k + 1)$st level. A branch representing the input symbol ξ_i is referred to as "branch ξ_i." The kth tree level is seen to consist of p^k branches. A sequence of l branches, such that the kth branch is in the kth level ($k = 1, 2, \ldots, l$), and such that the $(k + 1)$st branch is generated by the kth branch ($k = 1, 2, \ldots, l - 1$), is called a *tree path;* l is referred to as the *length* of the tree path. If the kth branch of this tree path is ξ_{i_k} ($k = 1, 2, \ldots, l$), the path is said to *describe* the input sequence $\xi_{i_1}\xi_{i_2} \cdots \xi_{i_l}$. Thus, the first $k + 1$ levels of a successor tree contain p^k paths, describing all p^k possible input sequences of length k which can be constructed with p input symbols.

Each branch in the successor tree constructed for M and $A(M)$ is associated with an A group. The A group with which the initial branch is associated is $A(M)$. If a branch b is associated with the A group G, then the branch ξ_i which b generates is associated with the ξ_i successor of G. Thus, the A groups associated with the kth-level branches ($k \geq 1$) can be determined from the A groups associated with the $(k - 1)$st-level branches. In this manner, any tree level can be constructed on the basis of the completed level which immediately precedes it. A tree path is said to *lead to* the A group G if its last branch is associated with G.

Figure 4.6 shows the first four levels of the successor tree constructed for machine $A17$ of Fig. 4.3 and the admissible set $\{2, 3, 4, 5\}$. Each branch is labeled with the input symbol which it represents and the A group with which it is associated. The A group associated with the initial branch is the admissible set $\{2, 3, 4, 5\}$. The remaining A groups

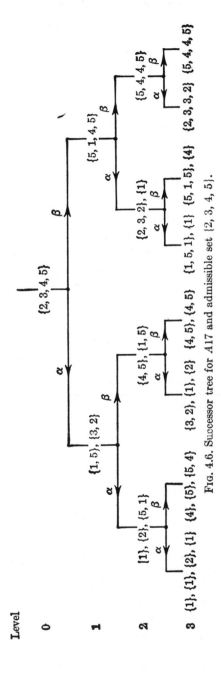

Level

0   {2, 3, 4, 5}

1   {1, 5}, {3, 2}   {5, 1, 4, 5}

2   {1}, {2}, {5, 1}   {4, 5}, {1, 5}   {2, 3, 2}, {1}   {5, 4, 4, 5}

3   {1}, {1}, {2}, {1}   {4}, {5}, {5, 4}   {3, 2}, {1}, {2}   {4, 5}, {4, 5}   {1, 5, 1}, {1}   {5, 1, 5}, {4}   {2, 3, 3, 2}   {5, 4, 4, 5}

FIG. 4.6. Successor tree for A17 and admissible set {2, 3, 4, 5}.

99

can be found with the aid of the transition table or diagram for $A17$. For example, when α is applied to states 2, 3, 4, and 5, the output symbols are 0, 0, 1, and 1, respectively, and the next states are 1, 5, 3, and 2, respectively; the α successor of the A group $\{2, 3, 4, 5\}$, then, consists of the σ sets $\{1, 5\}$ and $\{3, 2\}$. Consequently, branch α in the first level of the successor tree is associated with the A group $\{1, 5\}$, $\{3, 2\}$.

The following lemmas, which describe some properties of the successor tree for machine M and admissible set $A(M)$, are direct results of the foregoing rules and definitions:

LEMMA 4.1.   Let $A(M)$ be denoted by G_0, and let G_k be an A group associated with the kth branch of a tree path.   Then: (a) The resolution of G_k equals or exceeds the resolution of G_{k-1}.   (b) If G_{k-1} contains a multiple σ set, G_k must also contain a multiple σ set.

LEMMA 4.2.   Let $A(M) = \{\sigma_{i_1}, \sigma_{i_2}, \ldots, \sigma_{i_m}\}$, and let G be the A group led to by the tree path describing the input sequence ε.   Let σ'_{i_k} denote the successor of σ_{i_k} with respect to ε.   Then: (a) $\sigma'_{i_1}, \sigma'_{i_2}, \ldots, \sigma'_{i_m}$ are the m states contained in the σ sets of G.   (b) σ'_{i_k} and σ'_{i_l} are in different σ sets of G, if and only if σ_{i_k} and σ_{i_l} yield distinct output sequences when presented with the input sequence ε.

LEMMA 4.3.   Let b_1 and b_2 denote two branches associated with identical A groups.   Then a branch associated with any A group G is reachable from b_1 via l branches, if and only if a branch associated with the A group G is reachable from b_2 via l branches.

4.7. The Diagnosing Tree

The successor tree, as introduced in the preceding section, is infinite in extent, and as such is of no practical use.   In this section we shall define a "truncated" version of the successor tree by formulating a number of "termination rules."   A termination rule stipulates when a branch should be left as a *terminal branch*, i.e., as a branch which does not generate any next-level branches.   The following termination rules define a structure which will be referred to as a *diagnosing tree:*

DEFINITION 4.1.   A diagnosing tree is a successor tree in which a kth-level branch b becomes terminal, if one of the following conditions is met: (1) The A group associated with b contains a multiple σ set.   (2) The A group associated with b is associated with some branch in a level preceding the kth.   (3) There is a kth-level branch (possibly b itself) associated with a simple A group.

Rule (3) implies that the first level to contain a branch associated with a simple A group is also the last level in the diagnosing tree.   A tree whose last level is the kth is called a tree of *height k*.   Figure 4.7 demonstrates how the diagnosing tree is constructed for machine $A17$ of Fig. 4.3 and the admissible set $\{2, 3, 4, 5\}$.   The first-level branch associated with the A group $\{5, 1, 4, 5\}$ is terminal by virtue of rule 1. In the third level, the A group $\{1\}, \{1\}, \{2\}, \{1\}$ is seen to be simple; by virtue of rule 3, therefore, all the branches in the third level are terminal. As another example, Fig. 4.8 shows the diagnosing tree for $A17$ and the admissible

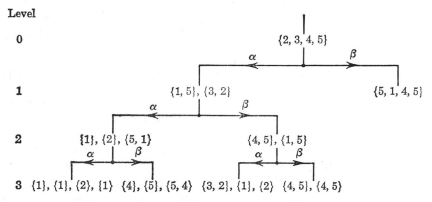

Fig. 4.7. Diagnosing tree for $A17$ and admissible set $\{2, 3, 4, 5\}$.

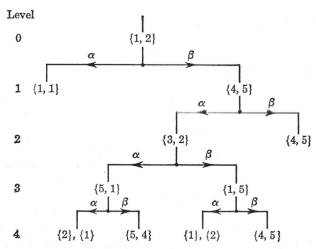

Fig. 4.8. Diagnosing tree for $A17$ and admissible set $\{1, 2\}$.

set $\{1, 2\}$. The first-level branch associated with the A group $\{1, 1\}$ is terminal by virtue of rule 1. The second-level branch associated with the A group $\{4, 5\}$ is terminal by virtue of rule 2, since the A group is already associated with a first-level branch. In the fourth level, the A group $\{2\}, \{1\}$ is seen to be simple; by virtue of rule 3, therefore, all the branches in the fourth level are terminal.

LEMMA 4.4. The height of a diagnosing tree constructed for an n-state machine M and an admissible set of size m is given by h, where

$$h \leq (m - 1)n^m \tag{4.3}$$

Proof. Let the A group G consist of the σ sets $g_1, g_2, \ldots, g_r$, where the size of g_i is m_i. The set of numbers $m_1, m_2, \ldots, m_r$ is called the *occupancy distribution* of G. The number of different A groups having the same occupancy distribution as G is at most

$$n^{m_1}n^{m_2} \cdots n^{m_r} = n^m \tag{4.4}$$

Now, if $A(M)$ is denoted by G_0 and G_k is an A group associated with the kth branch of a tree path, then either the occupancy distribution of G_k is the same as that of G_{k-1} or, by Lemma 4.1, the resolution of G_k exceeds that of G_{k-1}. Hence, if $G_j, G_{j+1}, \ldots, G_{j+n^m-1}$ are distinct and have the same resolution r, G_{j+n^m} must either be identical to one of the preceding A groups or have the resolution $r' \geq r + 1$. By induction, the number of successive A groups of resolution r or less, such that no two groups are identical, is at most rn^m. In particular, the number of successive A groups of resolution $m - 1$ or less, such that no two groups are identical, is at most $(m - 1)n^m$. Hence, if $G_0, G_1, \ldots, G_{(m-1)n^m-1}$ are distinct and not simple, $G_{(m-1)n^m}$ must either be identical to one of the preceding A groups or be simple. Thus, a path which does not terminate at the $[(m - 1)n^m]$th branch by virtue of rule 2 must terminate at this branch by virtue of rule 3. Consequently, no path in the diagnosing tree can consist of more than $(m - 1)n^m$ branches, which proves the lemma.

In all specific situations, h is considerably smaller than the bound expressed by (4.3), since in (4.3) we did not include the effect of rule 1 on the path length or the effect on the path length due to A groups associated with other paths. At any rate, Lemma 4.4 proves that the number of levels in a diagnosing tree is finite and that the construction of such a tree, therefore, is a finite process.

A *diagnosing path* will be any tree path in the diagnosing tree whose terminal branch is associated with a simple A group. A *diagnosing sequence* for M and $A(M) = \{\sigma_{i_1}, \sigma_{i_2}, \ldots, \sigma_{i_m}\}$ will be any input sequence which, when applied to $M|\sigma_{i_1}, M|\sigma_{i_2}, \ldots, M|\sigma_{i_m}$, results in m different output sequences. Lemma 4.2, then, yields:

LEMMA 4.5. The input sequence described by a diagnosing path in a diagnosing tree constructed for M and $A(M)$ is a diagnosing sequence for M and $A(M)$.

The *minimal diagnosing sequence* for M and $A(M)$, denoted by $\mathcal{E}(A)$, is the shortest diagnosing sequence for M and $A(M)$. The *truncated paths* of a diagnosing tree constructed for M and $A(M)$ are the paths included in the successor tree but absent from the diagnosing tree, by virtue of rule 1 or 2.

LEMMA 4.6. The truncated paths of a diagnosing tree constructed for M and $A(M)$ do not describe minimal diagnosing sequences.

Proof. If a path is truncated by virtue of rule 1, it terminates at some branch b associated with an A group which contains a multiple σ set. By Lemma 4.1, every path passing through b in the successor tree must lead to an A group which contains a multiple σ set. Such a path, then, cannot lead to a simple A group, and hence cannot be a diagnosing path. Now, consider a path truncated by virtue of rule 2, terminating at the jth level branch b_j which is associated with the A group G. Then there must be an ith-level branch b_i, where $i < j$, also associated with G. By Lemma 4.3, if in the successor tree a simple A group is reachable from b_j via l branches, a simple A group is also reachable from b_i via l branches. Hence, if a diagnosing path in the successor tree traverses b_j, one must also traverse b_i; moreover, the latter must be shorter than the former, since $i < j$. Consequently, if the successor tree contains a diagnosing path which traverses b_j, this path cannot describe a minimal diagnosing sequence.

THEOREM 4.2. The set of sequences described by the diagnosing paths in the diagnosing tree constructed for machine M and admissible set $A(M)$ is the set of all minimal diagnosing sequences for M and $A(M)$.

Proof. By Lemma 4.6, the set of diagnosing paths exhibited by the diagnosing tree must contain the paths which describe all minimal diagnosing sequences for M and $A(M)$. Since, by virtue of rule 3, all diagnosing paths exhibited by the tree have the same length, they all must be minimal. If the diagnosing tree exhibits no diagnosing paths, all its paths are terminated by virtue of rule 1 or 2, and hence, by Lemma 4.6, no diagnosing sequence exists for M and $A(M)$.

4.8. Simple Preset Diagnosing Experiments

The results obtained in the preceding section suggest a procedure for solving the m-wise diagnosing problem by the shortest simple preset experiment, whenever a solution by such an experiment exists:

ALGORITHM 4.2. Given machine M and its admissible set

$$A(M) = \{\sigma_{i_1}, \sigma_{i_2}, \ldots, \sigma_{i_m}\}$$

to find the initial state of M by the shortest simple preset experiment: (1) Construct the diagnosing tree for M and $A(M)$. (2) Choose any diagnosing sequence $\mathcal{E}(A)$ described by the tree. If none is described, no solution by a simple preset experiment exists. (3) List the responses of $M|\sigma_{i_1}, M|\sigma_{i_2}, \ldots, M|\sigma_{i_m}$ to $\mathcal{E}(A)$. (4) Apply $\mathcal{E}(A)$ to M and observe the response.   The initial state is the state σ_{i_k} for which the response listed in (3) is identical with the observed response.

Algorithm 4.2 can be demonstrated with machine $A17$ of Fig. 4.3 and the admissible set $\{2, 3, 4, 5\}$.   In this case, the diagnosing tree of Fig. 4.7 reveals the minimal diagnosing sequence to be $\alpha\alpha\alpha$.   Table 4.7 lists the responses of states 2, 3, 4, and 5 to $\alpha\alpha\alpha$.   These responses, as can be expected, are distinct and may serve as the criteria for identifying the initial state of $A17$, when subject to the specified admissible set.   As another example, the minimal diagnosing sequences for $A17$ and the admissible set $\{1, 2\}$ are revealed by Fig. 4.8 to be $\beta\alpha\alpha\alpha$ and $\beta\alpha\beta\alpha$.   For $m = 2$, the m-wise diagnosing problem reduces to the pairwise diagnosing problem for which, by Theorem 4.1, a solution through a simple preset experiment always exists.   In this case, the minimal diagnosing sequence can be more conveniently determined via the P_k tables, as described in

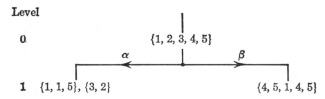

FIG. 4.9. Diagnosing tree for $A17$ and admissible set $\{1, 2, 3, 4, 5\}$.

Sec. 4.4.   For $m > 2$, a solution by a simple preset experiment does not always exist, as demonstrated by the diagnosing tree for $A17$ and the admissible set $\{1, 2, 3, 4, 5\}$, shown in Fig. 4.9.

Using Lemma 4.4, we can now summarize as follows:

TABLE 4.7. RESPONSES OF $A17$ TO $\alpha\alpha\alpha$

Initial state	Response to $\alpha\alpha\alpha$
2	000
3	010
4	101
5	100

THEOREM 4.3.   The diagnosing problem for an n-state machine with m admissible states, if at all solvable by simple preset experimentation, is solvable by a simple preset experiment of length l, where

$$l \le (m - 1)n^m \tag{4.5}$$

The solution of the m-wise diagnosing problem is directly applicable to the following problem: It is known that a given machine M is machine M_1 in a state belonging to the set $A(M_1)$, or machine M_2 in a state belonging to the set $A(M_2)$, . . . , or machine M_N in a state belonging to the set $A(M_N)$. It is desired to identify the machine and its initial state. Assuming that M_1, M_2, . . . , M_N are congruous and that their transition tables are available, the above problem is precisely the m-wise diagnosing problem for the disjunction machine $\Delta(M_1, M_2, . . . , M_N)$ and the admissible set $A(M_1) \cup A(M_2) \cup \cdot \cdot \cdot \cup A(M_N)$. The basic assumption that the given machine M is minimal implies, in this case, that every machine M_i is minimal and that no state in any machine M_i is equivalent to any state in machine M_j $(j \neq i)$.

4.9. Simple Adaptive Diagnosing Experiments

Consider a path in the diagnosing tree for M and $A(M)$, which leads to an A group G containing a simple σ set, say $\{\sigma_i'\}$ (since G may contain other σ sets which are not simple, G itself is not necessarily simple). If this path describes the input sequence $\mathcal{E}$, then $A(M)$ must contain a state, say σ_i, whose successor with respect to $\mathcal{E}$ is the state σ_i'. Since $\{\sigma_i'\}$ is a singleton in G, the response of σ_i to $\mathcal{E}$ cannot, by Lemma 4.2, be attributed to any state in $A(M)$ except σ_i. Thus, if σ_i is perchance the true initial state of M, it can be identified by an input sequence which is not necessarily described by a diagnosing path. Exploiting this fact, one can apply the minimal diagnosing sequence piecemeal, rather than in its entirety, with the expectation that the initial state is such that it can be identified with only a fraction of the total sequence. This scheme constitutes a solution to the m-wise diagnosing problem by a simple adaptive experiment.

The segmentation of the minimal diagnosing sequence into subsequences is done in the following manner: Let $\mathcal{E}_k$ be the kth subsequence, and let G_k be the A group led to by the path describing $\mathcal{E}_1\mathcal{E}_2 \cdot \cdot \cdot \mathcal{E}_k$; denote $A(M)$ by G_0. Then $\mathcal{E}_k$ is the subsequence described by the subpath which leads from G_{k-1} to the first A group which contains at least one more simple σ set than G_{k-1}. Since the resolution of G_0 is 1, and since the number of σ sets in an A group cannot exceed the size m of $A(M)$, the number of subsequences thus produced cannot exceed $m - 1$. As an example, machine $A17$ of Fig. 4.3 and the admissible set $\{2, 3, 4, 5\}$ yield $G_0 = \{2, 3, 4, 5\}$, $G_1 = \{1\}$, $\{2\}$, $\{5, 1\}$, $G_2 = \{1\}$, $\{1\}$, $\{2\}$, $\{1\}$; and hence $\mathcal{E}_1 = \alpha\alpha$ and $\mathcal{E}_2 = \alpha$ (see Fig. 4.7). Once the subsequences are determined, the adaptive experiment can be carried out as follows:

ALGORITHM 4.3. Given machine M, its admissible set

$$A(M) = \{\sigma_{i_1}, \sigma_{i_2}, . . . , \sigma_{i_m}\}$$

and the segmented diagnosing sequence $\mathcal{E}_1\mathcal{E}_2 \cdot \cdot \cdot \mathcal{E}_r$, to identify the initial state of M by a simple adaptive experiment: (1) List the responses of $M|\sigma_{i_1}$, $M|\sigma_{i_2}$, . . . , $M|\sigma_{i_m}$ to $\mathcal{E}_1\mathcal{E}_2 \cdots \mathcal{E}_r$.   Segment each response into r subsequences to correspond with the segmentation of the input sequence. Let $k = 1$.   (2) Apply $\mathcal{E}_k$ to M.   (3) (a) If the response of M to $\mathcal{E}_1\mathcal{E}_2 \cdots \mathcal{E}_k$ is attributable to only one state in the list compiled in (1), this state is the initial state of M.   (b) If the response of M to $\mathcal{E}_1\mathcal{E}_2$ $\cdots \mathcal{E}_k$ is attributable to two or more states in the list compiled in (1), increment k by 1 and return to (2).

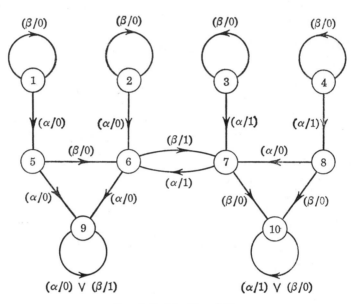

FIG. 4.10. Machine $A21$.

Algorithm 4.3 can be demonstrated with machine $A17$ and the admissible set $\{2, 3, 4, 5\}$, for which we have $\mathcal{E}_1 = \alpha\alpha$ and $\mathcal{E}_2 = \alpha$.   The list of responses to $\alpha\alpha\alpha$, segmented as specified in step 1, is given in Table 4.8. If the initial state of $A17$ happens to be 2, the response to $\alpha\alpha$ is 00, which is attributable only to state 2; hence, in this case the diagnosing experiment requires only two input symbols.   If the initial state happens to be 5, the response to $\alpha\alpha$ is 10, which cannot be uniquely attributed to state 5 (the initial state, on the basis of this response, may be either 4 or 5), and hence the second subsequence is required to complete the experiment.

It is seen that whenever the m-wise diagnosing problem is solvable by a simple preset experiment, it is also solvable by a simple adaptive experiment whose length is never greater than that of the preset one and whose order never exceeds $m - 1$.   The advantage of such an adaptive experiment is that it *may* terminate earlier than the preset experiment.   The exact length of the adaptive experiment cannot, of course, be estimated in advance, since it depends on the true initial state which remains unknown until the experiment terminates.

Although the solution of the m-wise diagnosing problem by simple preset experimentation implies a solution by simple adaptive experimentation, the converse is not true. There are cases where the initial state cannot be identified by any simple preset experiment, but can be identified by a simple adaptive experiment. An example is machine $A21$ of Fig. 4.10 and the admissible set $\{1, 2, 3, 4\}$. Clearly, any minimal diagnosing sequence for this problem must initiate with α. Now, any sequence starting with $\alpha\alpha$ yields identical responses if $A21$ is in state 1 or 2; any sequence starting with $\alpha\beta$ yields identical responses if $A21$ is in state 3 or 4. Consequently, no sequence exists to which the responses of all four admissible states are distinct. However, if α is applied and then the response is observed, it is possible to determine whether the initial state is in $\{1, 2\}$ (when the response is 0) or in $\{3, 4\}$ (when the response is 1). If it is found that the initial state is in $\{1, 2\}$, β can be applied, which yields 0 if the initial state is 1 and 1 if the initial state is 2; if it is found that the initial state is in $\{3, 4\}$, α can be applied, which yields 1 if the initial state is 3 and 0 if the initial state is 4. Thus, the initial state is identifiable by a simple adaptive experiment of order 2 and length 2. In conclusion, we have the following:

TABLE 4.8. SEGMENTED RESPONSES OF $A17$ TO $\alpha\alpha\alpha$

Initial state	Response to	
	$\alpha\alpha$	α
2	00	0
3	01	0
4	10	1
5	10	0

THEOREM 4.4. Every m-wise diagnosing problem solvable by a simple preset experiment of length l is solvable by a simple adaptive experiment of length l or less and of order $m - 1$ or less. There are m-wise diagnosing problems which are unsolvable by a simple preset experiment, but are solvable by a simple adaptive experiment.

The adaptive experiment described by Algorithm 4.3 is essentially a preset experiment, with the facility of early termination based on observed responses. Such an adaptive experiment, therefore, depends on the existence of a preset experiment and is by no means general. The most general adaptive experiment is one in which, after the application of every input symbol, as many admissible states are ruled out as possible on the basis of the observed response, i.e., only those admissible states are considered to which past responses can be attributed. In terms of the successor tree, this means that a path which leads to an A group containing a multiple σ set may still be used for designing a diagnosing experiment, since the multiple σ set may result from admissible states which were previously ruled out. This fact is demonstrated with the diagnosing tree for machine $A21$ and the admissible set $\{1, 2, 3, 4\}$, shown in Fig. 4.11. Although the paths describing $\alpha\alpha$ and $\alpha\beta$ lead to A groups containing multiple σ sets ($\{9, 9\}$ and $\{10, 10\}$, respectively), these σ sets are eliminable on the basis of the response to the first symbol α: after α is

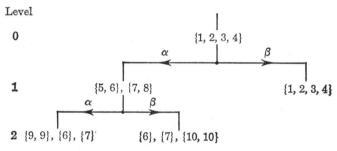

Fig. 4.11. Diagnosing tree for $A21$ and admissible set $\{1, 2, 3, 4\}$.

applied, either states 1 and 2 can be ruled out as admissible states (in which case $\{9, 9\}$ can be ignored), or states 3 and 4 can be ruled out (in which case $\{10, 10\}$ can be ignored).

Generalizing the foregoing remarks, it can be stated that a simple adaptive experiment for machine M and its admissible set

$$A(M) = \{\sigma_{i_1}, \sigma_{i_2}, \ldots, \sigma_{i_m}\}$$

is realizable if the successor tree for M and $A(M)$ contains m paths, whose nature is indicated in Fig. 4.12. In this figure, σ'_{i_h} denotes a successor of σ_{i_h}; any of the m paths shown in the figure may completely overlap any of the other paths. In addition to such paths, a simple adaptive experiment requires a set of rules, such that: (1) There is a rule for selecting the first input symbol in the experiment. (2) There is a rule for selecting the $(k + 1)$st input symbol in the experiment, given the response to the preceding k symbols. (3) If the true initial state is the state σ_{i_h} of $A(M)$, the set of rules must result in an input sequence described by the path terminating in $\{\sigma'_{i_h}\}$ ($h = 1, 2, \ldots, m$).

Through a proof similar to that employed in Lemma 4.4, it can be shown that if no set of paths of length $(m - 1)n^m$ or less has the properties depicted by Fig. 4.12, then no set of paths of any length has these properties. We thus have:

THEOREM 4.5. The diagnosing problems for an n-state machine with m admissible states, if at all solvable by simple adaptive experimentation, is solvable by a simple adaptive experiment of length l, where

$$l \leq (m - 1)n^m \qquad (4.6)$$

To determine whether a simple adaptive experiment is realizable for given M and $A(M)$, first determine whether the required set of paths

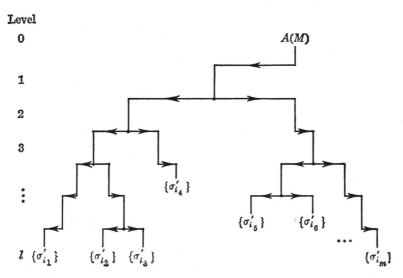

FIG. 4.12. Paths for a simple adaptive diagnosing experiment.

exists. If so, list all possible sets of rules for selecting the input sequence. If a set of rules exists which fulfills conditions 1, 2, and 3 stipulated above, then such an experiment exists, and this set can be used for its execution. If a set fulfilling these conditions does not exist, then the diagnosing problem for M and $A(M)$ cannot be solved by any simple adaptive experiment. By Theorem 4.4, this implies that the problem is not solvable by any simple experiment—preset or adaptive.

To verify that there are cases where the diagnosing problem is unsolvable by any simple experiment, either preset or adaptive, consider machine $A21$ of Fig. 4.10 and the admissible set $\{5, 6, 7, 8\}$. Any sequence or subsequence starting with α causes states 5 and 6 to pass into state 9 with identical responses; any sequence or subsequence starting with β causes states 7 and 8 to pass into state 10 with identical responses. Hence, once the first input symbol is applied (whether to initiate a preset or an adaptive experiment), there is no way of ever distinguishing either between states 5 and 6 or between states 7 and 8.   We thus have:

THEOREM 4.6.   There are m-wise diagnosing problems which are unsolvable by either simple preset experiments or simple adaptive experiments.

4.10. Multiple Preset Diagnosing Experiments

The obvious shortcoming of a simple experiment is that it is inherently destructive: when only one copy of the given machine is available, there is no way, in general, of knowingly recovering the initial state in order to conduct a new experiment, when the previous experiment proves to be a failure.   Thus, in simple experimentation, useful information conveyed by a failing experiment cannot always be exploited for future experimentation, since, by the time the information becomes available, the initial state may no longer be identifiable.   If a sufficient number of copies of the given machine is available, it is possible to conduct a number of experiments, each of which is by itself insufficient to solve the diagnosing problem, but which jointly supply sufficient information to identify the initial state.   For example, we concluded that there is no simple experiment which solves the diagnosing problem for machine $A21$ of Fig. 4.10 and the admissible set $\{5, 6, 7, 8\}$.   However, if two copies of $A21$ are available, a solution can be arrived at as follows: Apply $\alpha\alpha$ to the first copy of $A21$ and β to the second copy.   If the response of the first copy is 01, the initial state is 8; if the response is 10, the initial state is 7; if the response is 00, the initial state is either 5 or 6.   In the latter case, the response of the second copy is 0 if the initial state is 5 and 1 if the initial state is 6.   Thus, the diagnosing problem for $A21$ and the admissible set $\{5, 6, 7, 8\}$ is solvable by a multiple experiment of multiplicity 2 and length 3.

At this point it is useful to present the following theorem:

THEOREM 4.7.   In an n-state minimal machine, any set of r states $(2 \leq r \leq n)$ contains at least two states which are $(n - r + 1)$-distinguishable.

Proof.   By Lemma 3.9, the number of states in each class of P_k of a minimal n-state machine is at most $n - k$.   Hence, the number of states in each class of P_{n-r+1} is at most $n - (n - r + 1) = r - 1$.   Consequently, at least two states in the set of r states must be in two different classes of P_{n-r+1}, and hence $(n - r + 1)$-distinguishable.

For machine M and admissible set $A(M)$ of size m, let G_k be an A group, consisting of the σ sets $g_{k1}, g_{k2}, \ldots, g_{ku}$. G_0 consists of a single σ set g_{01}, where $g_{01} = A(M)$. G_{k+1} is constructed from G_k according to the following rules: If g_{ki} is of size $r \geq 2$, it must contain at least two states, say σ_j and σ_l, which are $(n - r + 1)$-distinguishable.   Partition g_{ki} into subsets, such that two states belong to the same subset if and only if they yield identical responses to $\mathcal{E}(\sigma_j, \sigma_l)$, that is, to the minimal diagnosing sequence for $\{\sigma_j, \sigma_l\}$. The response to $\mathcal{E}(\sigma_j, \sigma_l)$ of the states which belong to a given subset is called the *characteristic response* of this subset with respect to $\mathcal{E}(\sigma_j, \sigma_l)$. The σ sets of G_{k+1} are the singletons of G_k and all the subsets obtained through the foregoing rule. Since the responses of σ_j and σ_l to $\mathcal{E}(\sigma_j, \sigma_l)$ are distinct, if g_{ki} is not a singleton, it is always partitionable into at least two subsets. Thus, unless G_k is simple, G_{k+1} is always a proper refinement of G_k. Since the size of $A(M)$ is m, G_{m-1} must be simple.

The process described above can be displayed in a structure called the *multiple-experiment tree*, defined for M and $A(M)$.† Each kth-level branch in this tree represents some g_{ki}, with the initial branch representing g_{01}. A branch representing a simple g_{ki} is terminal. If g_{ki} is not simple and partitionable into, say, h subsets (in the manner described in the preceding paragraph), then the branch representing this g_{ki} splits into h next-level branches, which represent the h subsets resulting from the partitioning process. Using these rules, the entire tree can be developed, by constructing the kth level on the basis of the completed $(k-1)$st level. Since the g_{ki} sets represented in the kth level are σ sets of G_k, it follows that the height of the tree cannot exceed $m-1$. Also, the tree must exhibit exactly m terminal branches—one for each admissible state.

For reasons to become apparent presently, all branches in the multiple-experiment tree, except terminal branches, are drawn in the form of two-terminal boxes, representing copies of the given machine. Each branch is labeled with the g_{ki} which it represents. If g_{ki} is not a singleton, the branch is also labeled with the sequence $\mathcal{E}(\sigma_j, \sigma_l)$ employed in the partitioning of g_{ki} and with the characteristic response of g_{ki} with respect to the diagnosing sequence associated with the preceding branch.

As an example, Fig. 4.13 shows the multiple-experiment tree for machine $A17$ of Fig. 4.3 and the admissible set $\{1, 2, 3, 4, 5\}$. The initial branch represents $g_{01} = \{1, 2, 3, 4, 5\}$, which is the specified admissible set. The state pair $\{\sigma_j, \sigma_l\}$ used for the partitioning of g_{01} is $\{1, 4\}$. The state pair, in this case, is selected so as to result in the shortest possible $\mathcal{E}(\sigma_j, \sigma_l)$ (this selection rule, however, is not essential in this procedure). The selection can be made with the aid of the sequence list compiled in Table 4.6, where $\mathcal{E}(1, 4)$ is seen to be α. When α is applied to $A17$, the subset $\{1, 2, 3\}$ of g_{01} responds with 0, and the subset $\{4, 5\}$ with 1, as can be readily deduced from the transition table or diagram of $A17$. The initial branch, therefore, splits into two branches—a branch labeled 0, which is the characteristic response of $g_{11} = \{1, 2, 3\}$ with respect to $\mathcal{E}(1, 4) = \alpha$, and a branch labeled 1, which is the characteristic response

† The terminology to be employed for the multiple-experiment tree is the same as that employed for the diagnosing tree.

of $g_{12} = \{4, 5\}$ with respect to $\mathcal{E}(1, 4) = \alpha$. The state pair $\{1, 3\}$ is now selected from g_{11} in the same manner that $\{1, 4\}$ was selected from g_{01}. When $\mathcal{E}(1, 3) = \alpha\alpha$ is applied to $A17$, the subset $\{1, 2\}$ of g_{11} responds with 00 and the subset $\{3\}$ of g_{11} responds with 01. The branch representing g_{11}, therefore, splits into two branches—a branch labeled 00, which is the characteristic response of $g_{21} = \{1, 2\}$ with respect to $\mathcal{E}(1, 3) = \alpha\alpha$, and a

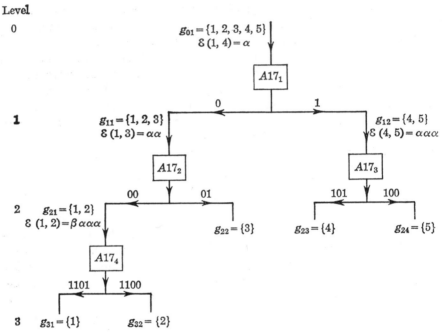

Fig. 4.13. Multiple-experiment tree for $A17$ and admissible set $\{1, 2, 3, 4, 5\}$.

branch labeled 01, which is the characteristic response of $g_{22} = \{3\}$ to $\mathcal{E}(1, 3) = \alpha\alpha$. The latter branch is a terminal one, since g_{22} is a singleton. The remainder of the tree is developed in an analogous fashion.

Once the multiple-experiment tree for M and $A(M)$ is constructed, the multiple experiment can be conducted by regarding every box in the tree as a different copy of M and applying to each copy the particular diagnosing sequence associated with the corresponding box. From the rules formulated for the construction of the tree it follows that, if the observed responses of all the copies of M which lie along a certain tree path match the responses listed for this path, then the initial state of M is the state represented by the terminal branch of the path. The initial state, then, can simply be identified by comparing the actual responses of the copies with the responses indicated along the m different paths.

For $A17$ and its admissible set $\{1, 2, 3, 4, 5\}$, four copies are employed. These copies, denoted by $A17_1$, $A17_2$, $A17_3$, and $A17_4$, are subjected to the diagnosing sequences α, $\alpha\alpha$, $\alpha\alpha\alpha$, and $\beta\alpha\alpha\alpha$, respectively, as prescribed by the multiple-experiment tree of Fig. 4.13. Now, if the initial state of $A17$ happens to be 2, $A17_1$ must yield 0, $A17_2$ must yield 00, and $A17_4$ must yield 1100. Since these responses match those indicated along the tree path terminating at $g_{32} = \{2\}$, the initial state is identifiable as 2.

It is seen that the effect of a copy of M associated with a set g_{ki} is to "split" this set into two or more subsets. Since the number of splitting operations required to refine $A(M)$ into m singletons is at most $m - 1$, the number of copies included in the multiple-experiment tree is at most $m - 1$. Since the length of a diagnosing sequence for a pair of states in an n-state machine cannot exceed $n - 1$, the total length of all the sequences included in the tree cannot exceed $(n - 1)(m - 1)$. We thus have:

THEOREM 4.8. The diagnosing problem for an n-state machine with m admissible states can always be solved by a multiple preset experiment of length l and multiplicity c, where

$$l \leq (n - 1)(m - 1) \tag{4.7}$$
$$c \leq m - 1 \tag{4.8}$$

The bound in (4.7) is considerably higher than the value of l encountered in most problems (although it is achievable with equality for $m = 2$) since, by Theorem 4.7, only a fraction of the employed sequences need be of length $n - 1$. The bound in (4.8), however, is achievable with equality with every n and $m \leq n$, as demonstrated by the n-state machine $A22$ of Table 4.9. Since every input symbol passes all the states of $A22$

TABLE 4.9. MACHINE $A22$

s_ν \ x_ν	z_ν						$s_{\nu+1}$					
	ξ_1	ξ_2	ξ_3	$\cdots$	ξ_{n-2}	ξ_{n-1}	ξ_1	ξ_2	ξ_3	$\cdots$	ξ_{n-2}	ξ_{n-1}
1	1	0	0		0	0	1	1	1		1	1
2	0	1	0		0	0	1	1	1		1	1
3	0	0	1		0	0	1	1	1		1	1
$\cdot$												
$\cdot$												
$\cdot$												
$n-2$	0	0	0		1	0	1	1	1		1	1
$n-1$	0	0	0		0	1	1	1	1		1	1
n	0	0	0		0	0	1	1	1		1	1

into state 1, all diagnosing sequences are limited to a single symbol. Since every input symbol is capable of performing exactly one "splitting" operation on the admissible set (regardless of the size of this set), the m-wise diagnosing experiment for $A22$ requires exactly $m - 1$ copies.

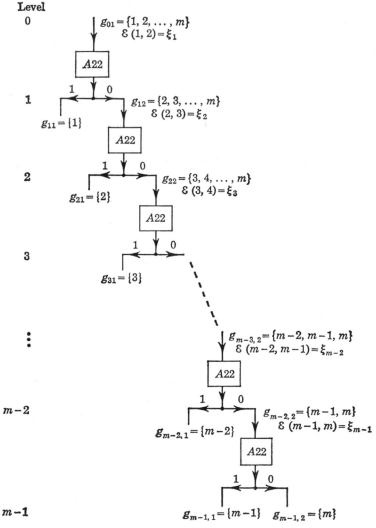

FIG. 4.14. Multiple-experiment tree for $A22$ and admissible set $\{1, 2, \ldots, m\}$.

The multiple-experiment tree for $A22$ and the admissible set $\{1, 2, \ldots, m\}$ is shown in Fig. 4.14.

It may be noted that, although the design procedure for the multiple experiment can minimize the length of the input sequence applied to each copy, it generally does not minimize the total length of the experiment or its multiplicity. In many cases both the length and multiplicity of an experiment can be reduced by exploiting the following obvious fact: Given two input sequences $\mathcal{E}_1$ and $\mathcal{E}_1\mathcal{E}_2$, the response of machine M to $\mathcal{E}_1$ can be deduced from the response of M to $\mathcal{E}_1\mathcal{E}_2$. Thus, if both $\mathcal{E}_1$ and $\mathcal{E}_1\mathcal{E}_2$ are diagnosing sequences to be employed in the multiple experiment, only $\mathcal{E}_1\mathcal{E}_2$ has to be actually applied. For example, in the multiple experiment described in Fig. 4.13, the responses of $A17_1$ to α and $A17_2$ to $\alpha\alpha$ can be deduced from the response of $A17_3$ to $\alpha\alpha\alpha$; consequently, only two copies of $A17$ are actually required for the experiment. As can be readily verified, the diagnosing problem for $A17$ and the admissible set $\{1, 2, 3, 4, 5\}$ cannot be solved by a simple experiment, and hence the above reduction achieves the lowest possible multiplicity for this problem.

4.11. Multiple Adaptive Diagnosing Experiments

Instead of applying simultaneously all the diagnosing sequences, which are required in the multiple experiment, they can be applied one at a time, each sequence (except the first) selected on the basis of the previously observed responses. Such an adaptive experiment may be performed as follows:

ALGORITHM 4.4. Given machine M, its admissible set $A(M) = \{\sigma_{i_1}, \sigma_{i_2}, \ldots, \sigma_{i_m}\}$ and the multiple-experiment tree for M and $A(M)$, to find the initial state of M by a multiple adaptive experiment: (1) Apply the input sequence indicated for the initial branch to the first copy of M. Let $k - 2$. (2) Proceed to the branch for which the listed output sequence coincides with the response yielded by the last applied input sequence. (3) (a) If the branch is not terminal, apply the input sequence indicated for this branch to the kth copy of M. Increment k by 1 and return to (2). (b) If the branch is terminal, the singleton $\{\sigma_{i_h}\}$ associated with this branch contains the initial state of M.

The effect of Algorithm 4.4 is to guide the experimenter along the particular path which terminates at $\{\sigma_{i_h}\}$, where σ_{i_h} is the true initial state of M. Consequently, the need for those copies of M which do not appear along this path is eliminated.

The algorithm can be demonstrated with the multiple-experiment tree of Fig. 4.13. If the true initial state of $A17$ is 3, applying α to the first copy of $A17$ yields 0, which leads to the branch associated with $\{1, 2, 3\}$. Accordingly, the sequence applied to the second copy is $\alpha\alpha$, which yields 01, and hence leads to the branch associated with $\{3\}$. The initial state of $A17$, then, can be deduced to be 3.

The maximum number of copies that may be needed for solving the diagnosing problem for an n-state machine with m admissible states is given by the number of copies appearing in the longest path of the corresponding multiple-experiment tree. This number, clearly, cannot exceed the total number of copies in the tree. By Theorem 4.8, then, the multiplicity of the multiple adaptive experiment is at most $m - 1$. By Theorem 4.7, if the individual diagnosing sequences are designed to be as short as possible, the length of the experiment cannot exceed

$$\sum_{r=2}^{m} (n - r + 1) = (n + 1)(m - 1) - \sum_{r=2}^{m} r$$
$$= \tfrac{1}{2}(2n - m)(m - 1) \tag{4.9}$$

We thus have:

THEOREM 4.9. The diagnosing problem for an n-state machine with m admissible states can always be solved by a multiple adaptive experiment of length l and multiplicity c, where

$$l \leq \tfrac{1}{2}(2n - m)(m - 1) \tag{4.10}$$
$$c \leq m - 1 \tag{4.11}$$

The bound in (4.10) is achievable with equality for $m = 2$ and any $n \geq 2$. The bound in (4.11) is achievable with equality for any n and $m \leq n$, as demonstrated by machine $A22$ of Table 4.9 and the multiple-experiment tree of Fig. 4.14: if the initial state of $A22$ is either $m - 1$ or m, exactly $m - 1$ copies are required for the diagnosing problem of $A22$ and the admissible set $\{1, 2, \ldots, m\}$.

The advantage of the multiple adaptive experiment over the multiple preset experiment may be measured by the extent to which the number of copies in the multiple-experiment tree exceeds the height of this tree. Table 4.10 represents an n-state machine $A23$, for which the advantage of the adaptive over the preset experiment, for any admissible set, is considerable. The multiple-experiment tree for $A23$ and the admissible set $\{1, 2, \ldots, m\}$ (where $2 < m < n - 1$, and where both m and n are even) is shown in Fig. 4.15. It is seen that the number of copies included in the multiple-experiment tree is $m/2 + 1$, and its height is 2. Thus, $m/2 + 1$ copies of $A23$ are required for solving the problem by a preset experiment and only 2 copies for solving the problem by an adaptive experiment.

It should be noted that the procedure given for designing the multiple adaptive experiment, like that given for the multiple preset experiment, does not generally minimize the length or multiplicity of the experiment. In many problems, both the length and multiplicity can be reduced by the technique described at the end of Sec. 4.10.

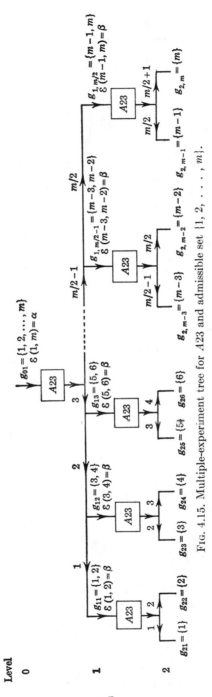

Fig. 4.15. Multiple-experiment tree for A23 and admissible set $\{1, 2, \ldots, m\}$.

117

TABLE 4.10. MACHINE $A23$

s_ν \ x_ν	z_ν		$s_{\nu+1}$	
	α	β	α	β
1	1	1	1	1
2	1	2	1	1
3	2	2	1	1
4	2	3	1	1
5	3	3	1	1
6	3	4	1	1
.				
.				
.				
$n-3$	$\dfrac{n}{2}-1$	$\dfrac{n}{2}-1$	1	1
$n-2$	$\dfrac{n}{2}-1$	$\dfrac{n}{2}$	1	1
$n-1$	$\dfrac{n}{2}$	$\dfrac{n}{2}$	1	1
n	$\dfrac{n}{2}$	1	1	1

4.12. The Homing Tree

The *homing tree*, like the diagnosing tree, is a truncated version of the successor tree, obtained by stipulating a number of termination rules:

DEFINITION 4.2.   A homing tree is a successor tree in which a kth-level branch b becomes terminal, if one of the following conditions is met: (1) The A group associated with b is associated with some branch in a level preceding the kth. (2) There is a kth-level branch (possibly b itself) associated with a homogeneous A group.

Rule 2 implies that the first level to contain a branch associated with a homogeneous A group is also the last level in the homing tree.   Figure 4.16 demonstrates how the homing tree is constructed for machine $A17$ of Fig. 4.3 and the admissible set $\{1, 2, 3, 4, 5\}$.   In the third level, the A group $\{1, 1\}$, $\{1\}$, $\{2\}$, $\{1\}$ is seen to be homogeneous; by virtue of rule 2, therefore, all the branches in the third level are terminal.

Through a proof analogous to that employed for Lemma 4.4, it can be shown that the length of any path in a homing tree for an n-state machine M and m admissible states cannot exceed $(m-1)n^m$.   The construction of the homing tree, therefore, is a finite process.   A bound which is considerably lower than $(m-1)n^m$ will be produced in a later section.

A *homing path* will be any path in the homing tree whose terminal

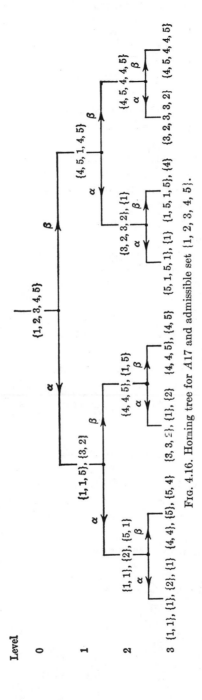

Fig. 4.16. Homing tree for A17 and admissible set $\{1, 2, 3, 4, 5\}$.

119

branch is associated with a homogeneous A group. A *homing sequence* for M and $A(M)$ will be any input sequence which, when applied to $M|\sigma_i$ and $M|\sigma_j$, where σ_i and σ_j are two states in $A(M)$, yields two distinct output sequences, if it passes σ_i and σ_j into two distinct states. Lemma 4.2, then, yields:

LEMMA 4.7. The input sequence described by a homing path in a homing tree constructed for M and $A(M)$ is a homing sequence for M and $A(M)$.

The *minimal homing sequence* for M and $A(M)$, denoted by $\mathcal{E}'(A)$, is the shortest homing sequence for M and $A(M)$. The *truncated paths* of a homing tree constructed for M and $A(M)$ are the paths included in the successor tree but absent from the homing tree, by virtue of rule 1. The following result can be proved in a manner entirely analogous to that employed in Lemma 4.6:

LEMMA 4.8. The truncated paths of a homing tree constructed for M and $A(M)$ do not describe minimal homing sequences.

We thus have the counterpart of Theorem 4.2:

THEOREM 4.10. The set of sequences described by the homing paths in the homing tree constructed for machine M and admissible set $A(M)$ is the set of all minimal homing sequences for M and $A(M)$.

4.13. Simple Preset Homing Experiments

The results obtained in the preceding section suggest a procedure for solving the m-wise homing problem by the shortest simple preset experiment:

ALGORITHM 4.5. Given machine M and its admissible set $A(M) = \{\sigma_{i_1}, \sigma_{i_2}, \ldots, \sigma_{i_m}\}$, to find the final state of M by the shortest simple preset experiment: (1) Construct the homing tree for M and $A(M)$. (2) Choose any homing sequence $\mathcal{E}'(A)$ described by the tree.[1]   (3) List the responses of $M|\sigma_{i_1}, M|\sigma_{i_2}, \ldots, M|\sigma_{i_m}$ to $\mathcal{E}'(A)$, and the states $\sigma'_{i_1}, \sigma'_{i_2}, \ldots, \sigma'_{i_m}$ into which $\sigma_{i_1}, \sigma_{i_2}, \ldots, \sigma_{i_m}$, respectively, pass when $\mathcal{E}'(A)$ is applied. (4) Apply $\mathcal{E}'(A)$ to M and observe the response. The final state is the state σ'_{i_k} for which the response listed in (3) is identical with the observed response.

Algorithm 4.5 can be demonstrated with machine $A17$ of Fig. 4.3 and the admissible set $\{1, 2, 3, 4, 5\}$. In this case, the homing tree of Fig. 4.16 reveals the minimal homing sequence to be $\alpha\alpha\alpha$. Table 4.11 lists the responses and final states for the initial states 1, 2, 3, 4, and 5, when $\alpha\alpha\alpha$ is applied. As can be expected, distinct final states correspond to distinct responses, and hence the responses may serve as the criteria for identifying the final state of $A17$, when subject to the specified admissible set.

[1] In Sec. 4.15 it will be shown that such a sequence always exists.

The solution to the homing problem is directly applicable to the following problem: It is known that a given machine M is machine M_1 in a state belonging to the set $A(M_1)$, or machine M_2 in a state belonging to the set $A(M_2)$, . . . , or machine M_N in a state belonging to the set $A(M_N)$. It is desired to identify the machine and its final state. Assuming that $M_1, M_2, \ldots, M_N$ are congruous and that their transition tables are available, the above problem is precisely the m-wise homing problem for the disjunction machine $\Delta(M_1, M_2, \ldots, M_N)$ and the admissible set $A(M_1) \cup A(M_2) \cup \cdots \cup A(M_N)$. The basic assumption that the given machine M is minimal implies, in this case, that every machine M_i is minimal and that no state in any machine M_i is equivalent to any state in machine M_j ($j \neq i$).

TABLE 4.11. RESPONSES OF $A17$ TO $\alpha\alpha\alpha$

Initial state	Response to $\alpha\alpha\alpha$	Final state
1	000	1
2	000	1
3	010	1
4	101	2
5	100	1

4.14. Simple Adaptive Homing Experiments

Consider a path in the homing tree for M and $A(M)$, which leads to an A-group G containing a homogeneous σ set, say $\{\sigma_i', \sigma_i', \ldots, \sigma_i'\}$, where σ_i' appears h times (since G may contain other σ sets which are not homogeneous, G itself is not necessarily homogeneous). If this path describes the input sequence $\mathcal{E}$, then $A(M)$ must contain some h states, say σ_{i_1}, $\sigma_{i_2}, \ldots, \sigma_{i_h}$, whose successors with respect to $\mathcal{E}$ are all σ_i'. Since $\{\sigma_i', \sigma_i', \ldots, \sigma_i'\}$ is homogeneous in G, the response of σ_{i_1}, or $\sigma_{i_2}, \ldots$, or σ_{i_h} to $\mathcal{E}$ cannot, by Lemma 4.2, be attributed to any *final* state except σ_i'. Thus, if σ_{i_1}, or $\sigma_{i_2}, \ldots$, or σ_{i_h} is perchance the true initial state of M, the final state of M can be identified by an input sequence which is not necessarily described by a homing path. Exploiting this fact, one can apply the minimal homing sequence piecemeal, rather than in its entirety, with the expectation that the final state is such that it can be identified with only a fraction of the total sequence. This scheme constitutes a solution to the m-wise diagnosing problem by a simple adaptive experiment.

The segmentation of the minimal homing sequence into subsequences is done in the following manner: Let $\mathcal{E}_k$ be the kth subsequence, and let

G_k be the A group led to by the path describing $\varepsilon_1\varepsilon_2 \cdots \varepsilon_k$; denote $A(M)$ by G_0. Then ε_k is the subsequence described by the subpath which leads from G_{k-1} to the first A group which contains at least one more homogeneous σ set than G_{k-1}. Since the resolution of G_0 is 1, and since the number of σ sets in an A group cannot exceed the size m of $A(M)$, the number of subsequences thus produced cannot exceed $m - 1$. As an example, machine $A17$ of Fig. 4.3 and the admissible set $\{1, 2, 3, 4, 5\}$ yield $G_0 = \{1, 2, 3, 4, 5\}$, $G_1 = \{1, 1\}, \{2\}, \{5, 1\}$, $G_2 = \{1, 1\}, \{1\}, \{2\}$, $\{1\}$, and hence $\varepsilon_1 = \alpha\alpha$ and $\varepsilon_2 = \alpha$ (see Fig. 4.16). Once the subsequences are determined, the adaptive experiment can be carried out as follows:

ALGORITHM 4.6.   Given machine M, its admissible set $A(M) = \{\sigma_{i_1}, \sigma_{i_2}, \ldots, \sigma_{i_m}\}$ and the segmented homing sequence $\varepsilon_1\varepsilon_2 \cdots \varepsilon_r$, to identify the final state of M by a simple adaptive experiment: (1) List the responses of $M|\sigma_{i_1}$, $M|\sigma_{i_2}$, $\ldots$, $M|\sigma_{i_m}$ to $\varepsilon_1\varepsilon_2 \cdots \varepsilon_r$. Segment each response into r subsequences to correspond with the segmentation of the input sequence. After each output subsequence, list the corresponding final state. Let $k = 1$. (2) Apply ε_k to M. (3) (a) If the response of M to $\varepsilon_1\varepsilon_2 \cdots \varepsilon_k$ is attributable to only one final state in the list compiled in (1), this state is the final state of M. (b) If the response of M to $\varepsilon_1\varepsilon_2 \cdots \varepsilon_k$ is attributable to two or more distinct final states in the list compiled in (1), increment k by 1 and return to (2).

Algorithm 4.6 can be demonstrated with machine $A17$ and the admissible set $\{1, 2, 3, 4, 5\}$, for which we have $\varepsilon_1 = \alpha\alpha$ and $\varepsilon_2 = \alpha$. The list of responses to $\alpha\alpha\alpha$, segmented as specified in step 1, and the corresponding final states are given in Table 4.12. If the initial state happens to be 1 or 2, the response to $\alpha\alpha$ is 00, which is attributable to the final state 1 only; hence, in this case the homing experiment requires only two input symbols. If the initial state happens to be 5, the response to $\alpha\alpha$ is 10, which cannot be uniquely attributable to any single final state (the final state, on the basis of this response, may be either 1 or 5), and hence the second subsequence is required to complete the experiment.

TABLE 4.12. SEGMENTED RESPONSES OF $A17$ TO $\alpha\alpha\alpha$

Initial state	Response to $\alpha\alpha$	Final state	Response to α	Final state
1	00	1	0	1
2	00	1	0	1
3	01	2	0	1
4	10	5	1	2
5	10	1	0	1

In conclusion, we can state:

THEOREM 4.11. Every m-wise homing problem solvable by a simple preset experiment of length l is solvable by a simple adaptive experiment of length l or less and order $m - 1$ or less.

Thus, the advantage of the adaptive experiment is that it *may* terminate earlier than the preset experiment. The exact length of the adaptive experiment cannot, of course, be estimated in advance, since it depends on the true initial state, which remains unknown until the experiment terminates.

4.15. Regular Preset Homing Experiments

The minimal length of the homing experiment is achieved at the cost of constructing a homing tree which, in problems involving large admissible sets, becomes quite cumbersome. If one is content with a homing experiment whose length is not necessarily minimal, simpler design procedures are available. A homing experiment designed through a procedure which does not guarantee a minimal length will be called a *regular homing experiment*.

Consider the successor tree for the n-state machine M and its admissible set $A(M)$. Let b be a branch associated with the A group G, consisting of the σ sets $g_1, g_2, \ldots, g_u$, in which at least one σ set, say g_h, is not homogeneous. If g_h contains r states, it must contain at least two states, say σ_i and σ_j, which are $(n - r + 1)$-distinguishable. Consequently, the subpath initiating with b and describing $\mathcal{E}(\sigma_i, \sigma_j)$ must lead to an A group G' which consists of at least $u + 1$ σ sets. Hence, if G is nonhomogeneous, a subpath of length $n - r + 1$ or less can always be found which leads from G to an A group whose resolution exceeds that of G. The subsequence described by this subpath is called a *regular subsequence* of G. We thus have a procedure by which we can trace a homing path in any given successor tree, and hence construct a homing sequence for any M and $A(M)$:

ALGORITHM 4.7. Given machine M and its admissible set $A(M)$, to find a homing sequence for M and $A(M)$: (1) Let $A(M)$ be G_0. Let $k = 0$. (2) (a) If G_k is not homogeneous, determine a regular subsequence, say $\mathcal{E}_k$, for G_k. Let the $\mathcal{E}_k$ successor of G_k be G_{k+1}. Increment k by 1 and return to (2). (b) If G_k is homogeneous, $\mathcal{E}_0 \mathcal{E}_1 \cdots \mathcal{E}_{k-1}$ is a homing sequence for M and $A(M)$.

Since the resolution of $A(M)$ is 1, and since the resolution of any A group cannot exceed the number of admissible states m, the number of subsequences produced by Algorithm 4.7 is at most $m - 1$. For an n-state machine, the length of a minimal diagnosing sequence for any pair of states cannot exceed $n - 1$; consequently, the length of each subsequence in the homing sequence produced by Algorithm 4.7 cannot exceed $n - 1$. We thus have:

THEOREM 4.12.   The homing problem for an n-state machine with m admissible states can always be solved by a simple preset experiment of length l, where

$$l \leq (n - 1)(m - 1) \qquad (4.12)$$

An alternative formulation of Theorem 4.12, which will be found useful in later discussions, is offered by the following:

COROLLARY 4.2.   Let M be a machine in which every pair of states is L-distinguishable.   The homing problem for M and m admissible states can always be solved by a simple preset experiment of length l, where

$$l \leq L(m - 1) \qquad (4.13)$$

Algorithm 4.7, which represents a method for designing regular preset homing experiments, does not necessitate the construction of any tree; it merely requires the determination of the various subsequences described by the various subpaths constituting a homing path, which, as shown above, can be done in a recursive manner.   The procedure is demonstrated in Table 4.13, where a regular preset homing experiment is

TABLE 4.13. REGULAR PRESET EXPERIMENT FOR $A17$ AND ADMISSIBLE SET $\{1, 2, 3, 4, 5\}$

k	G_k	σ_i, σ_j	$\mathcal{E}(\sigma_i, \sigma_j)$
0	$\{1, 2, 3, 4, 5\}$	1, 4	α
1	$\{1, 1, 5\}, \{3, 2\}$	1, 5	α
2	$\{1, 1\}, \{2\}, \{5, 1\}$	1, 5	α
3	$\{1, 1\}, \{1\}, \{2\}, \{1\}$		

designed for machine $A17$ of Fig. 4.3 and the admissible set $\{1, 2, 3, 4, 5\}$. G_0 is $\{1, 2, 3, 4, 5\}$, and G_k, for $k \geq 1$, is constructed on the basis of G_{k-1}, the previously determined subsequence (i.e., the subsequence listed in the last column of row $k - 1$), and the transition table or diagram of $A17$. The state pair $\{\sigma_i, \sigma_j\}$ is any pair of states in any nonhomogeneous σ set contained in G_k; $\mathcal{E}(\sigma_i, \sigma_j)$ is the minimal diagnosing sequence for $\{\sigma_i, \sigma_j\}$, which can be obtained by the method described in Sec. 4.4.   To minimize the length of the individual subsequences, σ_i and σ_j may be selected as to result in the shortest $\mathcal{E}(\sigma_i, \sigma_j)$.   For machine $A17$, this can be done with the aid of Table 4.6, which lists the minimal diagnosing sequences for all state pairs in $A17$.   It should be noted that this selection rule does not, in general, guarantee the minimality of the total length of the homing experiment (although, in our problem, the resulting homing sequence happens to be a minimal one). Row 3 in the table is the last row, since G_3 is a homogeneous A group. The homing sequence is constructed by writing the sequences $\mathcal{E}(\sigma_i, \sigma_j)$ in the order in which they appear in the last column. A regular homing experiment for $A17$ and the admissible set $\{1, 2, 3, 4, 5\}$, therefore, consists of applying $\alpha\alpha\alpha$ and observing the response. The responses of the states 1, 2, 3, 4, and 5, when $\alpha\alpha\alpha$ is applied, and the corresponding final states, are shown in Table 4.11.

Theorem 4.12 reveals the basic difference between the diagnosing problem and the homing problem: While the diagnosing problem cannot, in general, be solved by simple experimentation, the homing problem can always be solved by simple experimentation. Given a single copy of machine M, the initial state of M cannot always be identified; however, it is always possible to pass M into an identifiable state. Once the identifiable state is attained, future response of M to any specified excitation becomes, of course, predictable. Thus, there is always a way of forcing a machine, whose transition table is available but which is otherwise unpredictable, to become a predictable machine.

4.16. Regular Adaptive Homing Experiments

The regular preset homing experiments described in Sec. 4.15 can be modified into regular adaptive homing experiments by applying one subsequence at a time and selecting the next subsequence on the basis of the response to the preceding one. The procedure is the same as that outlined for the preset experiment, except that, on the basis of the observed response, all but one of the σ sets of G_k ($k \geq 1$) may be eliminated from further considerations.

ALGORITHM 4.8. Given machine M and its admissible set $A(M)$, to determine the final state of M by a simple adaptive experiment: (1) Let $A(M)$ be g_0. Let $k = 0$. (2) (a) If g_k is not homogeneous, determine a regular subsequence, say $\mathcal{E}_k$, of g_k. Apply $\mathcal{E}_k$ to M, and let g_k' be the subset of g_k to which the observed response is attributable. Let g_{k+1} be the $\mathcal{E}_k$ successor of g_k'. Increment k by 1 and return to (2). (b) If g_k is homogeneous, the final state of M is the state contained in g_k.

If g_k in Algorithm 4.8 is not homogeneous, the size of g_{k+1} must be smaller than that of g_k. Consequently, if the size of $A(M)$ is m, the number of subsequences is at most $m - 1$. For each g_k of size r, there is always a regular subsequence $\mathcal{E}_k$ whose length does not exceed $n - r + 1$, where n is the total number of states in M. Hence, the total length of the homing experiment cannot exceed

$$\sum_{r=2}^{m} (n - r + 1) = \tfrac{1}{2}(2n - m)(m - 1) \tag{4.14}$$

We thus have:

THEOREM 4.13. The homing problem for an n-state machine with m admissible states can always be solved by a simple adaptive experiment of length l and order d, where

$$l \le \tfrac{1}{2}(2n - m)(m - 1) \tag{4.15}$$
$$d \le m - 1 \tag{4.16}$$

It can be noted that the regular adaptive homing experiment, as designed through Algorithm 4.8, is never longer than the regular preset homing experiment, as designed through Algorithm 4.7.

Table 4.14 demonstrates the regular adaptive homing experiment for machine $A17$ of Fig. 4.3 and the admissible set $\{1, 2, 3, 4, 5\}$, when the true initial state is 4. The first column lists, for reference, the states through which $A17$ passes as the experiment progresses (these states, of course, are unknown to the experimenter). g_0 in this example is $\{1, 2, 3, 4, 5\}$, and $\mathcal{E}_0$ is α. When α is applied to $A17$, the observed response is 1, from which g_0' can be deduced to be $\{4, 5\}$. g_1, then, is the α successor of g_0', namely, $\{3, 2\}$. Applying $\mathcal{E}_1 = \alpha\alpha$ to $A17$ yields the response 01, from which g_1' can be deduced to be $\{3\}$. g_2, then, is the $\alpha\alpha$ successor of g_1', namely, $\{2\}$. Since g_2 is homogeneous, it can be concluded that the final state of $A17$ is 2.

TABLE 4.14. REGULAR ADAPTIVE EXPERIMENT FOR $A17$ AND
ADMISSIBLE SET $\{1, 2, 3, 4, 5\}$

True state	k	g_k	σ_i, σ_j	$\mathcal{E}(\sigma_i, \sigma_j)$	Response
4	0	$\{1, 2, 3, 4, 5\}$	1, 4	α	1
3	1	$\{3, 2\}$	2, 3	$\alpha\alpha$	01
2	2	$\{2\}$			

Figure 4.17 shows a machine labeled M^*, in which the bounds of Theorem 4.13 can be achieved with equality.[1] As indicated in the figure, the state set of M^* is $\{1, 2, \ldots, n\}$, the input alphabet is $\{\xi_1, \xi_2, \ldots, \xi_{n-1}\}$, and the output alphabet is $\{0, 1\}$. The output symbol 1 is generated only when ξ_{n-1} is applied to state n. From the structure of M^* it can be seen that if the states $1, 2, \ldots, i, j$ (any $j > i$) are subjected to any input symbol other than ξ_{j-1}, then the successor states are $1, 2, \ldots, i, j$, respectively, or $1, 2, \ldots, i, j - 1$, respectively. With respect to the homing tree for M^* and the admissible set $\{1, 2, \ldots, m\}$, this

[1] This machine is due to T. N. Hibbard (Least Upper Bounds on Minimal Terminal State Experiments for Two Classes of Sequential Machines, *J. Assoc. Comput. Mach.*, vol. 8, pp. 601–612, 1961).

implies that the shortest path leading from $\{1, 2, \ldots, m\}$ to an A group containing at least two σ sets is the path describing the input sequence $\xi_{m-1}\xi_m \cdots \xi_{n-1}$; the A group led to by this path is $\{1, 2, \ldots, m-1\}$, $\{n\}$. By induction, then, the shortest path leading

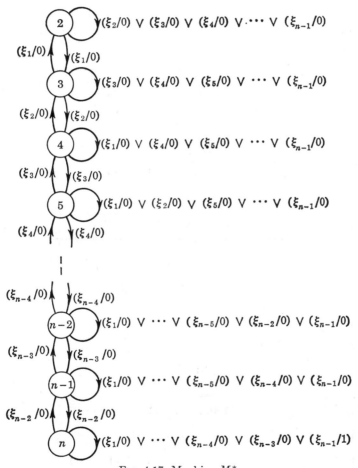

FIG. 4.17. Machine M^*.

from $\{1, 2, \ldots, m\}$ to a homogeneous A group is the path describing the input sequence $\xi_{m-1}\xi_m \cdots \xi_{n-1}$ (of length $n - m + 1$), followed by $\xi_{m-2}\xi_{m-1} \cdots \xi_{n-1}$ (of length $n - m + 2$), $\ldots$, followed by $\xi_1\xi_2 \cdots \xi_{n-1}$ (of length $n - 1$). By the identity (4.14), the length of

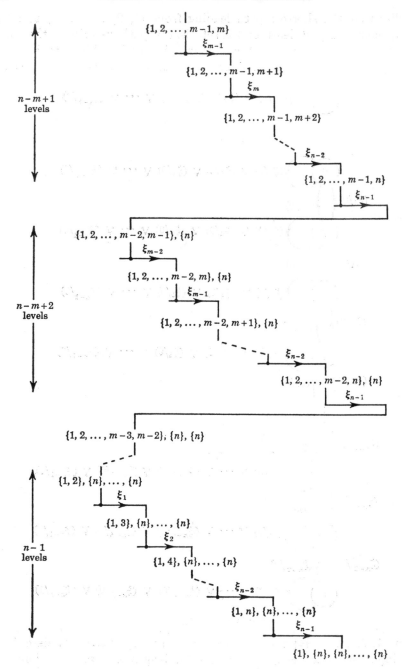

Fig. 4.18. Homing tree for M^* and admissible set $\{1, 2, \ldots, m\}$.

this sequence is $(2n - m)(m - 1)/2$. The path leads to the A group $\{1\}$, $\{n\}$, $\{n\}$, . . . , $\{n\}$ which contains m simple (and hence homogeneous) σ sets. Figure 4.18 shows the homing tree for machine M^* and the admissible set $\{1, 2, . . . , m\}$; in this figure, all terminal branches are omitted, and the only path shown is the one describing the minimal homing sequence cited above. Clearly, if the initial state of M^* happens to be 1, the shortest adaptive homing experiment for M^* and the admissible set $\{1, 2, . . . , m\}$ must consist of $m - 1$ subsequences, whose combined length is given by the upper bound in (4.15). Machine M^* also demonstrates that the shortest *preset* homing experiment may be $(2n - m)(m - 1)/2$ symbols long.

Notice that, since the terminal A group in Fig. 4.18 is a simple A group, the shown path describes a minimal diagnosing sequence (as well as a minimal homing sequence). Machine M^*, therefore, demonstrates that a simple preset or adaptive diagnosing experiment may be as long as the upper bound of l in (4.15).

4.17. Corollaries Regarding State Identification Experiments

A special case of the m-wise diagnosing or homing problem for machine M is the n-wise diagnosing or homing problem where n is the total number of states in M. This problem arises when no admissible states are specified for M, in which case one must assume that the initial state may be any of the n states of M. For this special case, the results obtained in preceding sections can be modified and summarized as follows:

COROLLARY 4.3. Let M be an n-state machine with a known transition table. The initial state of M, if at all identifiable by simple experimentation, is identifiable by a simple preset or a simple adaptive experiment of length l, where

$$l \leq (n - 1)n^n \qquad (4.17)$$

The initial state of M is always identifiable by a multiple preset experiment of length l and multiplicity c, where

$$l \leq (n - 1)^2 \qquad (4.18)$$
$$c \leq n - 1 \qquad (4.19)$$

and by a multiple adaptive experiment of length l and multiplicity c, where

$$l \leq \tfrac{1}{2}n(n - 1) \qquad (4.20)$$
$$c \leq n - 1 \qquad (4.21)$$

The final state of M is always identifiable by a simple preset experiment of length l, where

$$l \leq (n - 1)^2 \qquad (4.22)$$

and by a simple adaptive experiment of length l and order d, where

$$l \leq \tfrac{1}{2}n(n-1) \tag{4.23}$$
$$d \leq n-1 \tag{4.24}$$

Let M be a machine with the input alphabet $\{\xi_1, \xi_2, \ldots, \xi_p\}$ and the state set $\{\sigma_1, \sigma_2, \ldots, \sigma_n\}$. σ_j and σ_l ($l \neq j$) are called ξ_i-*mergeable* if the responses of $M|\sigma_j$ and $M|\sigma_l$ to ξ_i are identical and if σ_j and σ_l have the same successor with respect to ξ_i. A pair of ξ_i-mergeable states is depicted in Fig. 4.19.

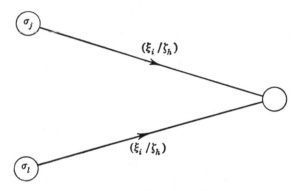

FIG. 4.19. A pair of ξ_i-mergeable states.

THEOREM 4.14. Let M be an n-state machine with the input alphabet $X = \{\xi_1, \xi_2, \ldots, \xi_p\}$. (a) If M contains a pair of ξ_i-mergeable states for every input symbol ξ_i in X, then the n-wise diagnosing problem for M is never solvable by a simple experiment. (b) If M does not contain a pair of ξ_i-mergeable states for any input symbol ξ_i in X, then the n-wise diagnosing problem for M is always solvable by a simple experiment.

Proof. (a) Applying any input symbol ξ_i to M causes a pair of states, say σ_j and σ_l, to pass into the same state with identical responses, and thus causes these states to become indistinguishable by any subsequent input symbols. (b) By Theorem 4.12, M can always be passed into a known final state. Let the homing sequence employed for this purpose be $\xi_{i_1}\xi_{i_2} \cdots \xi_{i_r}$; let the corresponding output sequence be $\zeta_{h_1}\zeta_{h_2} \cdots \zeta_{h_r}$ and the corresponding sequence of states be $\sigma_{j_1}, \sigma_{j_2}, \ldots, \sigma_{j_r}$. Now, suppose σ_{j_k}, ξ_{i_k}, and ζ_{h_k} are known for some $1 \leq k \leq r$; since, by assumption, no state in M has two converging branches bearing the same input-output pair (ξ_{i_k}/ζ_{h_k}), $\sigma_{j_{k-1}}$ can be uniquely determined. Denoting the initial state of M by σ_{j_0}, σ_{j_0} can be recursively determined, then, from the knowledge of the final state of M and the knowledge of the input and output sequences involved in the homing experiment.

From the transition table of a given machine M, it can be readily established whether M has the property cited in part a or the property cited in part b of Theorem 4.14. This theorem, therefore, can be conveniently applied to determine, in many cases, whether or not the initial state of a given machine is identifiable by a simple experiment. When a machine has neither the property of part a nor the property of part b, its initial state may or may not be identifiable by a simple experiment.

PROBLEMS

4.1. Outline a matrix procedure for solving the pairwise diagnosing problem.

4.2. Tables P 4.1 and P 4.2 represent machines A and B, respectively. List minimal diagnosing sequences for all pairs of states in which one state is selected from A and the other state from B.

TABLE P 4.1

s_ν \ x_ν	z_ν		$s_{\nu+1}$	
	α	β	α	β
1	0	1	2	3
2	1	0	3	4
3	0	1	1	4
4	1	0	4	3

TABLE P 4.2

s_ν \ x_ν	z_ν		$s_{\nu+1}$	
	α	β	α	β
1	0	1	1	3
2	0	1	2	2
3	1	0	3	1
4	1	0	4	2

4.3. Figure P 4.1 shows the transition diagrams of machines A and B. (*a*) A given machine is known to be A in state 3 or 4. Design a shortest preset experiment

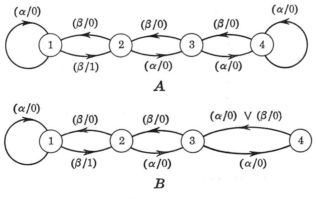

FIG. P 4.1

for identifying the initial state. (*b*) A given machine is known to be A in state 1, or B in state 1. Design a shortest preset experiment for identifying the machine and its initial state.

4.4. Specify a 6-state machine in which two states can be distinguished by an input sequence of length 5 but not less. Verify that the above requirement is satisfied.

4.5. Specify a 6-state machine and a 9-state machine in which two states (one in each machine) can be distinguished by an input sequence of length 14 but not less. Verify that the above requirement is satisfied.

4.6. Figure P 4.2 shows levels 0 to 3 of a partially labeled successor tree, where G_1, G_2, and G_3 are A groups. Show that tree paths passing through G_1, G_2, and G_3 in level 3 cannot represent minimal diagnosing sequences for M and $A(M)$.

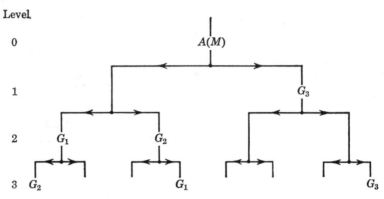

FIG. P 4.2

4.7. Show that the minimal diagnosing sequence for a machine with q output symbols and an admissible set of size m cannot be shorter than $(\log m)/(\log q)$ symbols.

4.8. Determine a minimal diagnosing sequence for the machine represented by Table P 4.3 and the admissible set $\{1, 2, 3, 4, 5\}$.

TABLE P 4.3   TABLE P 4.4

s_ν \ x_ν	z_ν α	β	$s_{\nu+1}$ α	β
1	0	0	2	3
2	0	0	3	2
3	0	0	8	5
4	0	0	5	8
5	1	1	6	7
6	1	1	7	6
7	1	1	4	1
8	1	1	1	4

s_ν \ x_ν	z_ν α	β	$s_{\nu+1}$ α	β
1	0	1	2	3
2	1	1	1	2
3	0	1	1	1

4.9. A given machine is known to be either the one specified by Table P 4.4 or the one specified by Table P 4.5. Design a shortest preset experiment for identifying the machine and its initial state.

4.10. For the machine specified by Table P 4.6: (a) Design preset diagnosing experiments, if the admissible sets are (i) $\{4, 5\}$, (ii) $\{1, 2, 5\}$, (iii) $\{1, 2, 3, 4, 5\}$.

(b) For cases ii and iii, describe an adaptive diagnosing experiment, if the true initial state is 1 (which is unknown at the outset).

TABLE P 4.5

s_ν x_ν	z_ν		$s_{\nu+1}$	
	α	β	α	β
1	1	1	1	3
2	1	1	2	2
3	0	1	2	1

TABLE P 4.6

s_ν x_ν	z_ν			$s_{\nu+1}$		
	α	β	γ	α	β	γ
1	1	0	0	2	2	3
2	0	1	1	1	2	2
3	1	0	0	4	2	3
4	0	1	1	1	5	4
5	0	1	1	3	5	3

4.11. A given machine is represented by the transition diagram of Fig. P 4.3. (a) Design a shortest preset experiment for identifying the initial state of the machine. (b) Design a shortest preset experiment for identifying the final state of the machine.

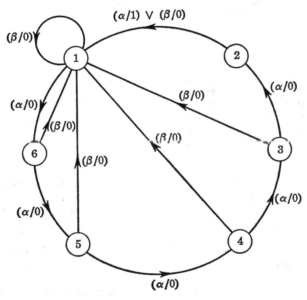

FIG. P 4.3

4.12. For the machine specified by Table P 4.6 and the admissible set $\{1, 2, 3, 4, 5\}$: (a) Design a shortest preset homing experiment. (b) Design a regular preset homing experiment. (c) Describe a regular adaptive homing experiment, if the true initial state is 5 (which is unknown at the outset).

4.13. For the machine described by Fig. P 4.4: (a) Design a regular preset homing experiment, if the true initial state is 7 (which is unknown at the outset).

4.14. The unknown initial state of the machine of Fig. P 4.4 is 1.   Describe an adaptive experiment that will pass the machine into state 7.

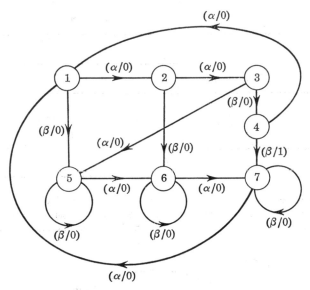

Fig. P 4.4

4.15. A given machine is known to be either A or B of Prob. 4.2.   Design a preset experiment for identifying the machine and its final state.

4.16. The P_1 partition of a minimal n-state machine M has u classes. (*a*) Show that any pairwise diagnosing problem for M is solvable by a simple preset experiment whose length is at most $n - u + 1$. (*b*) Show that any homing problem for M is solvable by a simple preset experiment whose length is at most $(n - 1)(n - u + 1)$. (*c*) Show that any homing problem for M is solvable by a simple adaptive experiment whose length is at most $u - 2 + [(n - u + 2)(n - u + 1)/2]$.

4.17. It can be shown that an n-state machine with an admissible set of size m can always be passed into a known state by a simple preset experiment of length l, where $l \leq (n - 1)(m - 1) + 2^{u+1} - 2 - um$ and where u is any positive integer.[1] (*a*) Find u (as a function of m) which minimizes the upper bound to l. (*b*) Evaluate the lowest upper bound to l, for $m = 2, 4, 8, 1024$.

4.18. The pairs table of the n-state machine M contains only distinct pairs.   Show that the initial state of M can always be identified by a simple preset experiment whose length is at most $(n - 1)^2$.

4.19. Without designing any diagnosing experiments, show that the 8-wise diagnosing experiment for the machine of Table P 4.3 is solvable by a simple experiment and that the 5-wise diagnosing experiment for the machine of Table P 4.6 is not solvable by a simple experiment.

4.20. (*a*) Construct a minimal (3, 2, 2) machine with the input alphabet $\{\alpha, \beta\}$, in which there is a pair of α-mergeable states and in which the 3-wise diagnosing

[1] This result is due to S. Ginsburg (On the Length of the Smallest Uniform Experiment Which Distinguishes the Terminal States of a Machine, *J. Assoc. Comput. Mach.*, vol. 5, pp. 266–280, 1958).

problem is solvable by a simple experiment. (*b*) Construct a minimal (3, 2, 2) machine with the input alphabet $\{\alpha, \beta\}$, in which there is a pair of α-mergeable states, but no pairs of β-mergeable states, and in which the 3-wise diagnosing problem is not solvable by a simple experiment.

4.21. It is known that in a given n-state machine, for every input sequence of a fixed length l, there exists a pair of states which pass into the same final state with identical responses. Show that the n-wise diagnosing problem for this machine is not solvable by a simple experiment.

4.22. Construct a 5-state machine where the 5-wise diagnosing and homing problems cannot be solved by any preset experiment of length less than 10. Construct the diagnosing and homing trees for this machine.

CHAPTER 5

MACHINE IDENTIFICATION EXPERIMENTS

5.1. Introduction

Our basic assumption in the preceding chapter was that every machine under investigation is provided with a complete transition table (or diagram, or matrix). The problems which concerned us had to do with the uncertainty as to the initial state of the machine. In the present chapter we shall concern ourselves with a broader problem—that of identifying an unknown machine, i.e., a machine whose transition table is not available.[1] Viewing a finite-state machine as a black box, the machine identification problem is essentially that of discovering the input-output characteristics of such a box, via external measurements. Inasmuch as no system can be effectively controlled and profitably utilized unless it is adequately characterized, this problem is one of the most fundamental as well as one of the most frequently encountered problems in system analysis.

To illustrate the difference between the state identification problems posed in Chap. 4 and the machine identification problems posed in the present chapter, let us consider the following crude example: A patient with an unknown disorder is admitted to a hospital for diagnosis and treatment. For our purpose, this patient may be regarded as a finite-state machine, with the input alphabet being the set of treatments that the patient may undergo, the output alphabet being the set of reactions that the patient may exhibit, and the state set being the set of physical conditions which the patient may attain. The diagnosing problem in this example is that of discovering the patient's initial disorder (i.e., "initial state"). As we previously established, this problem is not always solvable: it is conceivable that the nature of the disorder is such that, regardless of the treatments prescribed, the disorder disappears before it can be identified. The homing problem in this example is that of bringing the patient into a known physical condition (i.e., "final state"). As we previously established, this problem is always solvable:

---

[1] The material in this chapter is based in part on the work of E. F. Moore (Gedanken-Experiments on Sequential Machines, "Automata Studies," pp. 129–153, Princeton University Press, Princeton, N.J., 1956).

there is always a sequence of treatments which may be pursued to force the patient into an identifiable physical condition (not necessarily a desirable condition, to be sure). The machine identification problem in this example is that of determining how the patient's present reaction and next physical condition are related to the present treatment and present physical condition (i.e., determining the "transition table"). Clearly, no meaningful diagnosis procedures or improvement measures can be applied to the patient unless the above relationships are first established. The discovery of the patient's physiologic characteristics (which can be often estimated on the basis of age, sex, occupation, medical history, etc.) is, therefore, a prerequisite to any steps aimed at controlling the patient's health.

5.2. The General Machine Identification Problem

A machine will be said to be *identified* if its minimal form, up to isomorphism, is determined by external measurements. A machine will be

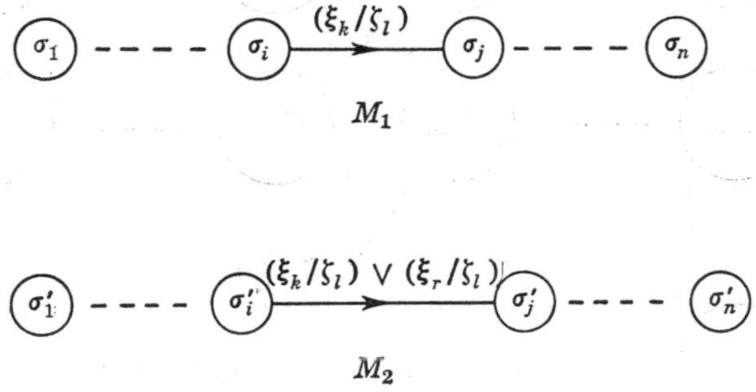

Fig. 5.1. Machines M_1 and M_2 for Theorem 5.1.

said to be *identifiable* if it can be identified regardless of its initial state. The machine identification problem, in its most general form, is simply the following: Identify a given machine M. In the remainder of this section we shall show that, if no information is available on M, the general machine identification problem is unsolvable.

THEOREM 5.1. Machine M is not identifiable unless the entire input alphabet of M is known in advance.

Proof. Suppose that only a subset of the input alphabet X of M, say X', is known to the investigator. Suppose also that an experiment employing the input sequence ε, where the symbols of ε are selected from X', reveals that M has the minimal form M_1, as represented in Fig. 5.1. Consider now a machine M_2 (also represented in Fig. 5.1), which is identical to M_1, except that the input-output pair (ξ_r/ζ_l), where ξ_r is in X but not in X', is added to a diverging or a reflecting branch of every state.

Since the responses of M_1 and M_2 to ε are identical, the above experiment can yield the conclusion that M is M_2 with the same assurance that M is M_1. Since M_1 and M_2 are not congruous, they are certainly not equivalent, and hence the assumption that the experiment reveals the minimal

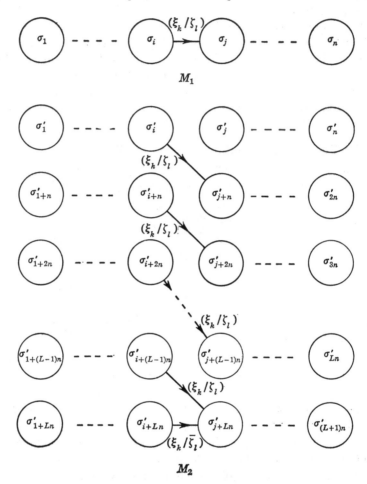

FIG. 5.2. Machines M_1 and M_2 for Theorem 5.2.

form of M cannot be justified. By contradiction, then, unless the input alphabet of M is completely known, M cannot be identified.

THEOREM 5.2. Machine M is not identifiable unless the maximum number of states contained in the minimal form of M is known in advance.

Proof. Suppose it is discovered, through an experiment of an arbitrarily great but finite length L, that M has the minimal form M_1, as represented in Fig. 5.2. If M_1 has the state set $\{\sigma_1, \sigma_2, \ldots, \sigma_n\}$, consider a machine M_2 (also represented in Fig. 5.2), which is constructed according to the following rules: M_2 has the $n(L + 1)$ states σ_1', σ_2', . . . , $\sigma_{n(L+1)}'$. If the input-output pair (ξ_k/ζ_l) labels the branch leading from σ_i to σ_j in M_1, then (ξ_k/ζ_l) also labels the branches leading from $\sigma_{i+(u-1)n}'$ to σ_{j+un}' in M_2, for $u = 1, 2, . . . , L$; when ξ_k is applied to σ_{i+Ln}' of M_2, the output symbol is $\bar{\zeta}_k \neq \zeta_k$, and the next state is σ_{j+Ln}'. By construction, then, every input sequence of length L or less yields identical output sequences in $M_1|\sigma_i$ and $M_2|\sigma_i'$. However, if any input sequence of length $L + 1$ is applied to $M_1|\sigma_i$ and $M_2|\sigma_i'$, the two output sequences must differ in the last symbol. Thus, the outcome of any finite experiment conducted on M can be equally attributed to M_1 as to M_2, although M_1 and M_2 are not equivalent; consequently, M cannot be identified by any finite experiment. Notice that when the maximum number of states $\hat{n}$ in M is known, machine M_2 is ruled out for every L such that $(L + 1)n > \hat{n}$. Thus, it is conceivable that when n is known, a sufficiently long experiment may identify M.

In conclusion, it can be stated that a necessary condition for the identification of a machine is the advance knowledge of its input alphabet and the bound on the number of states contained in its minimal form. As we shall see in a later chapter, the advance knowledge of the output alphabet of the machine is not a necessary condition for identification.

5.3. Identification of Machines of a Known Class

A machine identification problem most frequently encountered in practice is that of identifying an unknown machine which is known to belong to a specified finite class of machines.[1] In connection with this problem, we shall define an *exclusive class* as a class of machines $\{M_1, M_2, . . . , M_N\}$, such that no state in any M_i is equivalent to any state in M_j $(j \neq i)$.

THEOREM 5.3. A given machine M is known to belong to the finite class of machines $\mathfrak{M} = \{M_1, M_2, . . . , M_N\}$. Then a necessary and sufficient condition for M to be identifiable is that $\mathfrak{M}$ shall be exclusive.

Proof. If $\mathfrak{M}$ is not exclusive, then there is at least one pair of states, say $\sigma^{(i)}$ of M_i and $\sigma^{(j)}$ of M_j, which are equivalent. Hence, if M is either $M_i|\sigma^{(i)}$ or $M_j|\sigma^{(j)}$, no experiment can reveal its true identity. Thus, for M to be always identifiable, $\mathfrak{M}$ must be exclusive. To prove the sufficiency claim in the theorem, consider the disjunction machine $\Delta(M_1, M_2, . . . , M_N)$, in which each member of $\mathfrak{M}$ is included as an isolated submachine. Since $\mathfrak{M}$ is exclusive, $\Delta(M_1, M_2, . . . , M_N)$ is minimal, and hence there always exists a homing experiment which reveals its final state. Knowing the final state of $\Delta(M_1, M_2, . . . , M_N)$ implies the knowledge of the submachine containing the initial state of $\Delta(M_1, M_2,$

---

[1] Unless otherwise specified, a "class" of machines will be understood to consist of congruous, minimal machines, such that no two machines are equivalent.

. . . , M_N), and hence the machine M_h with which M can be identified. Thus, whenever $\mathfrak{M}$ is exclusive, M is identifiable.

Theorem 5.3 shows that two "distinguishable" machines, as defined in Sec. 3.9, are not necessarily distinguishable with respect to their external behavior, since such machines are not necessarily exclusive. For example, machines $A9$ and $A10$ of Figs. 3.6 and 3.7 are distinguishable, but not exclusive (states 1 and 2 of $A9$ are equivalent to states 1 and 2, respectively, of $A10$); consequently, if M is either $A9$ or $A10$, it cannot always be identified (it can be identified only if it happens to be $A10$ at state 3), and hence it is not "identifiable."

Let n_i denote the number of states in machine M_i, and let the machines in the exclusive class $\mathfrak{M} = \{M_1, M_2, \ldots, M_N\}$ be so labeled that $n_{i+1} \leq n_i$. $\Delta(M_1, M_2, \ldots, M_N)$, then, contains $\sum_{i=1}^{N} n_i$ states. By Theorem 4.1, any two states in machine M_i are $(n_i - 1)$-distinguishable. By Corollary 4.1, any two states, one of M_i and one of M_j ($j \neq i$), are $(n_i + n_j - 1)$-distinguishable. Since $n_i + n_j \leq n_1 + n_2$, any two states in $\Delta(M_1, M_2, \ldots, M_N)$ (whether in the same submachine or in two different submachines) must be $(n_1 + n_2 - 1)$-distinguishable. Using Corollary 4.2, with $L = n_1 + n_2 - 1$ and $m = \sum_{i=1}^{N} n_i$, it can be concluded that the homing problem for $\Delta(M_1, M_2, \ldots, M_N)$ is always solvable by a simple preset experiment of length $(n_1 + n_2 - 1)\left[\left(\sum_{i=1}^{N} n_i\right) - 1\right]$ or less. Since the solution to this homing problem is also the solution to the identification problem for M, we have:

THEOREM 5.4. A given machine M is known to belong to the exclusive class of machines $\{M_1, M_2, \ldots, M_N\}$, where M_i contains n_i states, and where $n_{i+1} \leq n_i$. Then M can always be identified by a simple preset experiment of length l, where

$$l \leq (n_1 + n_2 - 1)\left[\left(\sum_{i=1}^{N} n_i\right) - 1\right] \tag{5.1}$$

An important special case of Theorem 5.4 occurs when n_i, or the upper bound to n_i, is the same for all i:

COROLLARY 5.1. A given machine M is known to belong to the exclusive class of machines $\{M_1, M_2, \ldots, M_N\}$, where every machine contains at most n states. Then M can always be identified by a simple preset experiment of length l, where

$$l \leq (2n - 1)(Nn - 1) \tag{5.2}$$

The length of the machine identification experiment and the encumbrance involved in the design of this experiment are reduced considerably when, instead of a preset homing experiment, a series of regular adaptive homing experiments are conducted. This can be done in the following manner:

ALGORITHM 5.1. M is known to belong to the exclusive class of machines $\{M_1, M_2, \ldots, M_N\}$. To identify M by a simple adaptive experiment: (1) Let $k = 1$. (2) Conduct on M the regular adaptive homing experiment designed for M_k and the admissible set consisting of all the states of M_k. (3) (a) If $k < N$, increment k by 1 and return to (2). (b) If $k = N$, let $\sigma^{(i)}$, $i = 1, 2, \ldots, N$, denote the present state of M, under the assumption that M is M_i. Proceed to step 4. (4) Conduct on M the regular adaptive homing experiment designed for $\Delta(M_1, M_2, \ldots, M_N)$ and the admissible set $\{\sigma^{(1)}, \sigma^{(2)}, \ldots, \sigma^{(N)}\}$. If the final state of $\Delta(M_1, M_2, \ldots, M_N)$ is in the submachine M_h, then M is the machine M_h.

From Eq. (4.23) it follows that the execution of step 2 of the algorithm, for $k = 1, 2, \ldots, N$, requires at most $\sum_{i=1}^{N} \frac{1}{2} n_i(n_i - 1)$ input symbols, where n_i is the number of states in M_i. If $n_{i+1} \leq n_i$, it follows from Corollary 4.2 that the execution of step 4 requires at most $(n_1 + n_2 - 1)$ $(N - 1)$ steps. From Theorem 4.13 it follows that the order of the experiment described by the algorithm is at most

$$\sum_{i=1}^{N} (n_i - 1) + N - 1 = \left(\sum_{i=1}^{N} n_i \right) - 1 \tag{5.3}$$

We thus have:

THEOREM 5.5. A given machine M is known to belong to the exclusive class of machines $\{M_1, M_2, \ldots, M_N\}$, where M_i contains n_i states, and where $n_{i+1} \leq n_i$. Then M can always be identified by a simple adaptive experiment of length l and order d, where

$$l \leq \frac{1}{2} \left[\sum_{i=1}^{N} n_i(n_i - 1) \right] + (n_1 + n_2 - 1)(N - 1) \tag{5.4}$$

$$d \leq \left(\sum_{i=1}^{N} n_i \right) - 1 \tag{5.5}$$

It should be noted that in conducting the homing experiment for any particular machine M_k, as required in step 2 of Algorithm 5.1, the observed responses may be used to rule out one or more machines (possibly M_k itself) from further consideration as M. When step 2 in the algorithm is accompanied by such ruling-out operations, both the length and order of the experiment are considerably reduced.

When n_i, or the upper bound to n_i, is the same for all i, Theorem 5.5 yields:

COROLLARY 5.2. A given machine M is known to belong to the exclusive class of machines $\{M_1, M_2, \ldots, M_N\}$, where every machine contains at most n states. Then M can always be identified by a simple adaptive experiment of length l and order d, where

$$l \leq \tfrac{1}{2}N(n^2 + 3n - 2) - 2n + 1 \tag{5.6}$$
$$d \leq Nn - 1 \tag{5.7}$$

5.4. The Fault Identification Problem

A problem of considerable practical interest is that of identifying the fault of a failing machine. In connection with this problem, it is convenient to regard the faulty version of a machine as another machine. The task of identifying a faulty machine susceptible to a known class of faults reduces, then, to the task of identifying a machine which belongs to a known class of machines. From the results of Sec. 5.3, it follows that the fault can always be identified if the class of faulty machines is an exclusive class.

To illustrate the procedure for machine identification in general, and fault identification in particular, consider machine $A24$ of Table 5.1. It

TABLE 5.1. MACHINE $A24$

s_ν \ x_ν	z_ν α	z_ν β	$s_{\nu+1}$ α	$s_{\nu+1}$ β
1	1	0	2	4
2	0	1	3	1
3	0	0	4	2
4	0	1	1	3

TABLE 5.2. MACHINE $A24'$

s_ν \ x_ν	z_ν α	z_ν β	$s_{\nu+1}$ α	$s_{\nu+1}$ β
$1'$	1	0	$2'$	$4'$
$2'$	1	1	$3'$	$1'$
$3'$	0	0	$4'$	$2'$
$4'$	0	1	$1'$	$3'$

is known that $A24$ malfunctions and that the fault is such that at one of its states the machine, when excited with α, produces the output symbol 1 instead of 0. The faulty machine $A24$, then, may be one of the machines $A24'$, $A24''$, and $A24'''$, represented by Tables 5.2, 5.3, and 5.4, respec-

TABLE 5.3. MACHINE $A24''$

s_ν \ x_ν	z_ν α	z_ν β	$s_{\nu+1}$ α	$s_{\nu+1}$ β
$1''$	1	0	$2''$	$4''$
$2''$	0	1	$3''$	$1''$
$3''$	1	0	$4''$	$2''$
$4''$	0	1	$1''$	$3''$

TABLE 5.4. MACHINE $A24'''$

s_ν \ x_ν	z_ν α	z_ν β	$s_{\nu+1}$ α	$s_{\nu+1}$ β
$1'''$	1	0	$2'''$	$4'''$
$2'''$	0	1	$3'''$	$1'''$
$3'''$	0	0	$4'''$	$2'''$
$4'''$	1	1	$1'''$	$3'''$

tively. To determine whether $A24'$, $A24''$, and $A24'''$ constitute an exclusive class, the equivalence partition should be obtained for $\Delta(A24', A24'', A24''')$, i.e., for the disjunction machine of $A24'$, $A24''$, and $A24'''$. The partitioning can be performed with a pairs table, as shown in Table 5.5. The table reveals that the only equivalent pairs in $\Delta(A24', A24''$,

TABLE 5.5. PAIRS TABLE FOR $\Delta(A24', A24'', A24''')$

Pairs	α	β
$1', 1''$	$2', 2''$	$4', 4''$
$1', 3''$	$2', 4''$	$4', 2''$
$1', 1'''$	$2', 2'''$	$4', 4'''$
$1'', 3''$	$2'', 4''$	$4'', 2''$
$1'', 1'''$	$2'', 2'''$	$4'', 4'''$
$3'', 1'''$	$4'', 2'''$	$2'', 4'''$
$2', 4'''$	$3', 1'''$	$1', 3'''$
$3', 3'''$	$4', 4'''$	$2', 2'''$
$4', 2''$	$1', 3'''$	$3', 1''$
$4', 4''$	$1', 1''$	$3', 3''$
$4', 2'''$	$1', 3'''$	$3', 1'''$
$2'', 4''$	$3'', 1''$	$1'', 3''$
$2'', 2'''$	$3'', 3'''$	$1'', 1'''$
$4'', 2'''$	$1'', 3'''$	$3'', 1'''$

$A24'''$) are $\{1'', 3''\}$ and $\{2'', 4''\}$. Hence, $A24''$ is not minimal, but no state in any of the machines is equivalent to a state in any other machine. Thus, when $A24''$ is reduced to its minimal form, $\Delta(A24', A24'', A24''')$ becomes a minimal machine, which implies that $A24'$, $A24''$, and $A24'''$ (all in their minimal forms) constitute an exclusive class. The transition table and transition diagram of $\Delta(A24', A24'', A24''')$ are shown in Table 5.6 and Fig. 5.3 (with $A24''$ in its minimal form).

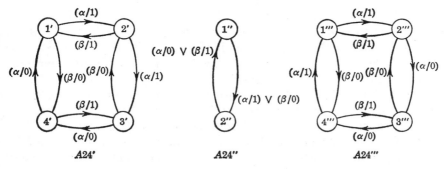

FIG. 5.3. Machine $\Delta(A24', A24'', A24''')$.

TABLE 5.6. MACHINE $\Delta(A24', A24'', A24''')$

x_ν / s_ν	z_ν		$s_{\nu+1}$	
	α	β	α	β
$1'$	1	0	$2'$	$4'$
$2'$	1	1	$3'$	$1'$
$3'$	0	0	$4'$	$2'$
$4'$	0	1	$1'$	$3'$
$1''$	1	0	$2''$	$2''$
$2''$	0	1	$1''$	$1''$
$1'''$	1	0	$2'''$	$4'''$
$2'''$	0	1	$3'''$	$1'''$
$3'''$	0	0	$4'''$	$2'''$
$4'''$	1	1	$1'''$	$3'''$

The problem of identifying the fault in $A24$ is now reduced to that of identifying the final state of the faulty machine $A24$ or to that of conducting a homing experiment for $\Delta(A24', A24'', A24''')$. The fault identification experiment is described in Table 5.7, where it is assumed that the initial state of $A24$ is 2 and that the true fault is the generation of 1 when α is applied at state 4. The true machine, then, is $A24'''$, and the true initial state is $2'''$ (this, of course, is unknown to the experimenter at the outset). The first column in Table 5.7 lists, as a guide to the reader, the true state of $A24'''$ at the various stages of the identification experiment. In accordance with Algorithm 5.1, we first conduct a regular adaptive homing experiment for $A24'$ and the admissible set $\{1', 2', 3', 4'\}$. At the end of this experiment it is established that, if the machine is $A24'$, its final state must be $2'$. Next, we conduct a regular adaptive homing experiment for $A24''$ and the admissible set $\{1'', 2''\}$, at the end of which it can be concluded that, if the machine is $A24''$, its final state must be $1''$. Next, we conduct a regular adaptive homing experiment for $A24'''$ and the admissible set $\{1''', 2''', 3''', 4'''\}$, which establishes that, if the machine is $A24'''$, its final state must be $1'''$. At the end of the third homing experiment, then, the given machine can be $A24'$ at state $1'$ ($\alpha\alpha\alpha$ passes $2'$ into $1'$), or $A24''$ at state $1''$ ($\alpha\alpha$ passes $1''$ into $1''$), or $A24'''$ at state $1'''$. Consequently, we conduct a regular adaptive homing experiment for $\Delta(A24', A24'', A24''')$ and the admissible set $\{1', 1'', 1'''\}$, which reveals the final state to be $4'''$. Since state $4'''$ is in submachine $A24'''$, the machine is identified as $A24'''$. Thus, it can be concluded that the fault is the one which causes the generation of 1 instead of 0, when α is applied to state 4 of machine $A24$.

Notice that a reduction in the length of the identification experiment is achieved if, after the application of each subsequence, as many states of $\Delta(A24', A24'', A24''')$ as possible are ruled out as final states. For example, after the first β is applied and the response 1 is observed, states $2''$, $2'''$, and $4'''$ (in addition to $2'$ and $4'$) may be ruled out as final states. As a result, the second homing experiment can be omitted and the third homing experiment shortened.

TABLE 5.7. FAULT-IDENTIFICATION EXPERIMENT FOR $A24$

True state	k	g_k	σ_i, σ_j	$\mathcal{E}(\sigma_i, \sigma_j)$	Response
Homing Experiment for $A24'$ and $\{1', 2', 3', 4'\}$					
$2'''$	0	$\{1', 2', 3', 4'\}$	$1', 2'$	β	1
$1'''$	1	$\{1', 3'\}$	$1', 3'$	α	1
$2'''$	2	$\{2'\}$			
Homing Experiment for $A24''$ and $\{1'', 2''\}$					
$2'''$	0	$\{1'', 2''\}$	$1'', 2''$	α	0
$3'''$	1	$\{1''\}$			
Homing Experiment for $A24'''$ and $\{1''', 2''', 3''', 4'''\}$					
$3'''$	0	$\{1''', 2''', 3''', 4'''\}$	$1''', 2'''$	α	0
$4'''$	1	$\{3''', 4'''\}$	$3''', 4'''$	α	1
$1'''$	2	$\{1'''\}$			
Homing Experiment for $\Delta(A24', A24'', A24''')$ and $\{1', 1'', 1'''\}$					
$1'''$	0	$\{1', 1'', 1'''\}$	$1', 1''$	$\alpha\alpha$	10
$3'''$	1	$\{1'', 3'''\}$	$1'', 3'''$	α	0
$4'''$	2	$\{4'''\}$			

5.5. Strongly Connected Machines

In this section we shall introduce an important class of machines, called "strongly connected machines":

DEFINITION 5.1.   Machine M, with the state set $\{\sigma_1, \sigma_2, \ldots, \sigma_n\}$, is said to be *strongly connected*, if an input sequence exists which passes M from any given state σ_i to any given state σ_j (where i may equal j).

From the definition it follows that a strongly connected machine cannot contain any transient, persistent, or isolated submachines. Conversely, any machine which contains a transient, persistent, or isolated submachine cannot be a strongly connected machine. Thus, a strongly connected machine is a machine in which every state can be attained regardless of the past history of the machine.

The cost and complexity of many machines which represent practical devices increase with their number of states. In many machines designed for practical use, therefore, transient and isolated submachines (which constitute a potential waste, since they may never be reachable) are avoided. Thus, strongly connected machines represent a class of machines which are often encountered in practice.

LEMMA 5.1. If M_1 and M_2 are strongly connected and distinguishable, then no state in M_1 is equivalent to any state in M_2.

Proof. Let the state set of M_1 be $\{\sigma_1, \sigma_2, \ldots, \sigma_{n_1}\}$ and the state set of M_2 be $\{\sigma'_1, \sigma'_2, \ldots, \sigma'_{n_2}\}$. Suppose there is a state σ_i of M_1 equivalent to some state σ'_j of M_2. Let $\mathcal{E}_1$ be the input sequence which passes σ_i to σ_1 and $\mathcal{E}_k$ the input sequence which passes σ_{k-1} to σ_k, for $k = 2, 3, \ldots, n_1$ (all these sequences exist, since M_1 is strongly connected). Apply the sequence $\mathcal{E}_1 \mathcal{E}_2 \cdots \mathcal{E}_{n_1}$ to $M|\sigma_i$ and $M_2|\sigma'_j$. After the application of $\mathcal{E}_1 \mathcal{E}_2 \cdots \mathcal{E}_k$, M_1 is in state σ_k and M_2 is in some state σ'_{j_k}. Since $\sigma_i = \sigma'_j$, their successors, with respect to any given input sequence, must be equivalent; hence, $\sigma_k = \sigma'_{j_k}$, for $k = 1, 2, \ldots, n_1$. Thus, for every state in M_1 there exists an equivalent state in M_2. Now, let $\mathcal{E}'_1$ be the input sequence which passes σ'_j to σ'_1 and $\mathcal{E}_k$ be the input sequence which passes σ'_{k-1} to σ'_k, for $k = 2, 3, \ldots, n_2$ (all these sequences exist, since M_2 is strongly connected). Apply the sequence $\mathcal{E}'_1 \mathcal{E}'_2 \cdots \mathcal{E}'_{n_2}$ to $M_1|\sigma_i$ and $M_2|\sigma'_j$. After the application of $\mathcal{E}'_1 \mathcal{E}'_2 \cdots \mathcal{E}'_k$, M_2 is in state σ'_k and M_1 is in some state σ_{i_k}. Since $\sigma_i = \sigma'_j$, we must have, as before, $\sigma'_k = \sigma_{i_k}$, for $k = 1, 2, \ldots, n_2$. Thus, for every state in M_2 there exists an equivalent state in M_1. Consequently, it is shown that, if $\sigma_i = \sigma'_j$, then $M_1 = M_2$, which is a contradiction. Hence, no state in M_1 can be equivalent to any state in M_2.

THEOREM 5.6. If $\mathfrak{M} = \{M_1, M_2, \ldots, M_N\}$ is a finite class of strongly connected machines, such that no two machines are equivalent, then $\mathfrak{M}$ is an exclusive class.

Proof. Suppose $\mathfrak{M}$ is not exclusive. Then there must be a state in some machine M_i equivalent to some state in machine M_j $(j \neq i)$. However, by Lemma 5.1, this is impossible, since M_i and M_j are distinguishable and strongly connected. By contradiction, then, $\mathfrak{M}$ must be exclusive.

Combining Theorems 5.3 and 5.6, we have:

COROLLARY 5.3. If a machine is known to belong to a specified finite class of strongly connected machines, it can always be identified.

The procedure for identifying a strongly connected machine and the bound to the length of the identification experiment are the same as those presented in the preceding sections.

5.6. Some Properties of Strongly Connected Machines

A *reversible machine* is a machine in which the initial state can always be recovered. Clearly, every strongly connected machine is reversible. The converse, however, is not true: a reversible machine need not be strongly connected.

THEOREM 5.7. A machine in which every isolated submachine is strongly connected is reversible.

Proof. Let the machine be M, which consists of the isolated submachines $M_1, M_2, \ldots, M_N$. If the initial state of M is σ_i in M_j, then its final state σ_i', for any input sequence, must also be in M_j. Since M_j is strongly connected, σ_i is always reachable from σ_i', which implies that M is reversible.

THEOREM 5.8. A reversible machine is strongly connected if and only if it contains no isolated submachines.

Proof. Clearly, if a reversible machine consists of two or more isolated submachines, it cannot be strongly connected. Now, suppose a reversible machine M has no isolated submachines, but contains a transient (and, therefore, a persistent) submachine. This implies that M may have an unrecoverable initial state, and hence that M is not reversible. By contradiction, then, M cannot have transient and persistent submachines. Since a machine is strongly connected if it has no transient, persistent, and isolated submachines, it follows that if a reversible machine has no isolated submachines, it must be strongly connected.

An important property of a strongly connected machine is that it can always be passed into any specified final state.

THEOREM 5.9. Let M be an n-state strongly connected machine. Then M can be passed into any specified state by a simple adaptive experiment of length l and order d, where

$$l \leq \tfrac{1}{2}(n + 2)(n - 1) \tag{5.8}$$
$$d \leq n \tag{5.9}$$

Proof. Using Eqs. (4.23) and (4.24), M can always be passed into a known final state (but not necessarily the specified one) by a simple adaptive experiment of length $n(n - 1)/2$ or less and order $n - 1$ or less. After the known state is attained, an additional sequence can be applied which would pass this state into any specified state (such a sequence always exists, since M, by assumption, is strongly connected). By Theorem 2.2, this additional sequence is of length $n - 1$ or less. Thus, the total length of the experiment is given by

$$l \leq \tfrac{1}{2}n(n - 1) + n - 1 = \tfrac{1}{2}(n + 2)(n - 1) \tag{5.10}$$

The total order is given by

$$d \leq n - 1 + 1 = n \tag{5.11}$$

5.7. Identification of Strongly Connected (n, p, q) Machines

In many cases a partial knowledge of the internal structure of a given machine reveals its input alphabet, output alphabet, and number of states. For example, if the machine represents a computing device, this information can be deduced from the input mechanism, output mechanism, and number of storage elements in the device. If the number of input symbols is p, the number of output symbols q, and the number of states n, this information is equivalent to the assertion that the given machine is an (n, p, q) machine. If, in addition, the machine is known to be strongly connected, it can be asserted that the given machine is a strongly connected (n, p, q) machine.

The class of strongly connected (n, p, q) machines, such that no two machines are equivalent, will be denoted by $C_{n,p,q}$. Clearly, $C_{n,p,q}$ is a subclass of the class of minimal (n, p, q) machines, such that no two machines are equivalent. By Theorem 3.7, the latter class is finite, and hence $C_{n,p,q}$ must also be finite. Using Eq. (3.21), the size of $C_{n,p,q}$, denoted by $|C_{n,p,q}|$, is subject to the following bound:

$$|C_{n,p,q}| \leq \frac{1}{n!} \prod_{r=0}^{n-1} [(qn)^p - r] \tag{5.12}$$

Since, by Theorem 5.6, $C_{n,p,q}$ is an exclusive class, any of its members can be identified by a simple preset experiment of length l, where, by Corollary 5.1,

$$l \leq (2n - 1)(|C_{n,p,q}|n - 1) \leq \frac{2n - 1}{(n - 1)!} \prod_{r=0}^{n-1} [(qn)^p - r]$$

$$= \frac{(2n - 1)(qn)^{pn}}{(n - 1)!} \prod_{r=0}^{n-1} \left[1 - \frac{r}{(qn)^p} \right]$$

$$\leq \frac{(2n - 1)(qn)^{pn}}{(n - 1)!} \exp \left[- \frac{n(n - 1)}{2(qn)^p} \right] \tag{5.13}$$

We thus have:

THEOREM 5.10. Machine M is known to be a strongly connected (n, p, q) machine. Then M can always be identified by a simple preset experiment of length l, where

$$l \leq \frac{(2n - 1)(qn)^{pn}}{(n - 1)!} \exp \left[- \frac{n(n - 1)}{2(qn)^p} \right] \tag{5.14}$$

For example, a strongly connected (2, 2, 2) machine can always be identified by a simple preset experiment whose length does not exceed 725 symbols.

5.8. Information-lossless Machines[1]

In Chap. 4 and the preceding sections of the present chapter, we studied the problems of identifying unknown states and unknown machines. In this section we shall discuss an identification problem of a different type—the problem of identifying unknown input sequences applied to a given finite-state machine. Specifically, the problem at hand is the following: An unknown finite input sequence $\mathcal{E}$ is applied to machine M, whose transition table and initial state σ_i (i.e., the state

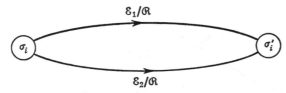

Fig. 5.4. A lossy state.

before $\mathcal{E}$ is applied) are known, and whose response to $\mathcal{E}$ can be observed; design an experiment which, when conducted on M after $\mathcal{E}$ terminates, identifies the sequence $\mathcal{E}$. Machines for which this problem can be solved regardless of $\mathcal{E}$ and σ_i are called *information-lossless machines*. While every finite-state machine has the property that, given the initial state and applied excitation, the response can always be determined, information-lossless machines have the additional property that, given the initial state and observed response, the excitation can always be determined.

A state σ_i in machine M will be said to *lead into state σ_i' via $\mathcal{E}/\mathcal{R}$* if applying the input sequence $\mathcal{E}$ to $M|\sigma_i$ yields the output sequence $\mathcal{R}$ and passes M into state σ_i'. State σ_i will be called a *lossy state* if it leads into some state σ_i' via $\mathcal{E}_1/\mathcal{R}$ and via $\mathcal{E}_2/\mathcal{R}$, where $\mathcal{E}_1$ and $\mathcal{E}_2$ are two different input sequences. The condition for lossiness is illustrated in Fig. 5.4.

THEOREM 5.11. A necessary and sufficient condition for machine M to be information-lossless is that M shall contain no lossy states.

Proof. Suppose M contains a lossy state σ_i, as shown in Fig. 5.4. Since the responses of $M|\sigma_i$ to $\mathcal{E}_1$ and $\mathcal{E}_2$ are identical, and since both sequences pass M into the same final state, no subsequent experimentation can reveal whether the response $\mathcal{R}$ is attributable to $\mathcal{E}_1$ or to $\mathcal{E}_2$. The

[1] The material in this section is based in part on the work of D. A. Huffman (Canonical Forms for Information-Lossless Finite-State Logical Machines, *IRE Trans.*, vol. CT-6, special supplement, pp. 41–59, 1959).

necessity assertion in the theorem is thus evident. Assume now that M contains no lossy states and that $\mathcal{R}$ is the response observed when an unknown input sequence $\mathcal{E}$ is applied to M at the known initial state σ_i. From the transition table, determine all the different input sequences, say $\mathcal{E}_1, \mathcal{E}_2, \ldots, \mathcal{E}_r$, to which the response $\mathcal{R}$ is equally attributable; one of these sequences must be $\mathcal{E}$. Denote the states into which σ_i leads via $\mathcal{E}_1/\mathcal{R}, \mathcal{E}_2/\mathcal{R}, \ldots, \mathcal{E}_r/\mathcal{R}$ by $\sigma_{i_1}, \sigma_{i_2}, \ldots, \sigma_{i_r}$, respectively. Since, by assumption, σ_i is not lossy, $\sigma_{i_1}, \sigma_{i_2}, \ldots, \sigma_{i_r}$ must be distinct, and hence there must exist a one-to-one relationship between the states σ_{i_k} and the input sequences $\mathcal{E}_k$. Now, apply a homing sequence, say $\mathcal{E}_H$, designed for M and the admissible set $\{\sigma_{i_1}, \sigma_{i_2}, \ldots, \sigma_{i_r}\}$. Denote the final state

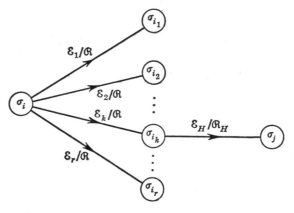

FIG. 5.5. Illustrating the proof of Theorem 5.11.

attained through $\mathcal{E}_H$ by σ_j and the response to $\mathcal{E}_H$ by $\mathcal{R}_H$. The excitation-response pair $\mathcal{E}_H/\mathcal{R}_H$ can be attributed only to one of the states $\sigma_{i_1}, \sigma_{i_2}, \ldots, \sigma_{i_r}$, for the following reason: Suppose $\mathcal{E}_H/\mathcal{R}_H$ is attributable to two states, say σ_{i_1} and σ_{i_2}; then σ_i leads to σ_j via $\mathcal{E}_1\mathcal{E}_H/\mathcal{R}\mathcal{R}_H$ and via $\mathcal{E}_2\mathcal{E}_H/\mathcal{R}\mathcal{R}_H$. However, since $\mathcal{E}_1$ and $\mathcal{E}_2$ are different sequences, this would imply that σ_i is lossy, which contradicts the assumption that M contains no lossy states. Consequently, $\mathcal{E}_H/\mathcal{R}_H$ uniquely determines the state into which σ_i passes when $\mathcal{E}$ is applied, and hence uniquely determines $\mathcal{E}$. The situation is depicted in Fig. 5.5, where $\mathcal{E}_k$ is assumed to be the true input sequence $\mathcal{E}$.

Let $S_j(\sigma_u)$ denote the set of states into which state σ_u of M passes with the output symbol ζ_j. If M is lossless and has p input symbols and q output symbols, the sets $S_1(\sigma_u), S_2(\sigma_u), \ldots, S_q(\sigma_u)$ must contain the total number of elements p. Now, let a "$D_k(\sigma_i)$ set" denote any set of states, say $\{\sigma_{i_1}, \sigma_{i_2}, \ldots, \sigma_{i_r}\}$, reachable from state σ_i with the same output sequence of length k. The set $S_j(\sigma_{i_1}) \cup S_j(\sigma_{i_2}) \cup \cdots \cup S_j(\sigma_{i_r})$, then, is a $D_{k+1}(\sigma_i)$ set. If M is lossless, the number of elements in $D_{k+1}(\sigma_i)$ must equal the total number of elements in $S_j(\sigma_{i_1})$, $S_j(\sigma_{i_2})$, . . . , $S_j(\sigma_{i_r})$, for any j. Thus, by recursively compiling all the $D_k(\sigma_i)$ sets for all k and i, one can establish whether or not M is information-lossless.

The above criterion can be readily applied through the so-called *lossiness test table*. In this table, each column represents a different output symbol ζ_j. The table is divided into successive subtables, the first of which contains the states of M, say σ_1, σ_2, . . . , σ_n, as stub entries, and the set $S_j(\sigma_u)$ as the entry common to row σ_u and column ζ_j. The stub entries in the $(k + 1)$st subtable are entries included in the kth subtable, but not included as stub entries in previously completed rows. The entry common to row $\{\sigma_{i_1}, \sigma_{i_2}, . . . , \sigma_{i_r}\}$ and column ζ_j of the $(k + 1)$st subtable is the set $S_j(\sigma_{i_1}) \cup S_j(\sigma_{i_2}) \cup \cdots \cup S_j(\sigma_{i_r})$, which can be compiled by inspection of the first subtable. Construction terminates when one of the following conditions is met: (1) The number of elements in some $S_j(\sigma_u)$ set (in the first subtable) is less than the size of the input alphabet. (2) The number of elements in some $S_j(\sigma_{i_1}) \cup S_j(\sigma_{i_2}) \cup \cdots \cup S_j(\sigma_{i_r})$ set (in the kth subtable, where $k > 1$) is less than the total number of elements in the sets $S_j(\sigma_{i_1})$, $S_j(\sigma_{i_2})$, . . . , $S_j(\sigma_{i_r})$. (3) No new stub entries can be added. If conditions 1 and 2 are not encountered, M is information-lossless. Clearly, the total number of rows in the lossiness test table cannot exceed

$$\sum_{r=1}^{n} \binom{n}{r} = 2^n - 1 \tag{5.15}$$

The process of establishing information-losslessness, therefore, is a finite process.

As an example, the lossiness test table for machine $A25$ of Fig. 5.6 and Table 5.8 is shown in Table 5.9. The first subtable of Table 5.9 is completed by inspection of Table 5.8. The stub entries $\{1, 3\}$, $\{1, 5\}$, and $\{2, 3\}$ in the second subtable are entries in the first subtable which have not yet appeared as stub entries. The entry common to row $\{1, 5\}$ and column 1, for example, is the union of the entries of rows 1 and 5 at column 1 of the first subtable, namely, $\{2, 3, 4\}$. The remainder of the table is completed in an analogous fashion. Since conditions 1 and 2 are not encountered in this table, $A25$ is information-lossless.

To illustrate how input sequences can be identified in information-lossless machines, suppose it is known that $A25$ was in state 1 before an unknown input sequence, yielding the output sequence 111, was applied to it. From Fig. 5.6 it can be deduced that 111 can be attributed to the input sequences $\alpha\beta\alpha$, $\alpha\beta\beta$, and $\alpha\alpha\beta$ which pass state 1 into states 2, 3, and 4, respectively. $\alpha\beta$ is a homing sequence for $A25$ and the admissible set

$\{2, 3, 4\}$. When $\alpha\beta$ is applied to states 2, 3, and 4, the output sequences are 11, 01, and 10, respectively. Consequently, the true input sequence is $\alpha\beta\alpha$, $\alpha\beta\beta$, or $\alpha\alpha\beta$, depending on whether the response to $\alpha\beta$ (applied after the unknown input sequence terminates) is 11, 01, or 10, respectively.

TABLE 5.8. MACHINE $A25$ TABLE 5.9. LOSSINESS TEST TABLE FOR $A25$

	z_ν		$s_{\nu+1}$	
s_ν \ x_ν	α	β	α	β
1	1	1	2	3
2	1	1	5	1
3	0	0	1	3
4	1	0	3	5
5	0	1	5	4

	0	1
1	—	2, 3
2	—	1, 5
3	1, 3	—
4	5	3
5	5	4
1, 3	1, 3	2, 3
1, 5	5	2, 3, 4
2, 3	1, 3	1, 5
2, 3, 4	1, 3, 5	1, 3, 5
1, 3, 5	1, 3, 5	2, 3, 4

An information-lossless machine M may be viewed as a communication channel, where messages transmitted at the input terminal are received in a coded form at the output terminal. The receiver's task of decoding the messages can be successfully carried out, provided the receiver knows the state of the channel before each message is transmitted, and provided the channel can be passed into a known final state after each message is transmitted. If the receiver has no control over the input terminal (as is

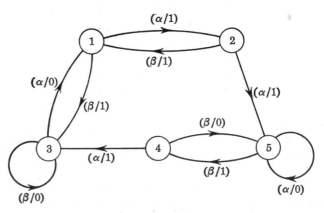

FIG. 5.6. Machine $A25$.

usually the case), the second condition may be met if the transmitter "agrees" to terminate every message with the sequence ε_H, i.e., with a predetermined homing sequence for M and the admissible set which consists of all the states of M. For example, a homing sequence for $A25$ and the admissible set $\{1, 2, 3, 4, 5\}$ is $\alpha\alpha\alpha$. If the transmitter consistently terminates every message with $\alpha\alpha\alpha$ (or transmits $\alpha\alpha\alpha$ at fixed, predetermined intervals), all transmitted messages can be decoded in the receiving end, without the need of having access to the input terminal. It can also be seen that if the transmitter agrees to transmit ε_H *before* every message, the receiver does not require the knowledge of the initial state of M (i.e., the state of M when the first message symbol is applied), since this knowledge can be derived from the observed response to ε_H. Thus, if every transmitted message is preceded and followed by ε_H, the message itself can be decoded on the basis of the transition table of M alone. In our example, this implies that every message is to initiate and terminate with the input sequence $\alpha\alpha\alpha$.

PROBLEMS

5.1. Construct a machine from which the machine of Fig. P 5.1 is indistinguishable by any experiment of length 4, but to which the machine of Fig. P 5.1 is not equivalent.

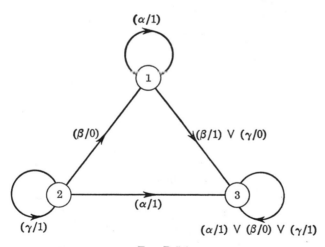

FIG. P 5.1

5.2. A minimal machine M is known to have two states, the input alphabet $\{\alpha, \beta\}$ and the output alphabet $\{0, 1\}$. It is also known that no state in the transition diagram of M has a reflecting branch. Describe the identification experiment for this machine, if its true representation is as shown in Table P 5.1 and if its true initial state is 1 (which are unknown at the outset).

5.3. It is known that the machine specified by Table P 5.2 malfunctions and that the nature of the fault is such that at least one "1" is generated as "0." Describe an experiment for identifying the fault, if the true fault is that the "1" in state 1 is generated as "0" and if the initial state of the machine is 3 (which are unknown at the outset).

TABLE P 5.1

s_ν \ x_ν	z_ν		$s_{\nu+1}$	
	α	β	α	β
1	0	1	2	2
2	1	1	1	1

TABLE P 5.2

s_ν \ x_ν	z_ν		$s_{\nu+1}$	
	α	β	α	β
1	0	1	1	3
2	0	0	3	3
3	1	0	2	1

5.4. Figure P 5.2 shows the incomplete transition diagram of a 2-state machine. Describe an experiment conducted on this machine, which serves to complete the diagram. Assume that the questionable branch is labeled $(\alpha/1)$ and terminates at state 1 and that the initial state is 1 (which are unknown at the outset).

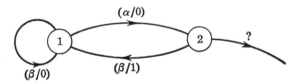

FIG. P 5.2

5.5. Show that machine M with the state set $S = \{\sigma_1, \sigma_2, \ldots, \sigma_n\}$ is strongly connected, if and only if $G(\sigma_i) = S$ for $i = 1, 2, \ldots, n$. [$G(\sigma_i)$ is as defined in Sec. 2.6.]

5.6. Show that a necessary and sufficient condition for the n-state machine M to be strongly connected is that $\sum_{k=1}^{n} [\tilde{M}]$ shall have no zero entries.

5.7. Machines M_1 and M_2 are strongly connected, and state σ_i of M_1 is equivalent to state σ_j of M_2. Show that $M_1 = M_2$.

5.8. Construct a general n-state machine which is strongly connected, but which contains no complete cycles.

5.9. Machine M has the state set $S = \{\sigma_1, \sigma_2, \ldots, \sigma_n\}$. Show that (a) M is reversible if, in every isolated submachine of M, there is a state σ_i such that $G(\sigma_i) = F(\sigma_i)$; (b) M is strongly connected, if it contains a state σ_i such that $G(\sigma_i) = F(\sigma_i) = S$. [$G(\sigma_i)$ is as defined in Sec. 2.6; $F(\sigma_i)$ is as defined in Prob. 2.10.]

5.10. Show that if machine M is strongly connected, then $\tilde{M}$ is strongly connected, but that the converse is not necessarily true.

5.11. Prove the following inequality, utilized in Eq. (5.13):

$$\prod_{r=0}^{n-1} \left[1 - \frac{r}{(qn)^p}\right] \le \exp\left[-\frac{n(n-1)}{2(qn)^p}\right]$$

5.12. Machine M is known to be a strongly connected $(n, 2, 2)$ machine. Show that M can always be identified by a simple preset experiment of length l, where

$$l \le \frac{(2n)^{2n+1}}{(n-1)!}$$

Evaluate the upper bound for l, when $n = 5$.

5.13. Machine M is known to be an (n, p, q) machine and to contain a complete cycle. Find an upper bound to the length of the identifying experiment for M (it may be assumed that $n \gg 1$).

5.14. Determine whether machine $A17$ of Fig. 4.3 is information-lossless.

5.15. Show that the machine represented by Fig. P 5.3 is information-lossless, and describe the identification of the input sequence $\alpha\alpha\beta$ applied to this machine at state 2.

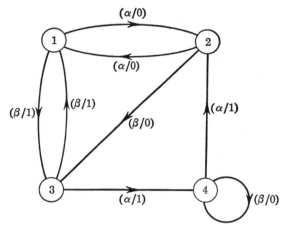

Fig. P 5.3

5.16. Show that machines having any of the following properties are information-lossless: (a) No row in the z_ν subtable contains two identical output symbols. (b) No column in the transition matrix contains two or more input-output pairs with the same output symbol.

CHAPTER 6

FINITE-MEMORY MACHINES

6.1. Introduction

The chief advantage in employing the finite-state model for the representation of a given system is that the prediction of the system response does not require any data concerning past performance of the system. To predict the response at any given time, it is sufficient to know the excitation and the state at that time. The present state of the machine, then, may be regarded as the particular "quantity" in which all past

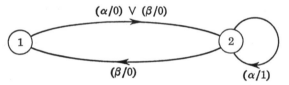

FIG. 6.1. Machine $A26$.

events relevant to the determination of the present response are implicitly incorporated. At this point, the following question may be raised: Can an explicit relationship be always established, relating the present response to the present excitation and to a finite number of past excitations and responses? The answer is "no," as can be readily demonstrated through the simple machine $A26$, shown in Fig. 6.1. In this machine, the final state remains unknown until the input α is applied and the response observed. Thus, the knowledge that the last l input symbols were β and the last l output symbols were 0 is not helpful in predicting the response of $A26$ to an applied α—regardless of the value of l. For this machine, therefore, the exploration of the past behavior does not always help in predicting the response to a present excitation. In general, then, no explicit relationship exists which expresses the present response as a function of the present excitation and of the past excitations and responses. In this connection, it can be concluded that a state in a finite-state machine may exhibit "infinite memory," in the sense that the existence of the machine in this state is the outcome of an event which occurred arbitrarily far in the past. For example, the state into which machine $A26$ passes after the application of the arbitrarily long sequence $\alpha\beta\beta\beta \cdots \beta$ is uniquely determined by the response to the *first* symbol included in this sequence.

In this chapter we shall deviate from the discussion of the general finite-state machine and study machines in which an explicit relationship *can* be established between past and present excitations and responses. Although such machines are of a rather restricted character, they are sufficiently common to warrant extensive discussion.[1]

6.2. Representation of Finite-memory Systems

A *finite-memory system* is a system representable by a finite-state machine, in which the response at any sampling time depends only on a finite, nonzero number of past excitations (and, possibly, on the present excitation)[2] and on a finite number of past responses. A finite-memory system, then, is representable by a finite-state machine whose input-output relationship can be written in the form

$$z_\nu = g(x_{\nu-i_1}, x_{\nu-i_2}, \ldots, x_{\nu-i_u}, z_{\nu-j_1}, z_{\nu-j_2}, \ldots, z_{\nu-j_v}) \tag{6.1}$$

where it is assumed that $0 \leq i_1 < i_2 < \cdots < i_u$ and $1 \leq j_1 < j_2 < \cdots < j_v$. By adding a number of dummy arguments[3] and letting $i_u = \mu_1$ and $j_v = \mu_2$, Eq. (6.1) can be written as

$$z_\nu = f(x_\nu, x_{\nu-1}, \ldots, x_{\nu-\mu_1}, z_{\nu-1}, z_{\nu-2}, \ldots, z_{\nu-\mu_2}) \tag{6.2}$$

To transform the above characterization into the standard characterizing functions f_z and f_s of a finite-state machine, a variable s is defined such that s_ν is the ordered $(\mu_1 + \mu_2)$-tuple $(x_{\nu-1}, x_{\nu-2}, \ldots, x_{\nu-\mu_1}, z_{\nu-1}, z_{\nu-2}, \ldots, z_{\nu-\mu_2})$. Equation (6.2) then becomes

$$z_\nu = f_z(x_\nu, s_\nu) \tag{6.3}$$

From the definition of s, $s_{\nu+1}$ is given by

$$(x_\nu, x_{\nu-1}, \ldots, x_{\nu-\mu_1+1}, z_\nu, z_{\nu-1}, \ldots, z_{\nu-\mu_2+1})$$
$$= (x_\nu, x_{\nu-1}, \ldots, x_{\nu-\mu_1+1}, f(x_\nu, x_{\nu-1}, \ldots, x_{\nu-\mu_1},$$
$$z_{\nu-1}, z_{\nu-2}, \ldots, z_{\nu-\mu_2}), z_{\nu-1}, \ldots, z_{\nu-\mu_2+1}) \tag{6.4}$$

Hence

$$s_{\nu+1} = h(x_\nu, x_{\nu-1}, \ldots, x_{\nu-\mu_1}, z_{\nu-1}, z_{\nu-2}, \ldots, z_{\nu-\mu_2}) \tag{6.5}$$

or

$$s_{\nu+1} = f_s(x_\nu, s_\nu) \tag{6.6}$$

---

[1] The material in this chapter is based in part on the work of J. M. Simon (A Note on the Memory Aspects of Sequence Transducers, *IRE Trans.*, vol. CT-6, pp. 26–29, 1959) and L. A. Zadeh (unpublished notes on discrete-state systems and automata, University of California, Berkeley, 1960).

[2] Machines in which the response is independent of the excitation are said to be *autonomous*. Autonomous machines will not be discussed in this book.

[3] A *dummy argument* is an argument which leaves the value of the function unchanged, regardless of the value assumed by this argument.

Equations (6.3) and (6.6) can be recognized as the characterizing functions of a finite-state machine. Consequently, the set of ordered $(\mu_1 + \mu_2)$-tuples $(x_{\nu-1}, x_{\nu-2}, \ldots, x_{\nu-\mu_1}, z_{\nu-1}, z_{\nu-2}, \ldots, z_{\nu-\mu_2})$ is an adequate state set for the system represented by Eq. (6.2). If the sizes of the input and output alphabets of the system are p and q, respectively, the size of the state set is given by

$$n = p^{\mu_1} q^{\mu_2} \tag{6.7}$$

As an example, consider a device, labeled $A27$, which is periodically fed with the digits 0 and 1 and whose output at time t_ν equals the sum modulo 2 of the output at time $t_{\nu-1}$ and the input at time $t_{\nu-2}$. Designating modulo-2 addition by $\oplus$,† $A27$ can be characterized by

$$z_\nu = x_{\nu-2} \oplus z_{\nu-1} = g(x_{\nu-2}, z_{\nu-1}) \tag{6.8}$$

Adding the dummy arguments x_ν and $x_{\nu-1}$, (6.8) becomes

$$z_\nu = f(x_\nu, x_{\nu-1}, x_{\nu-2}, z_{\nu-1}) \tag{6.9}$$

The input alphabet in this case is

$$X = \{0, 1\}$$

The output alphabet is

$$Z = \{0, 1\}$$

The state set is the set of all ordered 3-tuples $(x_{\nu-1}, x_{\nu-2}, z_{\nu-1})$:

$$S = \{(0, 0, 0), (0, 0, 1), (0, 1, 0), (0, 1, 1)\ (1, 0, 0), (1, 0, 1), (1, 1, 0),$$
$$(1, 1, 1)\}$$

The relationship between x_ν, s_ν, $s_{\nu+1}$, and z_ν can be displayed in a tabular form, as shown in Table 6.1. The columns under the heading "s_ν" represent all ordered 3-tuples—each 3-tuple written twice (once for each possible value of x_ν). The columns under the heading "$s_{\nu+1}$" can be completed by reproducing previously completed columns (such as columns x_ν and $x_{\nu-1}$) and by utilizing the defining relationship (6.8) (for column z_ν). The shown table can be conveniently used for determining the characterizing functions f_z and f_s for $A27$. For example, from the

---

† Summation modulo 2 is defined by $0 \oplus 0 = 0, 0 \oplus 1 = 1, 1 \oplus 0 = 1, 1 \oplus 1 = 0$. If y is either 0 or 1, we have $y \oplus y = 0$.

fourth row it can be deduced that when the input symbol 1 is applied at state (0, 0, 1), the output symbol is 1 and the next state is (1, 0, 1). Similar deductions with respect to the other rows result in the transition table for $A27$, shown in Table 6.2.

In general, the machine obtained by the above procedure is not minimal. The minimal form, however, can always be determined by any of the minimization techniques described in Chap. 3. The minimal form

TABLE 6.1. RELATIONSHIP BETWEEN x_ν, s_ν, $s_{\nu+1}$, AND z_ν OF $A27$

x_ν	s_ν			$s_{\nu+1}$			z_ν
	$x_{\nu-1}$	$x_{\nu-2}$	$z_{\nu-1}$	x_ν	$x_{\nu-1}$	z_ν	
0	0	0	0	0	0	0	0
1	0	0	0	1	0	0	0
0	0	0	1	0	0	1	1
1	0	0	1	1	0	1	1
0	0	1	0	0	0	1	1
1	0	1	0	1	0	1	1
0	0	1	1	0	0	0	0
1	0	1	1	1	0	0	0
0	1	0	0	0	1	0	0
1	1	0	0	1	1	0	0
0	1	0	1	0	1	1	1
1	1	0	1	1	1	1	1
0	1	1	0	0	1	1	1
1	1	1	0	1	1	1	1
0	1	1	1	0	1	0	0
1	1	1	1	1	1	0	0

TABLE 6.2. MACHINE $A27$

s_ν \ x_ν	z_ν		$s_{\nu+1}$	
	0	1	0	1
(0, 0, 0)	0	0	(0, 0, 0)	(1, 0, 0)
(0, 0, 1)	1	1	(0, 0, 1)	(1, 0, 1)
(0, 1, 0)	1	1	(0, 0, 1)	(1, 0, 1)
(0, 1, 1)	0	0	(0, 0, 0)	(1, 0, 0)
(1, 0, 0)	0	0	(0, 1, 0)	(1, 1, 0)
(1, 0, 1)	1	1	(0, 1, 1)	(1, 1, 1)
(1, 1, 0)	1	1	(0, 1, 1)	(1, 1, 1)
(1, 1, 1)	0	0	(0, 1, 0)	(1, 1, 0)

of machine $A27$ is shown in Fig. 6.2, where states 1, 2, 3, and 4 represent
the equivalence classes $\{(1, 0, 0), (1, 1, 1)\}$, $\{(0, 0, 1), (0, 1, 0)\}$, $\{(0, 0, 0)$,
$(0, 1, 1)\}$, and $\{(1, 0, 1), (1, 1, 0)\}$, respectively.

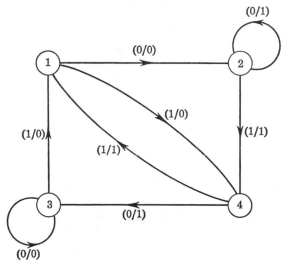

FIG. 6.2. Machine $A27$.

6.3. Properties of Finite-memory Machines

A finite-state machine representing a finite-memory system will be
called a *finite-memory machine*. A finite-memory machine M, then, is
any machine in which

$$z_\nu = f(x_\nu, x_{\nu-1}, \ldots, x_{\nu-\mu_1}, z_{\nu-1}, z_{\nu-2}, \ldots, z_{\nu-\mu_2}) \qquad (6.10)$$

where any of the arguments (except one of the x_i) may be a dummy argument. μ_1 and μ_2 are called the *x memory* and *z memory* of M, respectively.
The integer

$$\mu = \max (\mu_1, \mu_2) \qquad (6.11)$$

is called the *maximal memory* of M. If, in addition to (6.10), we have

$$f(x_\nu, x_{\nu-1}, \ldots, x_{\nu-\mu}, z_{\nu-1}, z_{\nu-2}, \ldots, z_{\nu-\mu})$$
$$\neq f(x_\nu, x_{\nu-1}, \ldots, x_{\nu-\mu+1}, z_{\nu-1}, z_{\nu-2}, \ldots, z_{\nu-\mu+1}) \qquad (6.12)$$

then M is said to have the *memory* μ. Thus, μ is the memory of the
machine, if the prediction of the response to at least one excitation at
time t_ν requires the knowledge of the excitation and/or the response at
time $t_{\nu-\mu}$ (and, possibly, excitations and responses which occur at later
times) but does not require the knowledge of any excitations and responses
at times earlier than $t_{\nu-\mu}$.

In what follows, $(\xi_{i_1}/\zeta_{j_1})(\xi_{i_2}/\zeta_{j_2}) \cdots (\xi_{i_l}/\zeta_{j_l})$ will be called an *input-output sequence*, if the input sequence $\xi_{i_1}\xi_{i_2} \cdots \xi_{i_l}$ causes the machine to generate the output sequence $\zeta_{j_1}\zeta_{j_2} \cdots \zeta_{j_l}$. A path in a transition diagram will be said to *describe* the input-output sequence $(\xi_{i_1}/\zeta_{j_1})(\xi_{i_2}/\zeta_{j_2})$ $\cdots (\xi_{i_l}/\zeta_{j_l})$, if its kth branch, for $k = 1, 2, \ldots, l$, is labeled with the input-output pair (ξ_{i_k}/ζ_{j_k}) (and, possibly other input-output pairs). Paths will be called $(\xi_{i_1}/\zeta_{j_1})\ (\xi_{i_2}/\zeta_{j_2}) \cdots (\xi_{i_l}/\zeta_{j_l})$-*coincident* if every one of them describes the input-output sequence $(\xi_{i_1}/\zeta_{j_1})(\xi_{i_2}/\zeta_{j_2}) \cdots (\xi_{i_l}/\zeta_{j_l})$.

LEMMA 6.1. In a minimal machine of memory μ,

$$s_\nu = g(x_{\nu-1}, x_{\nu-2}, \ldots, x_{\nu-\mu}, z_{\nu-1}, z_{\nu-2}, \ldots, z_{\nu-\mu}) \tag{6.13}$$

Proof. Assuming the converse, the machine must contain at least two paths which are $(\xi_{i_1}/\zeta_{j_1})(\xi_{i_2}/\zeta_{j_2}) \cdots (\xi_{i_\mu}/\zeta_{j_\mu})$-coincident, for some input-output sequence $(\xi_{i_1}/\zeta_{j_1})(\xi_{i_2}/\zeta_{j_2}) \cdots (\xi_{i_\mu}/\zeta_{j_\mu})$, and which terminate at two distinguishable states. Let the initial states in these paths be σ_{k_0} and σ'_{k_0} and the final states be σ_{k_μ} and σ'_{k_μ}; let the minimal diagnosing sequence for σ_{k_μ} and σ'_{k_μ} be $\xi_{i_{\mu+1}}\xi_{i_{\mu+2}} \cdots \xi_{i_{\mu+r}}$ $(r \geq 1)$. Then σ_{k_0} and σ'_{k_0} yield identical responses to $\xi_{i_1}\xi_{i_2} \cdots \xi_{i_\mu}\xi_{i_{\mu+1}} \cdots \xi_{i_{\mu+r-1}}$, but different responses to $\xi_{i_1}\xi_{i_2} \cdots \xi_{i_\mu}\xi_{i_{\mu+1}} \cdots \xi_{i_{\mu+r}}$. However, this is impossible, since, by assumption, the machine has the memory μ, and hence

$$z_\nu = f(x_\nu, x_{\nu-1}, \ldots, x_{\nu-\mu}, z_{\nu-1}, z_{\nu-2}, \ldots, z_{\nu-\mu}) \tag{6.14}$$

which implies that the present response can be uniquely determined by any past input-output sequence of length μ. The lemma, then, follows by contradiction.

In what follows, two or more paths will be said to *intersect* at state σ_k, if σ_k (the "intersection") is reachable from the initial states of these paths with the same input-output sequence. Lemma 6.1 implies that the transition diagram of a machine of memory μ must have the following properties: Paths which are $(\xi_{i_1}/\zeta_{j_1})(\xi_{i_2}/\zeta_{j_2}) \cdots (\xi_{i_\mu}/\zeta_{j_\mu})$-coincident must intersect at their final states. In addition, there must be at least one pair of $(\xi_{i_1}/\zeta_{j_2})(\xi_{i_2}/\zeta_{j_2}) \cdots (\xi_{i_\mu}/\zeta_{j_\mu})$-coincident paths which intersect at their final states, but have no other intersections. Such a pair of paths is shown in Fig. 6.3.

LEMMA 6.2. If in a given machine M,

$$s_\nu = g(x_{\nu-1}, x_{\nu-2}, \ldots, x_{\nu-\mu}, z_{\nu-1}, z_{\nu-2}, \ldots, z_{\nu-\mu}) \tag{6.15}$$

then M is a machine of maximal memory μ.

Proof. For any finite-state machine,

$$z_\nu = f_z(x_\nu, s_\nu) \tag{6.16}$$

For M, then,

$$z_\nu = f_z(x_\nu, g(x_{\nu-1}, x_{\nu-2}, \ldots, x_{\nu-\mu}, z_{\nu-1}, z_{\nu-2}, \ldots, z_{\nu-\mu}))$$
$$= f(x_\nu, x_{\nu-1}, \ldots, x_{\nu-\mu}, z_{\nu-1}, z_{\nu-2}, \ldots, z_{\nu-\mu}) \qquad (6.17)$$

Hence, by definition, M is a machine of maximal memory μ.

In connection with the preceding lemmas, it is important to notice the following basic difference between an arbitrary finite-state machine and a finite-memory machine: In every finite-state machine there is at least one *specially designed* input sequence (namely, a homing sequence) which, when applied to the machine, uniquely determines the final state. In a

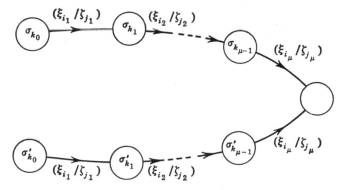

FIG. 6.3. $(\xi_{i_1}/\zeta_{j_1})(\xi_{i_2}/\zeta_{j_2}) \cdots (\xi_{i_\mu}/\zeta_{j_\mu})$-coincident paths.

finite-memory machine of memory μ, this is true for *every* input sequence of length μ or greater (whether a specially designed one or not).

THEOREM 6.1. Let M be a minimal n-state machine of memory μ. Then

$$\mu \leq \tfrac{1}{2}n(n-1) \qquad (6.18)$$

Proof. If M is minimal and of memory μ, it must exhibit a pair of paths which intersect at their final states, but not before, as shown in Fig. 6.3. Let $\{\sigma_{k_l}, \sigma'_{k_l}\}$ be the lth pair of states and $\{\sigma_{l+h}, \sigma'_{k_{l+h}}\}$ the $(l+h)$th pair of states $(l+h \leq \mu)$ in these paths. Suppose that σ_{k_l} and $\sigma_{k_{l+h}}$ are identical and that σ'_{k_l} and $\sigma'_{k_{l+h}}$ are identical. Then the paths which start at σ_{k_l} and σ'_{k_l}, each describing the input-output sequence $(\xi_{i_l}/\zeta_{j_l})(\xi_{i_{l+1}}/\zeta_{j_{l+1}}) \cdots (\xi_{i_{l+h-1}}/\zeta_{j_{l+h-1}})$, constitute two closed paths which are $(\xi_{i_l}/\zeta_{j_l})(\xi_{i_{l+1}}/\zeta_{j_{l+1}}) \cdots (\xi_{i_{l+h-1}}/\zeta_{j_{l+h-1}})$-coincident, and hence two paths of infinite length which describe the same input-output sequence, but which do not intersect (see Fig. 6.4). From Lemma 6.1, such paths cannot exist in a finite-memory machine. Now, suppose that σ_{k_l} and $\sigma'_{k_{l+h}}$ are identical and that σ'_{k_l} and $\sigma_{k_{l+h}}$ are identical. Then the paths which start at σ_{k_l} and σ'_{k_l}, each describing the input-output sequence $(\xi_{i_l}/\zeta_{j_l})(\xi_{i_{l+1}}/\zeta_{j_{l+1}}) \cdot \cdot \cdot (\xi_{i_{l+h-1}}/\zeta_{j_{l+h-1}})(\xi_{i_l}/\zeta_{j_l}) \cdot \cdot \cdot (\xi_{i_{l+h-1}}/\zeta_{j_{l+h-1}})$, constitute two closed paths which are $(\xi_{i_l}/\zeta_{j_l})(\xi_{i_{l+1}}/\zeta_{j_{l+1}}) \cdot \cdot \cdot (\xi_{i_{l+h-1}}/\zeta_{j_{l+h-1}})(\xi_{i_l}/\zeta_{j_l}) \cdot \cdot \cdot (\xi_{i_{l+h-1}}/\zeta_{j_{l+h-1}})$-coincident, and hence two paths of infinite length which describe the same input-output sequence, but which do not intersect (see Fig. 6.5). Again, by Lemma 6.1, such paths

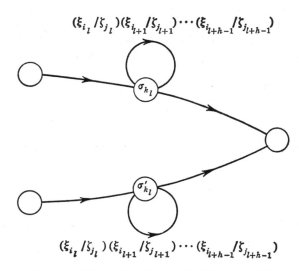

FIG. 6.4. Illustrating the proof of Theorem 6.1.

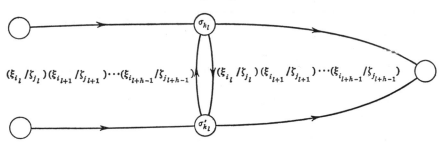

FIG. 6.5. Illustrating the proof of Theorem 6.1.

cannot exist. Thus, the unordered lth pair $\{\sigma_{k_l}, \sigma'_{k_l}\}$ and the unordered $(l + h)$th pair $\{\sigma_{k_{l+h}}, \sigma'_{k_{l+h}}\}$ cannot be identical unordered pairs. The length μ of any of the paths shown in Fig. 6.3 cannot, therefore, exceed the number of unordered pairs of states which can be selected in the n-state machine M. This number is given by

$$\binom{n}{2} = \tfrac{1}{2}n(n - 1) \qquad (6.19)$$

from which Eq. (6.18) follows.

6.4. Determination of Machine Memory

In this section we shall study the following problem: Given the characterizing functions f_z and f_s of a machine (in a tabular, diagrammatic, or matrix form), how can one determine whether the machine is a finite-memory machine, and if so, how can one determine its memory?

Consider a machine M, with the state set $\{\sigma_1, \sigma_2, \ldots, \sigma_n\}$. Let $Q_k^{(i)}$ denote the set of all input-output sequences described by paths of length k which terminate at state σ_i. By Lemma 6.1, if M is of memory μ, then

$$\bar{Q}_{\mu-1}^{(i)} \cap Q_{\mu-1}^{(j)} \neq 0 \text{ for some } i \text{ and } j \neq i \tag{6.20}$$

$$Q_{\mu}^{(i)} \cap Q_{\mu}^{(j)} = 0 \text{ for all } i \text{ and } j \neq i \tag{6.21}$$

By Theorem 6.1, if M is not a finite-memory machine, then

$$Q_{n(n-1)/2}^{(i)} \cap Q_{n(n-1)/2}^{(j)} \neq 0 \text{ for some } i \text{ and } j \neq i \tag{6.22}$$

Consequently, the following procedure can be formulated for determining the memory of a machine:

ALGORITHM 6.1. Given machine M with the state set $\{\sigma_1, \sigma_2, \ldots, \sigma_n\}$, to find the memory of M: (1) Let $k = 1$. (2) Compile the sets $Q_k^{(1)}$, $Q_k^{(2)}, \ldots, Q_k^{(n)}$. (3) (a) If $Q_k^{(i)} \cap Q_k^{(j)} \neq 0$ for some i and $j \neq i$, proceed to (4). (b) If $Q_k^{(i)} \cap Q_k^{(j)} = 0$ for all i and $j \neq i$, k is the memory of M. (4) (a) If $k < n(n-1)/2$, increment k by 1 and return to (2). (b) If $k = n(n-1)/2$, M is not a finite-memory machine.

The execution of Algorithm 6.1 is facilitated by using the higher-order transition matrices, introduced in Chap. 2. The (i, j) entry in the kth-order transition matrix $[\bar{M}]^k$ represents all paths of length k leading from state σ_i to state σ_j. The entries in the jth column of $[\bar{M}]^k$, therefore,

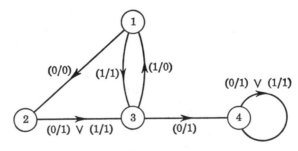

FIG. 6.6. Machine $A28$.

represent all paths of length k terminating at state σ_j. Consequently, the input-output sequences described by the paths listed in the jth column of $[\bar{M}]^k$ are the members of the set $Q_k^{(j)}$. From $[\bar{M}]^k$ and the transition diagram of M, a table can be constructed in which the jth column contains the members of $Q_k^{(j)}$; if no two columns have a common member, k must be the memory of M.

As an example, consider machine $A28$ of Fig. 6.6. The transition matrix of $A28$ is given by (6.23), and the first-order transition matrix of $A28$ is given by (6.24). From (6.24) and (6.23), one can construct Table 6.3, which lists $Q_1^{(1)}$, $Q_1^{(2)}$, $Q_1^{(3)}$, and $Q_1^{(4)}$. Since the input-output sequences (0/1) and (1/1) appear in two different columns of this table, the memory of $A28$ must exceed 1. Equation (6.25) shows the second-order transition matrix of $A28$. From (6.25) and (6.23), one can construct Table 6.4, which lists $Q_2^{(1)}$, $Q_2^{(2)}$, $Q_2^{(3)}$, and $Q_2^{(4)}$. Since no input-output sequence appears in two different columns of this table, $A28$ must have the memory 2. If $A28$ were not a finite-memory machine, this fact would have been revealed by the table listing $Q_6^{(1)}$, $Q_6^{(2)}$, $Q_6^{(3)}$, and $Q_6^{(4)}$.

$$[A28] = \begin{array}{c} \\ 1 \\ 2 \\ 3 \\ 4 \end{array} \begin{array}{cccc} 1 & 2 & 3 & 4 \\ \left[\begin{array}{cccc} 0 & (0/0) & (1/1) & 0 \\ 0 & 0 & (0/1) \vee (1/1) & 0 \\ (1/0) & 0 & 0 & (0/1) \\ 0 & 0 & 0 & (0/1) \vee (1/1) \end{array}\right] \end{array} \qquad (6.23)$$

$$[\overline{A28}] = \begin{array}{c} \\ 1 \\ 2 \\ 3 \\ 4 \end{array} \begin{array}{cccc} 1 & 2 & 3 & 4 \\ \left[\begin{array}{cccc} 0 & \pi_{12} & \pi_{13} & 0 \\ 0 & 0 & \pi_{23} & 0 \\ \pi_{31} & 0 & 0 & \pi_{34} \\ 0 & 0 & 0 & \pi_{44} \end{array}\right] \end{array} \qquad (6.24)$$

TABLE 6.3. THE $Q_1^{(j)}$ SETS FOR $A28$

$Q_1^{(1)}$	$Q_1^{(2)}$	$Q_1^{(3)}$	$Q_1^{(4)}$
(1/0)	(0/0)	(1/1) (0/1)	(0/1) (1/1)

$$[\overline{A28}]^2 = \begin{array}{c} \\ 1 \\ 2 \\ 3 \\ 4 \end{array} \begin{array}{cccc} 1 & 2 & 3 & 4 \\ \left[\begin{array}{cccc} \pi_{13}\pi_{31} & 0 & \pi_{12}\pi_{23} & \pi_{13}\pi_{34} \\ \pi_{23}\pi_{31} & 0 & 0 & \pi_{23}\pi_{34} \\ 0 & \pi_{31}\pi_{12} & \pi_{31}\pi_{13} & \pi_{34}\pi_{44} \\ 0 & 0 & 0 & \pi_{44}\pi_{44} \end{array}\right] \end{array} \qquad (6.25)$$

TABLE 6.4. THE $Q_2^{(j)}$ SETS FOR $A28$

$Q_2^{(1)}$	$Q_2^{(2)}$	$Q_2^{(3)}$	$Q_2^{(4)}$
(1/1)(1/0)	(1/0)(0/0)	(0/0)(0/1)	(1/1)(0/1)
(0/1)(1/0)		(0/0)(1/1)	(0/1)(0/1)
		(1/0)(1/1)	(0/1)(1/1)
			(1/1)(1/1)

6.5. The Minimal x-z Function

Once the memory μ of a finite-state machine M is determined, the machine can be characterized by an equation of the form

$$z_\nu = f(x_\nu, x_{\nu-1}, \ldots, x_{\nu-\mu}, z_{\nu-1}, z_{\nu-2}, \ldots, z_{\nu-\mu}) \tag{6.26}$$

f, as defined by (6.26), will be called the x-z *function* of M. The x-z function often contains a number of dummy arguments and can be reduced to the form

$$z_\nu = \check{f}(x_{\nu-i_1}, x_{\nu-i_2}, \ldots, x_{\nu-i_u}, z_{\nu-j_1}, z_{\nu-j_2}, \ldots, z_{\nu-j_v}) \tag{6.27}$$

where $0 \le i_1 < i_2 < \cdots < i_u$, $1 \le j_1 < j_2 < \cdots < j_v$, and where $i_u = \mu$ and/or $j_v = \mu$. $\check{f}$ is called a *minimal x-z function* of M, if $u + v$ is the smallest number of x_i and z_i arguments required to express z as a function of excitations and responses, in the form indicated by (6.27). Thus, the minimal x-z function is obtained from the x-z function by deleting from the latter as many x_i and z_i arguments as possible. Obtaining the minimal x-z function, or *minimizing* the x-z function, is of interest in a number of analysis and synthesis problems, where the most compact terminal characterization, in the form (6.27), is desired for given finite-state machines.

The problem of minimizing the x-z function can be expressed more precisely through the x-z *table*, whose general format is shown in Table 6.5. The table is divided into q groups of rows, one group for every output symbol in the output alphabet $\{\zeta_1, \zeta_2, \ldots, \zeta_q\}$ of the n-state machine M. The group of rows corresponding to the z_ν entry ζ_k will be called the ζ_k *group*. The columns $x_{\nu-\mu}, z_{\nu-\mu}, x_{\nu-\mu+1}, z_{\nu-\mu+1}, \ldots, x_{\nu-1}, z_{\nu-1}, x_\nu$ are completed as follows: Let (ξ_l/ζ_k) be an input-output pair associated with a branch originating at state σ_i, and let $(\xi_{l_1}/\zeta_{k_1})(\xi_{l_2}/\zeta_{k_2}) \cdots (\xi_{l_\mu}/\zeta_{k_\mu})$ be an input-output sequence in the set $Q_\mu^{(i)}$ (such sequences can be read off the table listing $Q_\mu^{(1)}, Q_\mu^{(2)}, \ldots, Q_\mu^{(n)}$, constructed for the determination of μ through Algorithm 6.1). Then $\xi_{l_1}, \zeta_{k_1}, \xi_{l_2}, \zeta_{k_2}, \ldots, \xi_{l_\mu}, \zeta_{k_\mu}, \xi_l$ (written in this order) is a row in the ζ_k group. The entire table can be completed by following these rules with respect to all n states. If the number of input-output sequences in $Q_\mu^{(i)}$ is r_i, and if the size of the input alphabet is p, the number of rows in the x-z table is $p \sum\limits_{i=1}^{n} r_i$. The x-z table, then, is the tabular display of the x-z function, where z_ν is listed for every ordered $(2\mu + 1)$-tuple $(x_{\nu-\mu}, z_{\nu-\mu}, x_{\nu-\mu+1}, z_{\nu-\mu+1}, \ldots, x_{\nu-1}, z_{\nu-1}, x_\nu)$ which can occur in the given machine.   As an example, Table 6.6 shows the x-z table for machine $A28$ of Fig. 6.6.   From matrix (6.23) it is seen that the input-output pair $(0/0)$ is associated with a branch originating at state 1.   From Table 6.4, the set $Q_2^{(1)}$ is seen to consist of the input-output sequences $(1/1)(1/0)$ and $(0/1)(1/0)$.   Consequently, the 0 group in the x-z table must contain the rows 1, 1, 1, 0, 0 and 0, 1, 1, 0, 0.   The remaining rows in Table 6.6 are completed in an analogous fashion. Serial numbers are attached to the rows and columns of this table, to facilitate subsequent discussion.

TABLE 6.5. A GENERAL x-z TABLE

z_ν	$x_{\nu-\mu}$	$z_{\nu-\mu}$	$x_{\nu-\mu+1}$	$z_{\nu-\mu+1}$	$\cdots$	$x_{\nu-1}$	$z_{\nu-1}$	x_ν
ζ_1								
ζ_2								
$\cdot$ $\cdot$ $\cdot$								
ζ_q								

In terms of the x-z table, the problem of minimizing the x-z function can be formulated as follows: Delete the maximum number of columns from the table, such that no row in any group would become identical to any row in any other group.   Let the columns which remain after this deletion be $x_{\nu-i_1}, x_{\nu-i_2}, \ldots, x_{\nu-i_u}, z_{\nu-j_1}, z_{\nu-j_2}, \ldots, z_{\nu-j_v}$.   Since $u + v$ is necessarily the minimum number of arguments, and since no ordered $(u + v)$-tuple appears in two different ζ_k groups of the x-z table, we have

$$z_\nu = \check{f}(x_{\nu-i_1}, x_{\nu-i_2}, \ldots, x_{\nu-i_u}, z_{\nu-j_1}, z_{\nu-j_2}, \ldots, z_{\nu-j_v}) \qquad (6.28)$$

where $\check{f}$ is the minimal x-z function.

TABLE 6.6. x-z TABLE FOR $A28$

		1	2	3	4	5
	z_ν	$x_{\nu-2}$	$z_{\nu-2}$	$x_{\nu-1}$	$z_{\nu-1}$	x_ν
1		1	1	1	0	0
2		0	1	1	0	0
3	0	0	0	0	1	1
4		0	0	1	1	1
5		1	0	1	1	1
6		1	1	1	0	1
7		0	1	1	0	1
8		1	0	0	0	0
9		1	0	0	0	1
10		0	0	0	1	0
11		0	0	1	1	0
12		1	0	1	1	0
13	1	1	1	0	1	0
14		0	1	0	1	0
15		0	1	1	1	0
16		1	1	1	1	0
17		1	1	0	1	1
18		0	1	0	1	1
19		0	1	1	1	1
20		1	1	1	1	1

To find the minimal x-z function, then, the following procedure can be used:

ALGORITHM 6.2. Given the x-z table for machine M, to determine the minimal x-z function of M: (1) Let $h = 1$. (2) For every combination of h columns, check whether the deletion of the remaining columns does or does not render rows in different ζ_k groups identical. (3) (a) If every combination renders rows in different ζ_k groups identical, increment h by 1 and return to (2). (b) If there is a combination which does not render rows in different ζ_k groups identical, let this combination correspond to the columns $x_{\nu-i_1}, x_{\nu-i_2}, \ldots, x_{\nu-i_u}, z_{\nu-j_1}, z_{\nu-j_2}, \ldots, z_{\nu-j_v}$. The minimal x-z function is given by (6.28).

The execution of Algorithm 6.2 becomes considerably simpler, when the following facts are exploited: (1) Every combination of h columns to be considered must include either column $x_{\nu-\mu}$ or column $z_{\nu-\mu}$. (2) If two rows appearing in two different ζ_k groups differ in a single column, this column must be included in every combination of h columns to be considered. (3) A column which contains the same symbol in every row need not be included in any considered combination of h columns.

(4) Two identical columns need not be included in any combination of h columns to be considered.

In Table 6.6, for example, it can be noticed that rows 3 and 18 differ in column 2 only; rows 1 and 16 differ in column 4 only; rows 1 and 6 differ in column 5 only. Consequently, columns 2, 4, and 5 must appear in any combination of h columns to be considered in the execution of Algorithm 6.2. Checking the rows at these three columns, it is seen that no row in the 0 group is identical to any row in the 1 group. We can thus conclude that, for machine $A28$,

$$z_\nu = \check{f}(x_\nu, z_{\nu-1}, z_{\nu-2}) \tag{6.29}$$

where the number of arguments is the smallest possible.

The minimal x-z function can be displayed in a tabular form by deleting from the x-z table all the columns found deletable through Algorithm 6.2 and merging all identical rows. The resulting table is called the *minimal x-z table*. The minimal x-z table for machine $A28$ is shown in Table 6.7.

TABLE 6.7. MINIMAL x-z TABLE FOR $A28$

z_ν	$z_{\nu-2}$	$z_{\nu-1}$	x_ν
0	1	0	0
	0	1	1
1	1	0	1
	0	0	0
	0	0	1
	0	1	0
	1	1	0
	1	1	1

6.6. Linear Binary Machines[1]

In this and the following two sections we shall study a special class of finite-memory machines, called *linear binary machines*, which, because of their interesting and useful properties, warrant special attention. In linear binary machines the input and output alphabets are {0, 1}, and the output at any sampling time equals the sum modulo 2 of selected past (and possibly present) input symbols and past output symbols.

---

[1] The material on linear binary machines is based in part on the work of D. A. Huffman (The Synthesis of Sequential Coding Networks, "Information Theory," pp. 77–95, Academic Press, Inc., New York, 1956; An Algebra for Periodically Time-varying Linear Binary Sequence Transducers, Annals of the Computation Laboratory, vol. 29, pp. 189–203, Harvard University Press, Cambridge, Mass., 1959).

Designating modulo-2 addition by $\oplus$, a linear binary machine is characterizable by the relationship

$$
\begin{aligned}
z_\nu &= f(x_{\nu-i_1}, x_{\nu-i_2}, \ldots, x_{\nu-i_u}, z_{\nu-j_1}, z_{\nu-j_2}, \ldots, z_{\nu-j_v}) \\
&= x_{\nu-i_1} \oplus x_{\nu-i_2} \oplus \cdots \oplus x_{\nu-i_u} \oplus z_{\nu-j_1} \oplus z_{\nu-j_2} \oplus \cdots \oplus z_{\nu-j_v} \quad (6.30)
\end{aligned}
$$

where $0 \le i_1 < i_2 < \cdots < i_u$ and $1 \le j_1 < j_2 < \cdots < j_v$. The *ground state* of a linear binary machine will be defined as the state of the machine when

$$
x_{\nu-i_1} = x_{\nu-i_2} = \cdots = x_{\nu-i_u} = z_{\nu-j_1} = z_{\nu-j_2} = \cdots = z_{\nu-j_v} = 0
$$

A machine will be said to be *quiescent* when it is in the ground state.

THEOREM 6.2.   Let M be a linear binary machine, quiescent at time t_0, and let $x_0 x_1 \cdots x_k$ be any input-output sequence applied to M at time t_0.   Then the response of M at time t_k ($k \ge 0$) is given by

$$
z_k = c_{k0} x_0 \oplus c_{k1} x_1 \oplus \cdots \oplus c_{kk} x_k \quad (6.31)
$$

where the c_{ki} coefficients are either 0 or 1.

Proof.   Let M be of memory μ. M, then, can be characterized by the equation

$$
\begin{aligned}
z_\nu = \delta_0 x_\nu \oplus \delta_1 x_{\nu-1} \oplus \cdots \oplus \delta_\mu x_{\nu-\mu} \\
\oplus \epsilon_1 z_{\nu-1} \oplus \epsilon_2 z_{\nu-2} \oplus \cdots \oplus \epsilon_\mu z_{\nu-\mu} \quad (6.32)
\end{aligned}
$$

where the δ_i and the ϵ_i coefficients are either 0 or 1.   If M is quiescent at t_0,

$$
x_{-1} = x_{-2} = \cdots = x_{-\mu} = z_{-1} = z_{-2} = \cdots = z_{-\mu} = 0 \quad (6.33)
$$

Hence,

$$
z_0 = \delta_0 x_0 \quad (6.34)
$$

which proves the theorem for $k = 0$.   Suppose the theorem is true for $k = 0, 1, \ldots, l$.   Then

$$
\begin{aligned}
z_{l+1} &= \delta_0 x_{l+1} \oplus \delta_1 x_l \oplus \cdots \oplus \delta_\mu x_{l-\mu+1} \\
&\quad \oplus \epsilon_1 z_l \oplus \epsilon_2 z_{l-1} \oplus \cdots \oplus \epsilon_\mu z_{l-\mu+1} \\
&= \delta_0 x_{l+1} \oplus \delta_1 x_l \oplus \cdots \oplus \delta_\mu x_{l-\mu+1} \\
&\quad \oplus \epsilon_1 (c_{l0} x_0 \oplus c_{l1} x_1 \oplus \cdots \oplus c_{ll} x_l) \\
&\quad \oplus \epsilon_2 (c_{l-1,0} x_0 \oplus c_{l-1,1} x_1 \oplus \cdots \oplus c_{l-1,l-1} x_{l-1}) \\
&\quad \oplus \cdots \\
&\quad \oplus \epsilon_\mu (c_{l-\mu+1,0} x_0 \oplus c_{l-\mu+1,1} x_1 \oplus \cdots \oplus c_{l-\mu+1,l-\mu+1} x_{l-\mu+1}) \quad (6.35)
\end{aligned}
$$

Since, by (6.33), all x_i variables with negative subscripts are 0, (6.35) can be written as

$$
z_{l+1} = a_0 x_0 \oplus a_1 x_1 \oplus \cdots \oplus a_l x_l \oplus a_{l+1} x_{l+1} \quad (6.36)
$$

where the a_i coefficients are either 0 or 1. Hence, if the theorem is true for $k = 0, 1, \ldots, l$, it must be true for $k = l + 1$. By induction, the theorem is true for all $k \geq 0$.

Theorem 6.2 states, in effect, that the response of a quiescent linear binary machine can be expressed as a linear combination of present and past excitations. Let $\xi'_{i_0}\xi'_{i_1} \cdots \xi'_{i_k}$ be an input sequence applied to the quiescent binary machine M, and let ζ'_{j_k} be the response of M to ξ'_{i_k}. Then

$$\zeta'_{j_k} = c_{k0}\xi'_{i_0} \oplus c_{\kappa 1}\xi'_{i_1} \oplus \cdots \oplus c_{kk}\xi'_{i_k} \tag{6.37}$$

Similarly, let $\xi''_{i_0}\xi''_{i_1} \cdots \xi''_{i_k}$ be an input sequence applied to the quiescent M and ζ''_{j_k} be the response to ξ''_{i_k}. Then,

$$\zeta''_{j_k} = c_{k0}\xi''_{i_0} \oplus c_{k1}\xi''_{i_1} \oplus \cdots \oplus c_{kk}\xi''_{i_k} \tag{6.38}$$

Consider now the input sequence $(\xi'_{i_0} \oplus \xi''_{i_0})(\xi'_{i_1} \oplus \xi''_{i_1}) \cdots (\xi'_{i_k} \oplus \xi)''_{i_k}$ constructed by adding (modulo 2) corresponding symbols of the previous two sequences. Let ζ_{j_k} denote the response to $(\xi'_{i_k} \oplus \xi''_{i_k})$. Then,

$$
\begin{aligned}
\zeta_{j_k} &= c_{k0}(\xi'_{i_0} \oplus \xi''_{i_0}) \oplus c_{k1}(\xi'_{i_1} \oplus \xi''_{i_1}) \oplus \cdots \oplus c_{kk}(\xi'_{i_k} \oplus \xi''_{i_k}) \\
&= (c_{k0}\xi'_{i_0} \oplus c_{k1}\xi'_{i_1} \oplus \cdots \oplus c_{kk}\xi'_{i_k}) \\
&\qquad\qquad \oplus (c_{k0}\xi''_{i_0} \oplus c_{k1}\xi''_{i_1} \oplus \cdots \oplus c_{kk}\xi''_{i_k}) \\
&= \zeta'_{j_k} \oplus \zeta''_{j_k} \tag{6.39}
\end{aligned}
$$

A quiescent linear binary machine, therefore, obeys the principle of superposition: The response to a sum (modulo 2) of excitations is given by the sum (modulo 2) of the responses to the individual excitations.

We shall now introduce a *delay operator* D, defined by

$$D^r y = y_{\nu - r} \qquad r = 0, 1, 2, \ldots \tag{6.40}$$

where y may refer to either x or z. D^0 will be written as I. In terms of this delay operator, (6.30) can be expressed as

$$Iz = D^{i_1}x \oplus D^{i_2}x \oplus \cdots \oplus D^{i_u}x \oplus D^{j_1}z \oplus D^{j_2}z \oplus \cdots \oplus D^{j_v}z \tag{6.41}$$

Adding $D^{j_1}z \oplus D^{j_2}z \oplus \cdots \oplus D^{j_v}z$ to both sides of (6.41) (modulo 2), yields

$$Iz \oplus D^{j_1}z \oplus D^{j_2}z \oplus \cdots \oplus D^{j_v}z = D^{i_1}x \oplus D^{i_2}x \oplus \cdots \oplus D^{i_u}x \tag{6.42}$$

or

$$(D^{j_v} \oplus \cdots \oplus D^{j_2} \oplus D^{j_1} \oplus I)z = (D^{i_u} \oplus \cdots \oplus D^{i_2} \oplus D^{i_1})x \tag{6.43}$$

The input-output characteristics of a linear binary machine M can be expressed in terms of a *transfer ratio*, denoted by $T(M)$:

$$T(M) = \frac{D^{i_u} \oplus \cdots \oplus D^{i_2} \oplus D^{i_1}}{D^{j_v} \oplus \cdots \oplus D^{j_2} \oplus D^{j_1} \oplus I} \tag{6.44}$$

Given the transfer ratio of a machine, the function f, as defined by (6.30), can always be determined by reversing the process described by Eqs. (6.41) to (6.44).

From the definition of D, Eq. (6.41) implies that

$$D^r z = D^r(D^{i_1}x \oplus D^{i_2}x \oplus \cdots \oplus D^{i_u}x$$
$$\oplus D^{j_1}z \oplus D^{j_2}z \oplus \cdots \oplus D^{j_v}z) \quad (6.45)$$

From (6.45) and the superposition property it follows that if the machine characterized by (6.41) is quiescent, both sides of (6.41) can be multiplied by an arbitrary polynomial in D, with no risk of destroying the equality:

$$(D^k \oplus D^{k-1} \oplus \cdots \oplus I)z = (D^k \oplus D^{k-1} \oplus \cdots \oplus I)$$
$$(D^{i_1}x \oplus D^{i_2}x \oplus \cdots \oplus D^{i_u}x \oplus D^{j_1}z \oplus D^{j_2}z \oplus \cdots \oplus D^{j_v}z) \quad (6.46)$$

Consequently, if a given linear binary machine M is quiescent, the numerator and denominator of its transfer ratio may be multiplied by an arbitrary polynomial in D. Moreover, if M is quiescent, and if the numerator and denominator polynomials in its transfer ratio contain a common factor, this common factor can be canceled from the ratio, without destroying the usefulness of the transfer ratio for predicting the behavior of M. The cancellation of a common factor, which can be carried out via the Euclidean algorithm, reduces the orders of the numerator and denominator polynomials in the transfer ratio, thereby simplifying both the analysis and synthesis of the machine at hand.

As an example, consider the linear binary machine $A29$, specified by

$$z_\nu = x_{\nu-1} \oplus x_{\nu-3} \oplus x_{\nu-5} \oplus x_{\nu-6} \oplus x_{\nu-7} \oplus x_{\nu-8} + z_{\nu-1} \oplus z_{\nu-6} \oplus z_{\nu-7} \quad (6.47)$$

or $\quad z_{\nu-7} \oplus z_{\nu-6} \oplus z_{\nu-1} \oplus z_\nu$
$$= x_{\nu-8} \oplus x_{\nu-7} \oplus x_{\nu-6} \oplus x_{\nu-5} \oplus x_{\nu-3} \oplus x_{\nu-1} \quad (6.48)$$

The transfer ratio for $A29$ is, therefore,

$$T(A29) = \frac{D^8 \oplus D^7 \oplus D^6 \oplus D^5 \oplus D^3 \oplus D}{D^7 \oplus D^6 \oplus D \oplus I} \quad (6.49)$$

To determine the highest common factor of the numerator and denominator polynomials, we apply the Euclidean algorithm, replacing subtraction by modulo-2 addition (and noting that $D^r \oplus D^r = 0$):

$$
\begin{array}{r}
D \\
D^7 \oplus D^6 \oplus D \oplus I \,\overline{)\, D^8 \oplus D^7 \oplus D^6 \oplus D^5 \oplus D^3 \oplus D} \\
\underline{D^8 \oplus D^7 \oplus D^2 \oplus D} \\
D^6 \oplus D^5 \oplus D^3 \oplus D^2
\end{array}
\quad (6.50)
$$

$$
\begin{array}{r}
D \\
D^6 \oplus D^5 \oplus D^3 \oplus D^2 \,\overline{)\, D^7 \oplus D^6 \oplus D \oplus I} \\
\underline{D^7 \oplus D^6 \oplus D^4 \oplus D^3} \\
\mathrm{HCF} \to D^4 \oplus D^3 \oplus D \oplus I \,\overline{)\, D^6 \oplus D^5 \oplus D^3 \oplus D^2} \\
\underline{D^6 \oplus D^5 \oplus D^3 \oplus D^2} \\
0
\end{array}
$$

The last divisor (indicated by an arrow) is the highest common factor. To reduce the transfer ratio, both the numerator and denominator are now divided by this factor:

$$D^4 \oplus D^3 \oplus D \oplus I \,\overline{\big)\, \begin{array}{l} \, D^4 \oplus D^2 \oplus D \\ \hline D^8 \oplus D^7 \oplus D^6 \oplus D^5 \oplus D^3 \oplus D \\ D^8 \oplus D^7 \oplus D^5 \oplus D^4 \\ \hline D^6 \oplus D^4 \oplus D^3 \oplus D \\ D^6 \oplus D^5 \oplus D^3 \oplus D^2 \\ \hline D^5 \oplus D^4 \oplus D^2 \oplus D \\ D^5 \oplus D^4 \oplus D^2 \oplus D \\ \hline 0 \end{array}} \qquad (6.51)$$

$$D^4 \oplus D^3 \oplus D \oplus I \,\overline{\big)\, \begin{array}{l} \, D^3 \oplus I \\ \hline D^7 \oplus D^6 \oplus D \oplus I \\ D^7 \oplus D^6 \oplus D^4 \oplus D^3 \\ \hline D^4 \oplus D^3 \oplus D \oplus I \\ D^4 \oplus D^3 \oplus D \oplus I \\ \hline 0 \end{array}} \qquad (6.52)$$

From (6.51) and (6.52),

$$T(A29) = \frac{(D^4 \oplus D^2 \oplus D)(D^4 \oplus D^3 \oplus D \oplus I)}{(D^3 \oplus I)(D^4 \oplus D^3 \oplus D \oplus I)}$$

$$= \frac{D^4 \oplus D^2 \oplus D}{D^3 \oplus I} \qquad (6.53)$$

The quiescent $A29$, therefore, can be characterized by

$$z_{\nu-3} \oplus z_\nu = x_{\nu-4} \oplus x_{\nu-2} \oplus x_{\nu-1} \qquad (6.54)$$

or

$$z_\nu = x_{\nu-1} \oplus x_{\nu-2} \oplus x_{\nu-4} \oplus z_{\nu-3} \qquad (6.55)$$

For example, when $A29$ is quiescent, its response to the input sequence 100111001010 is, by (6.55), 011011010001. It can be readily verified that this response is the same as that obtained via the original (long-version) relationship (6.47).

In general, not all the states of a linear binary machine are reachable from its ground state. When the machine is known to be in the ground state, all the states which are not reachable from this state can be ignored, thus simplifying the representation of the given machine and hence its analysis. The cancellation of a common factor in the transfer ratio of a machine effects precisely this simplification. The machine represented by the reduced ratio contains all those states reachable from the ground state of the original machine. Inasmuch as most linear binary machines encountered in practice are operated with the ground state as an initial state, such a reduction is in most cases justified and desirable.

6.7. Time Response of Linear Binary Machines

The *free response* of a linear binary machine M will be defined as the response of M to the infinite input sequence $000 \cdot \cdot \cdot$. The response of a machine will be said to be *periodic* if the output symbol at time t_ν is the same as the output symbol at time $t_{\nu+\rho}$ for all ν; ρ, a nonzero and finite integer, is called the *period* of the free response. If the response is constant, its period is taken as 1.

THEOREM 6.3. Let M be a linear binary machine of memory μ and z memory μ'. Then the free response of M becomes periodic after at most $2^{\mu'} + \mu - 1$, with the period

$$\rho \leq 2^{\mu'} - 1 \tag{6.56}$$

Proof. M can be characterized by

$$z_\nu = \delta_0 x_\nu \oplus \delta_1 x_{\nu-1} \oplus \cdot \cdot \cdot \oplus \delta_{\mu''} x_{\nu-\mu''}$$
$$\oplus \epsilon_1 z_{\nu-1} \oplus \epsilon_2 z_{\nu-2} \oplus \cdot \cdot \cdot \oplus \epsilon_{\mu'} z_{\nu-\mu'} \tag{6.57}$$

where the δ_i and the ϵ_i coefficients are either 0 or 1. Suppose that the observation of the free response starts at time $t_{1-\mu}$, where $\mu = \max{(\mu', \mu'')}$. Hence, for all $\nu \geq 1$,

$$z_\nu = \epsilon_1 z_{\nu-1} \oplus \epsilon_2 z_{\nu-2} \oplus \cdot \cdot \cdot \oplus \epsilon_{\mu'} z_{\nu-\mu'} \tag{6.58}$$

After at most μ symbols, then, every output symbol is uniquely determined by the previous μ' output symbols. Consequently, the response becomes periodic with the period ρ, if for any $\nu \geq 1$ the ordered μ'-tuple $(z_{\nu-1}, z_{\nu-2}, \ldots, z_{\nu-\mu'})$ becomes identical to the ordered μ'-tuple $(z_{\nu-1+\rho}, z_{\nu-2+\rho}, \ldots, z_{\nu-\mu'+\rho})$. Since only $2^{\mu'}$ such μ'-tuples exist, the last segment of length μ' in the output sequence $z_1 z_2 \cdot \cdot \cdot z_{2^{\mu'}+\mu'}$, namely, $z_{2^{\mu'}+1} z_{2^{\mu'}+2} \cdot \cdot \cdot z_{2^{\mu'}+\mu'}$, must be the same as some previous segment of length μ'. Hence, the period cannot exceed $2^{\mu'}$. Now, suppose the period is exactly $2^{\mu'}$; then the sequence must contain a segment which consists of μ' zeros. However, from (6.58) it can be deduced that such a segment must be followed by an infinite sequence of zeros, which implies that the period is 1 rather than $2^{\mu'}$. By contradiction, then, the period cannot exceed $2^{\mu'} - 1$. The periodicity starts at some time t_ν, where $1 \leq \nu \leq 2^{\mu'}$, and hence after at most $\mu + 2^{\mu'} - 1$ symbols.

The infinite portion of the response which exhibits a periodic behavior is called the *periodic portion* of the response; the finite portion which precedes the periodic portion is called the *transient portion* of the response. If the observation of the free response starts at time t_ν, and if the machine memory is μ, both periodic and transient portions of the response depend on the values of $x_{\nu-1}, x_{\nu-2}, \ldots, x_{\nu-\mu}$ and $z_{\nu-1}, z_{\nu-2}, \ldots, z_{\nu-\mu}$, which constitute the *initial conditions* of the machine. Let ρ be the period of the free response, and let $\zeta_{i_1}\zeta_{i_2} \cdot \cdot \cdot \zeta_{i_\rho}$ be any sequence of ρ symbols contained in the periodic portion of the response. Then, from the proof to Theorem 6.3, it follows that the ρ subsequences of length μ' (where μ' is the z memory) which start with the symbols $\zeta_{i_1}, \zeta_{i_2}, \ldots, \zeta_{i_\rho}$ must be distinct. If ρ has the maximal value $2^{\mu'} - 1$, these sequences constitute all μ'-digit binary numbers, with the exception of the μ'-digit number $00 \cdot \cdot \cdot 0$.

As an example, consider the linear binary machine $A30$, of memory 5 and z memory 3, specified by

$$z_\nu = x_{\nu-5} \oplus z_{\nu-1} \oplus z_{\nu-3} \tag{6.59}$$

Equation (6.60) shows the free response of this machine, starting at time t_ν, when the initial conditions are $x_{\nu-5} = x_{\nu-4} = x_{\nu-3} = x_{\nu-1} = z_{\nu-1} = 1$ and $x_{\nu-2} = z_{\nu-3} = z_{\nu-2} = 0$. $\mathcal{E}$ and $\mathcal{R}$ denote the input and output sequences, respectively. The length of the transient portion in this case is seen to be 2. The period is 7, which is the maximal value for the specified z memory ($2^3 - 1 = 7$). Starting at the third output symbol, the seven consecutive subsequences of length 3 are 111, 110, 101, 010, 100, 001, and 011, which constitute all 3-digit binary numbers, except 000.

$$\begin{array}{llccc} \mathcal{E}: & 11101 & 00 & 0000000 & 0000000 \cdot \cdot \cdot \\ \mathcal{R}: & 001 & 01 & 1110100 & 1110100 \cdot \cdot \cdot \\ & \underbrace{} & \underbrace{} & \underbrace{} & \underbrace{} \\ & \text{Ini-} & \text{Tran-} & \text{Period 1} & \text{Period 2} \\ & \text{tial} & \text{sient} \\ & \text{condi-} \\ & \text{tions} \end{array} \tag{6.60}$$

One convenient way of characterizing the behavior of a linear binary machine, operated from its ground state, is through its *impulse response*. The impulse response of machine M is defined as the response of the quiescent M to the infinite input sequence $1000 \cdot \cdot \cdot$. Such a sequence is referred to as an *impulse*. Clearly, the impulse response of a machine, starting at time t_ν, is the same as its free response, starting at time $t_{\nu+1}$, and subject to the initial conditions $x_\nu = 1$, $z_\nu = 0$ or 1, and all preceding input and output symbols equal 0. From Theorem 6.3, then, the impulse response becomes periodic after at most $2^{\mu'} + \mu$ symbols, where μ is the memory and μ' the z memory of M. The period of the impulse response cannot exceed $2^{\mu'} - 1$. As an example, the impulse response of machine $A30$, specified by (6.59), is shown in (6.61).

$$\begin{array}{lccc} \mathcal{E}: & 100 & 0000000 & 0000000 \cdot \cdot \cdot \\ \mathcal{R}: & 000 & 0011101 & 0011101 \cdot \cdot \cdot \\ & \underbrace{} & \underbrace{} & \underbrace{} \\ & \text{Tran-} & \text{Period 1} & \text{Period 2} \\ & \text{sient} \end{array} \tag{6.61}$$

An input sequence which is 0 at all times except at time t_ν will be denoted by $\mathfrak{D}_\nu$. The response of a machine to $\mathfrak{D}_\nu$ will be denoted by $\mathfrak{R}_\nu$. $\mathfrak{R}_\nu$, then, is the impulse response of the machine, where the impulse is applied at time t_ν. A sequence $\mathcal{E}$ will be said to be the *sum* of the sequences $\mathcal{E}_1, \mathcal{E}_2, \ldots, \mathcal{E}_r$, written as $\mathcal{E}_1 \oplus \mathcal{E}_2 \oplus \cdots \oplus \mathcal{E}_r$, if the symbol of $\mathcal{E}$ at time t_ν is equal to the sum modulo 2 of the symbols of $\mathcal{E}_1, \mathcal{E}_2, \ldots,$ $\mathcal{E}_r$ at the same time t_ν. Thus, if $\mathcal{E}$ is 0 at all times except $t_{i_1}, t_{i_2}, \ldots, t_{i_l}$, it can be written as

$$\mathcal{E} = \mathfrak{D}_{i_1} \oplus \mathfrak{D}_{i_2} \oplus \cdots \oplus \mathfrak{D}_{i_l} \tag{6.62}$$

By virtue of the superposition property, if $\mathcal{E}$ is applied to a quiescent linear binary machine M, the response of M, denoted by $\mathfrak{R}$, is given by

$$\mathfrak{R} = \mathfrak{R}_{i_1} \oplus \mathfrak{R}_{i_2} \oplus \cdots \oplus \mathfrak{R}_{i_l} \tag{6.63}$$

The response, then, can be obtained by adding (modulo 2) the impulse responses of M, starting at $t_{i_1}, t_{i_2}, \ldots, t_{i_l}$. Clearly, if the excitation becomes periodic after a finite number of symbols, so does the response. As an example, (6.64) shows the response of machine $A30$ to a sequence which becomes periodic (with the period 1) after four symbols.

$$
\begin{array}{llll}
\mathcal{E}: & 101100 & 0000000 & 0000000 \cdots \\
\mathfrak{R}_1: & 000001 & 1101001 & 1101001 \cdots \\
\mathfrak{R}_3: & 000000 & 0111010 & 0111010 \cdots \\
\mathfrak{R}_4: & 000000 & 0011101 & 0011101 \cdots \\
\mathfrak{R}: & 000001 & 1001110 & 1001110 \cdots
\end{array} \tag{6.64}
$$

$$\underbrace{\qquad}_{\text{Transient}} \quad \underbrace{\qquad}_{\text{Period 1}} \quad \underbrace{\qquad}_{\text{Period 2}}$$

Every sequence $\mathfrak{R}$ of 1's and 0's, which becomes periodic with period ρ after τ symbols, can be written in the form

$$\mathfrak{R} = \mathfrak{R}_T \oplus \mathfrak{R}_P \tag{6.65}$$

where $\mathfrak{R}_T$ is an infinite sequence which becomes $000 \cdots$ after at most τ symbols, and where $\mathfrak{R}_P$ is an infinite periodic sequence of period ρ and with no transient portion. $\mathfrak{R}_T$ and $\mathfrak{R}_P$ are called the *transient component* and *periodic component* of $\mathfrak{R}$, respectively. $\mathfrak{R}_P$ is constructed as follows: If $\tau = \eta + k\rho$, where $0 \leq \eta \leq \rho$ and k is a nonnegative integer, delete the transient portion and the first $\rho-\eta$ symbols of the periodic portion from $\mathfrak{R}$; the resulting infinite sequence is $\mathfrak{R}_P$. $\mathfrak{R}_T$ is then given by

$$\mathfrak{R}_T = \mathfrak{R} \oplus \mathfrak{R}_P \tag{6.66}$$

As an example, for $\mathcal{R}$ as given in Eq. (6.64),

$$\mathcal{R}_P: \quad \underbrace{0011101}_{\text{Period 1}} \quad \underbrace{0011101}_{\text{Period 2}} \cdots$$

$$\mathcal{R}_T: \quad \underbrace{001111}_{\text{Transient}} \quad 00000000 \cdots$$

(6.67)

It can be readily verified that the sequences of (6.67) satisfy Eq. (6.65).

6.8. Identification of Linear Binary Machines

As was pointed out in the preceding section, given the impulse response of a linear binary machine, the response of the quiescent machine to any excitation can be readily determined. The impulse response, therefore, is sufficient to characterize an unknown quiescent machine. In this section we shall see how the impulse-response characterization can be employed to derive the x-z characterization. Once the x-z function is obtained, the characterizing functions f_z and f_s of the given machine can be constructed as outlined in Sec. 6.2.

Consider a quiescent linear binary machine M whose transfer ratio is given by

$$T(M) = I\eta_1 \oplus D\eta_2 \oplus D^2\eta_3 \oplus \cdots \oplus D^{l-1}\eta_l \qquad (6.68)$$

where the η_i coefficients may be either 0 or 1. For the quiescent M, then,

$$z_\nu = \eta_1 x_\nu \oplus \eta_2 x_{\nu-1} \oplus \eta_3 x_{\nu-2} \oplus \cdots \oplus \eta_l x_{\nu-l+1} \qquad (6.69)$$

Suppose now that the infinite input sequence $1000 \cdots$ (i.e., an impulse) is applied to M at time t_1. We thus have $x_1 = 1$, and $x_k = 0$ for all $k \neq 1$. From (6.69), then, $z_1 = \eta_1$, $z_2 = \eta_2$, . . . , $z_l = \eta_l$, and $z_k = 0$ for all $k > l$. The impulse response of a machine characterized by $T(M)$, as given in (6.68), is, therefore, $\eta_1\eta_2 \cdots \eta_l 000 \cdots$. Conversely, if a machine exhibits the impulse response $\eta_1\eta_2 \cdots \eta_l 000 \cdots$, it can be characterized by $T(M)$, as given in (6.68).

The above result enables us to find the transfer ratio of a machine which exhibits an arbitrary impulse response. As was established in Sec. 6.7, the impulse response $\mathcal{R}$ of every linear binary machine can be expressed as the sum of transient and periodic components $\mathcal{R}_T$ and $\mathcal{R}_P$, respectively. Let

$$\mathcal{R}_T = \delta_1\delta_2 \cdots \delta_r 000 \cdots \qquad (6.70)$$
$$\mathcal{R}_P = \epsilon_1\epsilon_2 \cdots \epsilon_p\epsilon_1\epsilon_2 \cdots \epsilon_p \cdots \qquad (6.71)$$

The machine which realizes $\mathfrak{R}_T$ has the transfer ratio

$$T_T = I\delta_1 \oplus D\delta_2 \oplus \cdots \oplus D^{r-1}\delta_r \tag{6.72}$$

The machine which realizes $\mathfrak{R}_P$ has the transfer ratio

$$
\begin{aligned}
T_P &= I\epsilon_1 \oplus D\epsilon_2 \oplus \cdots \oplus D^{\rho-1}\epsilon_\rho \\
&\quad \oplus D^\rho\epsilon_1 \oplus D^{\rho+1}\epsilon_2 \oplus \cdots \oplus D^{2\rho-1}\epsilon_\rho \\
&\quad \oplus D^{2\rho}\epsilon_1 \oplus D^{2\rho+1}\epsilon_2 \oplus \cdots \oplus D^{3\rho-1}\epsilon_\rho \\
&\quad \oplus \cdots \\
&= (I\epsilon_1 \oplus D\epsilon_2 \oplus \cdots \oplus D^{\rho-1}\epsilon_\rho)(I \oplus D^\rho \oplus D^{2\rho} \oplus \cdots) \\
&= (I\epsilon_1 \oplus D\epsilon_2 \oplus \cdots \oplus D^{\rho-1}\epsilon_\rho)\frac{I}{D^\rho \oplus I} \tag{6.73}
\end{aligned}
$$

By virtue of the superposition property, the machine M which realizes the impulse response $\mathfrak{R} = \mathfrak{R}_T \oplus \mathfrak{R}_P$ has the transfer ratio

$$T(M) = T_T \oplus T_P = I\delta_1 \oplus D\delta_2 \oplus \cdots \oplus D^{r-1}\delta_r$$
$$\oplus \frac{I\epsilon_1 \oplus D\epsilon_2 \oplus \cdots \oplus D^{\rho-1}\epsilon_\rho}{D^\rho \oplus I} \tag{6.74}$$

$T(M)$ can be written as a ratio of two polynomials in D, where common factors may be canceled as explained in Sec. 6.6. Thus, once the impulse response of M is observed, its transfer ratio can always be determined. The construction of the x-z function from the transfer ratio, and the characterizing functions f_z and f_s from the x-z function, is straightforward.

As an example, suppose the linear binary machine $A31$ exhibits the impulse response

$$\mathfrak{R} = 111011101001110100111 \cdots \tag{6.75}$$

Hence

$$\mathfrak{R}_P = 010011101001110100111 \cdots \tag{6.76}$$
$$\mathfrak{R}_T = 101000000000000000000 \cdots \tag{6.77}$$

By (6.72), (6.73), and (6.74),

$$T_T = I \oplus D^2 \tag{6.78}$$
$$T_P = (D \oplus D^4 \oplus D^5 \oplus D^6)\frac{I}{D^7 \oplus I} \tag{6.79}$$
$$T(A31) = I \oplus D^2 \oplus \frac{D \oplus D^4 \oplus D^5 \oplus D^6}{D^7 \oplus I}$$
$$= \frac{D^9 \oplus D^7 \oplus D^6 \oplus D^5 \oplus D^4 \oplus D^2 \oplus D \oplus I}{D^7 \oplus I} \tag{6.80}$$

Application of the Euclidean algorithm to (6.80) reveals that the numerator and denominator polynomials have a common factor $(D^4 \oplus D^2 \oplus D \oplus I)$ and that $T(A31)$ can be written as

$$T(A31) = \frac{(D^4 \oplus D^2 \oplus D \oplus I)(D^5 \oplus I)}{(D^4 \oplus D^2 \oplus D \oplus I)(D^3 \oplus D \oplus I)}$$

$$= \frac{D^5 \oplus I}{D^3 \oplus D \oplus I} \tag{6.81}$$

The quiescent machine $A31$, therefore, is characterized by

$$z_\nu = x_\nu \oplus x_{\nu-5} \oplus z_{\nu-1} \oplus z_{\nu-3} \tag{6.82}$$

As can be readily verified, the machine characterized by (6.82) indeed exhibits the impulse response (6.75).

It should be noticed that the identification of a linear binary machine through its impulse response, as outlined above, hinges on the ability of the investigator to detect the transient and periodic portions of the response after a finite number of observed symbols. This ability, in turn, requires the advance knowledge of the maximal memory of the machine, through which the upper bounds to the length of the transient portion and the period can be determined (see Theorem 6.3). Alternatively, it is sufficient to know the maximum number of states in the machine, since this number may be used, via Theorem 6.1, to compute the maximal memory. Notice also that the number of states n in a linear binary machine of memory μ cannot exceed 4^μ. The knowledge of μ, therefore, is equivalent to the knowledge of the upper bound to n, as can be expected in view of Theorem 5.2.

6.9. Output-independent Machines

A finite-memory machine in which the z memory is 0 is called an *output-independent machine*. An output-independent machine, then, is any machine in which

$$z_\nu = f(x_\nu, x_{\nu-1}, \ldots, x_{\nu-\mu}) \tag{6.83}$$

where any of the arguments may be a dummy argument. Output-independent machines, constituting a subclass of the class of finite-memory machines, exhibit all the properties previously derived for the latter class. In particular, from Lemma 6.1, we have:

THEOREM 6.4. In a minimal output-independent machine of memory μ,

$$s_\nu = g(x_{\nu-1}, x_{\nu-2}, \ldots, x_{\nu-\mu}) \tag{6.84}$$

The state of an output-independent machine, then, is completely determined by the applied input sequence of length μ, and hence can be controlled directly by the source of excitation. If in machine M,

$$\sigma_i = g(\xi_{j_1}, \xi_{j_2}, \ldots, \xi_{j_\mu}) \tag{6.85}$$

then all that is required to pass M into state σ_i is to apply the input sequence $\xi_{j_1}\xi_{j_2} \cdots \xi_{j_\mu}$. Since such a sequence can be applied at any state, it follows that any state in an output-independent machine can be reached from any other state, and hence that an output-independent machine is equivalent to a strongly connected one.

Given an output-independent machine M, with memory μ and input alphabet $\{\xi_1, \xi_2, \ldots, \xi_p\}$, the x-z function (6.83) of M can always be established by applying, successively, all possible p^μ sequences $\xi_{j_1}\xi_{j_2} \cdots \xi_{j_\mu}$. Once the x-z function is determined, the transition table (or diagram, or matrix) of M can, of course, be constructed. Thus, an output-independent machine with known memory and input alphabet can always be identified by a simple preset experiment. Notice that the output alphabet is not needed for designing the experiment, and hence that, at the outset, the known machine belongs to an infinite class of machines. However, since every output-independent machine is strongly connected, this class is exclusive and meets the identifiability requirement of Theorem 5.3.

The sequence which contains all possible p^μ μ-symbol subsequences $\xi_{j_1}\xi_{j_2} \cdots \xi_{j_\mu}$ is called a (p, μ) sequence. The shortest (p, μ) sequence is one in which every symbol, except the last $\mu - 1$ symbols, initiates a different subsequence of length μ. Such a sequence, whose length is necessarily $p^\mu + \mu - 1$, is called a compact (p, μ) sequence. The following procedure, which will be presented without proof, can be used for constructing compact (p, μ) sequences for every specified p and μ:[†]

ALGORITHM 6.3. To construct a compact (p, μ) sequence for an output-independent machine with memory μ and input alphabet $\{\xi_1, \xi_2, \ldots, \xi_p\}$: (1) Let $\xi_{j_1} = \xi_{j_2} = \cdots = \xi_{j_\mu} = \xi_p$. Let $k = \mu + 1$. (2) Considering the input alphabet as an ordered set (with ξ_1 being the first symbol, ξ_2 the second symbol, $\ldots$, ξ_p the pth symbol), let ξ_{j_k} be the symbol with the lowest subscript, such that the subsequence $\xi_{j_{k-\mu+1}}\xi_{j_{k-\mu+2}} \cdots \xi_{j_k}$ is not included anywhere in the sequence $\xi_{j_1}\xi_{j_2} \cdots \xi_{j_{k-1}}$. (3) (a) If $k < p^\mu + \mu - 1$, increment k by 1 and return to (2). (b) If $k = p^\mu + \mu - 1$, then $\xi_{j_1}\xi_{j_2} \cdots \xi_{j_k}$ is a compact (p, μ) sequence.

As an example, (6.86) shows the construction of a compact $(3, 3)$ sequence for an output-independent machine with memory 3 and input

[†] The procedure is due to B. Lippel and I. J. Epstein (A Method for Obtaining Complete Digital Coding Chains, *IRE Trans.*, vol. EC-6, p. 121, 1957).

alphabet $\{\alpha,\ \beta,\ \gamma\}$. Successive rows show successive subsequences of length 3 (there are 27 of those). The last row shows the total sequence, whose length is $3^3 + 3 - 1 = 29$.

$$
\begin{array}{c}
\gamma\gamma\gamma \\
\gamma\gamma\alpha \\
\gamma\alpha\alpha \\
\alpha\alpha\alpha \\
\alpha\alpha\beta \\
\alpha\beta\alpha \\
\beta\alpha\alpha \\
\alpha\alpha\gamma \\
\alpha\gamma\alpha \\
\gamma\alpha\beta \\
\alpha\beta\beta \\
\beta\beta\alpha \\
\beta\alpha\beta \\
\alpha\beta\gamma \\
\beta\gamma\alpha \\
\gamma\alpha\gamma \\
\alpha\gamma\beta \\
\gamma\beta\alpha \\
\beta\alpha\gamma \\
\alpha\gamma\gamma \\
\gamma\gamma\beta \\
\gamma\beta\beta \\
\beta\beta\beta \\
\beta\beta\gamma \\
\beta\gamma\beta \\
\gamma\beta\gamma \\
\beta\gamma\gamma \\
\hline
\gamma\gamma\gamma\alpha\alpha\alpha\beta\alpha\alpha\gamma\alpha\beta\beta\alpha\beta\gamma\alpha\gamma\beta\alpha\gamma\gamma\beta\beta\beta\gamma\beta\gamma\gamma
\end{array}
$$

(6.86)

The sequences produced by Algorithm 6.3 have the following property: If the first p^μ symbols are placed around a circle, then every sequence constructed by reading off $p^\mu + \mu - 1$ consecutive symbols around this circle constitutes a compact $(p,\ \mu)$ sequence (regardless of the starting point, and regardless of whether the symbols are read off in the clockwise or in the counterclockwise direction). Since sequences constructed by selecting different starting points on the circle (but proceeding in the same direction) are necessarily distinct, each application of Algorithm 6.3 can yield p^μ different compact $(p,\ \mu)$ sequences. The number $W_{p,\mu}$ of different compact $(p,\ \mu)$ sequences is given by[1]

$$
W_{p,\mu} = (p!)^{p^{\mu-1}} \tag{6.87}
$$

[1] This result is due to T. van Aardenne-Ehrenfest and N. G. de Bruijn (Circuits and Trees in Oriented Linear Graphs, *Simon Stevin*, vol. 28, pp. 203–217, 1950–1951).

In conclusion, we have:

THEOREM 6.5. An output-independent machine with known memory μ and input alphabet of size p can always be identified by a simple preset experiment of length l, where

$$l \leq p^\mu + \mu - 1 \tag{6.88}$$

PROBLEMS

6.1. Which of the systems described in Probs. 1.2 to 1.9 represent finite-memory systems? Tabulate the x-z functions of those systems which have a finite memory.

6.2. Show that a machine of memory 0 is a trivial machine.

6.3. Construct the transition table (in a minimal form) of the finite-memory machine whose input and output alphabets are $\{0, 1\}$ and which is characterized by

$$z_\nu = x_{\nu-2} \times z_{\nu-1}$$

6.4. The machine specified by Table P 6.1 is of finite memory μ. (a) Find the upper bound to μ. (b) Determine μ.

TABLE P 6.1

x_ν / s_ν	z_ν		$s_{\nu+1}$	
	α	β	α	β
1	1	1	1	2
2	0	0	3	2
3	0	1	1	1

6.5. For the machine shown in Fig. P 6.1, (a) determine the memory; (b) construct the minimal x-z table.

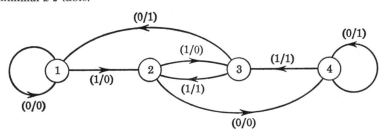

FIG. P 6.1

6.6. Show that the memory of a minimal finite-memory (n, p, q) machine cannot be less than $(\log n)/(\log pq)$.

6.7. Machine M is known to have p input symbols, n states, and memory μ. Find the lower bound to the size of the output alphabet.

6.8. Show that the length of the preset homing experiment for a machine of memory μ is at most μ.

6.9. The linear binary machine A is specified by

$$z_\nu = x_\nu \oplus x_{\nu-1} \oplus z_{\nu-1}$$

(*a*) Draw the transition diagram of the minimal form of A, and identify the ground state. (*b*) Find the transfer ratio of A, and reduce it by canceling the common factor of the numerator and denominator polynomials. (*c*) Show that the quiescent A can be represented by $z_\nu = x_\nu \oplus z_{\nu-1}$. (*d*) Draw the transition diagram of the quiescent A, as represented in part *c*. Verify that this machine constitutes the set of states of A which are reachable from the ground state. (*e*) Find the response of the quiescent A to the input sequence 101100011100.

6.10. A linear binary machine is specified by

$$z_\nu = x_\nu \oplus x_{\nu-1} + \cdots \oplus x_{\nu-\mu} \oplus z_{\nu-1} \oplus z_{\nu-2} \oplus \cdots \oplus z_{\nu-\mu}$$

Show that the machine, when operated from its ground state, is a trivial machine.

6.11. (*a*) Show that $D \oplus I$ is a factor in $D^r \oplus I$, for any $r \geq 1$. (*b*) Show that any modulo-2 polynomial in D which contains an even number of terms has a factor $D \oplus I$. (*c*) Show that $D^{2r_1} \oplus D^{2r_2} \oplus \cdots \oplus D^{2r_2} = (D^{r_1} \oplus D^{r_2} \oplus \cdots \oplus D^{r_k})^2$.

6.12. Given

$$T(M) = \frac{D^{10} \oplus D^9 \oplus D^8 \oplus D^7 \oplus D}{D^7 \oplus D^4 \oplus D^2 \oplus D \oplus I}$$

Find the x-z function for the quiescent machine M.

6.13. Given

$$T(M) = \frac{D^{i_u} \oplus D^{i_{u-1}} \oplus \cdots \oplus D^{i_1}}{D^{j_v} \oplus D^{j_{v-1}} \oplus \cdots \oplus D^{j_1}}$$

where $i_u > i_{u-1} > \cdots > i_1$ and $j_v > j_{v-1} > \cdots > j_1$. (*a*) Show that $T(M)$ characterizes a linear binary machine only if $j_1 \leq i_1$. (*b*) Show that if $i_1 = j_1 = 0$, then there exists a machine M^{-1}, such that $T(M)T(M^{-1}) = I$ (i.e., if M and M^{-1} are connected in cascade, the input and output of the combined machine are identical at all times).[1] (*c*) Determine the $x-z$ function of M^{-1}, if M is specified by

$$z_\nu = x_\nu \oplus x_{\nu-1} \oplus x_{\nu-2} \oplus x_{\nu-4} \oplus z_{\nu-1} \oplus z_{\nu-3}$$

6.14. Show that the period of the free response of a 4-state linear binary machine cannot exceed 63.

6.15. The linear binary machine M of memory μ is excited with an input sequence of period ρ_0. Show that the response becomes periodic after a finite number of symbols and that the period does not exceed $\rho_0(2^\mu - 1)$.

6.16. The impulse response of a quiescent linear binary machine is 1011001001001 $\cdots$. Find the response of the quiescent machine to the input sequences (*a*) 110101000000000 $\cdots$, (*b*) 101101101101101 $\cdots$. Decompose the resulting responses into transient and periodic components.

6.17. The impulse response of a quiescent linear binary machine is

$$101010011101001110100111010011 \cdots$$

Determine the $x-z$ function of this machine.

6.18. A linear binary machine is specified by

$$z_\nu = x_\nu \oplus x_{\nu-1} \oplus x_{\nu-3} \oplus z_{\nu-2} \oplus z_{\nu-3}$$

[1] Both M and M^{-1}, therefore, are information-lossless (see Sec. 5.8).

The initial conditions at time t_ν are $x_{\nu-1} = x_{\nu-2} = x_{\nu-3} = z_{\nu-1} = z_{\nu-2} = z_{\nu-3} = 1$. Construct a sequence which, when applied to the machine at time t_ν, maintains a constant output composed of 0's only.

6.19. An output-independent machine is known to have the memory 5 and the input alphabet $\{0, 1\}$. Design a shortest preset experiment for identifying the machine.

6.20. A given machine M is known to be an output-independent (n, p, q) machine. Show that M can be identified by a simple preset experiment of length l, where

$$l \leq p^{n(n-1)/2} + \tfrac{1}{2}n^2 - \tfrac{1}{2}n - 1$$

6.21. Construct 2-state machines meeting the following requirements: (a) not finite-memory, (b) finite-memory but not output-independent, (c) output-independent.

6.22. Show that the following characterizing functions represent an output-independent machine of memory 1:

$$z_\nu = f_z(x_\nu, s_\nu)$$
$$s_{\nu+1} = f_s(x_\nu)$$

CHAPTER 7

INPUT-RESTRICTED MACHINES

7.1. Introduction

In our study of finite-state machines we focused our attention on the properties of the machines themselves, and were not concerned with the properties of the sources which excite these machines. We consistently assumed that the machines under discussion can be excited by any source whatsoever, as long as the symbols generated by this source belong to the input alphabet of the machine. In this chapter we shall abandon this assumption and discuss a more general class of machines, where the source may be subject to some known constraints. Specifically, we shall discuss a class of machines, known as *input-restricted machines*, in which not every input symbol can be applied at every state. Such restrictions invariably arise because of some interdependence between the internal structure of the machine and the source of excitation. As an illustration, consider Example 2 of Sec. 1.7, where an English text, composed of the 26 letters of the alphabet and spaces, is scanned with the purpose of counting the number of words starting with "*un*" and ending with "*d*." When the machine is in state "Mark *u-n-d*," for example, the input symbol "*p*" cannot be applied, since no English word contains the sequence of letters "*undp*" (or the probability of occurrence of such a sequence is extremely small). For all practical purposes, therefore, the symbol "*p*" (as well as many other symbols) can be ruled out as a possible excitation when the machine that describes this text-scanning system is in state "Mark *u-n-d*."

In the following sections we shall see how some of the notions and techniques developed in preceding chapters can be extended to the class of input-restricted machines.[1]

[1] The material in this chapter is based in part on the work of D. D. Aufenkamp (Analysis of Sequential Machines, *IRE Trans.*, vol. EC-7, pp. 299–306, 1958), S. Ginsburg (A Technique for the Reduction of a Given Machine to a Minimal-State Machine, *IRE Trans.*, vol. EC-8, pp. 346–355, 1959; On the Reduction of Superfluous States in a Sequential Machine, *J. Assoc. Comput. Mach.*, vol. 6, pp. 259–282, 1959), and M. C. Paull and S. H. Unger (Minimizing the Number of States in Incompletely Specified Sequential Switching Functions, *IRE Trans.*, vol. EC-8, pp. 356–367, 1959).

7.2. State Compatibility

In postulating the finite-state model (see Sec. 1.6), it was tacitly assumed that the characterizing functions f_z and f_s of a finite-state machine are defined for every pair (x_ν, s_ν). In the study of input-restricted machines, it is convenient to modify this model and permit (x_ν, s_ν) pairs for which both f_z and f_s remain undefined. Specifically, we can assume that f_z and f_s of machine M are undefined for the pair (ξ_j, σ_i),

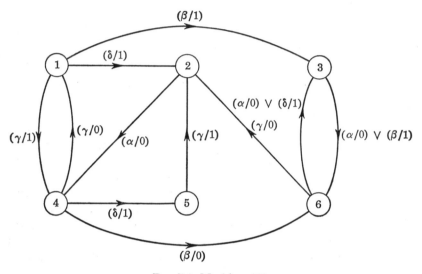

FIG. 7.1. Machine $A32$.

where ξ_j is an input symbol and σ_i a state of M, if under no circumstances can ξ_j be applied to $M|\sigma_i$; M is then said to exhibit an *input restriction* in state σ_i. In the transition table of M, such a restriction is manifested by the fact that the entry common to row σ_i and column ξ_j in both the z_ν and $s_{\nu+1}$ subtables is empty (or filled with dashes). An input sequence is said to be *acceptable* to state σ_i if, when applied to $M|\sigma_i$, it does not violate the input restrictions in any of the states of M. As an example, Fig. 7.1 and Table 7.1 represent the input-restricted machine $A32$.

States σ_i and σ_j of an input-restricted machine M are said to be *compatible* if $M|\sigma_i$ and $M|\sigma_j$, when excited by any input sequence acceptable to both σ_i and σ_j, yield identical output sequences. σ_i and σ_j are *incompatible* if there is at least one input sequence, acceptable to both σ_i and σ_j, which yields different output sequences when applied to $M|\sigma_i$ and $M|\sigma_j$. Compatibility is seen to obey the reflexive and symmetric laws, but not the transitive law, since the sequences acceptable to σ_i and σ_j are not necessarily the sequences acceptable to σ_j and σ_k. Compatibility, therefore, cannot be treated as an ordinary equivalence relation, and must be confined to pairs of states only.

TABLE 7.1. MACHINE $A32$

s_ν \ x_ν	z_ν				$s_{\nu+1}$			
	α	β	γ	δ	α	β	γ	δ
1	—	1	1	1	—	3	4	2
2	0	—	—	—	4	—	—	—
3	0	1	—	—	6	6	—	—
4	—	0	0	1	—	6	1	5
5	—	—	1	—	—	—	2	—
6	0	—	0	1	3	—	2	3

It can be noticed that the definition of a compatible pair of states becomes identical with the definition of an equivalent pair of states, when no input restrictions are imposed on the machine at hand. Thus, the definition of state-pair compatibility can be obtained from that of state-pair equivalence, if in the latter (see Definition 3.1) the phrase "any input sequence" is changed into "any input sequence acceptable to both states" (this change, of course, has no effect on the validity of Definition 3.1, since in a nonrestricted machine the set of acceptable sequences constitutes the set of *all* input sequences). The process of establishing whether a pair of states is compatible or not is, therefore, the same as that of establishing whether a pair of states is equivalent or not, with the only difference that all sequences not acceptable to both states in the pair are ignored.

In Sec. 3.7 a method, referred to as the *pairs table* method, was described for determining all equivalent pairs of states in a given machine. In accordance with the foregoing remarks, this method can also be used for determining all compatible pairs of states, provided the first version of the pairs table is modified as follows: (1) The entries in the pairs column are pairs of states which yield the same output symbol when excited by any input symbol acceptable to both states. (2) If the input symbol ξ_h is not acceptable to both σ_i and σ_j, the entry common to row $\{\sigma_i, \sigma_j\}$ and column ξ_h in the pairs table is left blank (or filled with a dash). The construction of successive versions of the pairs table may then be carried out in the same manner as described in Sec. 3.7. Uncircled stub entries in the final version represent all the compatible pairs of states for the given machine.

As an example, Table 7.2 shows the final version of the pairs table for machine $A32$ of Fig. 7.1. The compatible pairs in $A32$, then, are $\{1, 2\}$, $\{1, 3\}$, $\{1, 5\}$, $\{2, 3\}$, $\{2, 4\}$, $\{2, 5\}$, $\{3, 5\}$, $\{3, 6\}$, and $\{4, 6\}$.

TABLE 7.2. PAIRS TABLE FOR $A32$

Pairs	α	β	γ	δ
1, 2	—	—	—	—
1, 3	—	3, 6	—	—
1, 5	—	—	2, 4	—
2, 3	4, 6	—	—	—
2, 4	—	—	—	—
2, 5	—	—	—	—
⟨2, 6⟩	3, 4	—	—	—
3, 5	—	—	—	—
3, 6	3, 6	—	—	—
4, 6	—	—	1, 2	3, 5

7.3. Quasi-equivalent Machines

State σ_j in machine M' is said to be *quasi-equivalent* to state σ_i of machine M if any input sequence acceptable to σ_i yields identical responses, when applied to $M|\sigma_i$ and $M'|\sigma_j$. Machine M' is said to be *quasi-equivalent* to machine M if to every state σ_i of M there corresponds at least one state σ_j of M', such that σ_j is quasi-equivalent to σ_i. On the basis of this definition, M' can be interpreted in the following manner: Given an unknown machine, which could be either M or M', and the response of this machine to any input sequence *acceptable to some state in* M, there is no way of finding whether the unknown machine is M or M'. Thus, M' is quasi-equivalent to M, if there is no way of distinguishing between M and M', via external experiments which employ only those input sequences which are acceptable to states of M. Notice that quasi-equivalence is a nonsymmetric relation: the fact that M' is quasi-equivalent to M does not imply that M is quasi-equivalent to M'.

Let $\Sigma_1, \Sigma_2, \ldots, \Sigma_n$ be sets of states of machine M, such that every state of machine M is included in at least one Σ_i set. The set of sets $\Sigma_1, \Sigma_2, \ldots, \Sigma_n$ is called a *grouping; n* is referred to as the *size* of the grouping. Two states which appear together in at least one Σ_i set constitute an *adjoint pair;* a pair of states which is not adjoint constitutes a *disjoint pair*. A grouping is said to be *proper* if it fulfills the following two conditions: (1) The responses of the states in any adjoint pair, say σ_{i_1} and σ_{i_2}, to any input symbol ξ_j acceptable to both σ_{i_1} and σ_{i_2} must be identical. (2) The first successors of σ_{i_1} and σ_{i_2} with respect to ξ_j must either be identical or constitute an adjoint pair.

Let machine M have the state set $\{\sigma_1, \sigma_2, \ldots, \sigma_r\}$. Let machine M'

be quasi-equivalent to machine M and have the state set $\{\sigma_1', \sigma_2', \ldots, \sigma_n'\}$. By definition of quasi-equivalence, to every state σ_i in M there must correspond at least one state in M' which is quasi-equivalent to σ_i. Group the states of M into the sets $\Sigma_1, \Sigma_2, \ldots, \Sigma_n$, such that Σ_i is the set of all states to which σ_i' is quasi-equivalent. These sets constitute a grouping, since they include every state of M at least once. Let σ_{i_1} and σ_{i_2} be any pair of states in set Σ_i, and let ξ_j be any input symbol acceptable to both σ_{i_1} and σ_{i_2}. The responses of $M|\sigma_{i_1}$ and $M|\sigma_{i_2}$ to ξ_j must be the same as the response of $M'|\sigma_i'$ to ξ_j. The responses of $M|\sigma_{i_1}$ and $M|\sigma_{i_2}$ to ξ_j, therefore, must be identical. Suppose that the first successors of σ_{i_1} and σ_{i_2} with respect to ξ_j are σ_{k_1} and σ_{k_2} and that the first successor of σ_i' with respect to ξ_j is σ_k'. Since σ_i' is quasi-equivalent to σ_{i_1} and σ_{i_2}, σ_k' must be quasi-equivalent to σ_{k_1} and σ_{k_2}. σ_{k_1} and σ_{k_2}, therefore, cannot be disjoint and must be included in the same set Σ_k. In conclusion, the grouping $\Sigma_1, \Sigma_2, \ldots, \Sigma_n$ of M, constructed as described above, must be a proper grouping.

Given machine M, with a proper grouping $\Sigma_1, \Sigma_2, \ldots, \Sigma_n$, a machine M' can be constructed according to the following rules: M' has n states, labeled $\sigma_1', \sigma_2', \ldots, \sigma_n'$. If, in M, a state belonging to the set Σ_u passes into a state belonging to the set Σ_v, yielding the output symbol ζ_k when the input symbol ξ_j is applied, then, in M', the state σ_u' passes into the state σ_v', yielding the output symbol ζ_k when the input symbol ξ_j is applied. No ambiguity is encountered in this construction, since, if any state of M, belonging to Σ_u, passes into any state belonging to Σ_v, yielding ζ_k to the input symbol ξ_j, then *every* state of M, which belongs to Σ_u and to which ξ_j is acceptable, passes into a state which belongs to Σ_v, yielding ζ_k to the input symbol ξ_j. From the construction of M' it follows that state σ_i' of M' is quasi-equivalent to every state of M which belongs to the set Σ_i. M', therefore, is quasi-equivalent to M. We thus have the following result:

THEOREM 7.1. To every n-state machine M', which is quasi-equivalent to machine M, there corresponds in M a proper grouping of size n. To every proper grouping of size n in machine M, there corresponds a machine M', which is quasi-equivalent to M.

The construction of the proper grouping of M, when M' is given, and the construction of M', when the proper grouping of M is given, can be carried out as outlined above. If M is an r-state machine, and if $n < r$, then M' is said to be a *reduced form* of M. If no reduced form of M has less than n states, M' is said to be a *minimal form* of M, denoted by $\check{M}$. The minimal form $\check{M}$ of a given machine M has the same significance in the input-restricted case as in the nonrestricted case: $\check{M}$ is the smallest machine which exhibits the same behavior as the given machine M. It should be borne in mind, however, that in the input-restricted case the behaviors of M and $\breve{M}$ are to be compared only with respect to excitations acceptable to the states of the original machine M.

Theorem 7.1 suggests that $\breve{M}$ can be determined from the r-state machine M by listing all the proper groupings of M, having the size r or less, and selecting the smallest one. Given the smallest proper grouping, or the *minimal proper grouping*, a machine quasi-equivalent to M can always be constructed, as previously described; this machine is the minimal form of M. Although this method assures a solution, it is quite laborious in all but the most trivial cases, because of the required enumeration of proper groupings. In the following section we shall produce a number of results which will somewhat facilitate this enumeration task.

7.4. Determination of Minimal Forms

A set Σ_i appearing in a proper grouping $\Sigma_1, \Sigma_2, \ldots, \Sigma_n$, will be called a *compatible set*.

LEMMA 7.1. Every pair of states in a compatible set must be compatible.

Proof. Consider the states σ_{i_1} and σ_{i_2} in set Σ_1 of the proper grouping $\Sigma_1, \Sigma_2, \ldots, \Sigma_n$. By Theorem 7.1, there exists a machine M' in which one state, labeled σ_i', is quasi-equivalent to σ_{i_1} and σ_{i_2}. The responses of σ_{i_1} and σ_{i_2} to any input sequence $\mathcal{E}$ acceptable to both states, then, must be identical, since both responses must be the same as the response of σ_i' to $\mathcal{E}$. Hence, by definition, σ_{i_1} and σ_{i_2} must be compatible.

In what follows, a C *set* for machine M will be a set of states in M which meets the following two conditions: (1) Every pair of states in a C set is compatible. (2) The set is not included in any C set containing a larger number of states. Lemma 7.1, then, yields:

THEOREM 7.2. Every set in a proper grouping for machine M must be either a C set or a subset of a C set for M.

The construction of a minimal form, then, can be carried out by listing all possible C sets and then forming all possible groupings from the listed C sets or subsets of these C sets. The smallest grouping which proves to be proper is the minimal proper grouping, which results in the minimal form of the given machine.

The list of all possible C sets can be readily compiled when the list of all compatible pairs is given. The list of all compatible pairs, in turn, can be produced via the pairs table, as described in Sec. 7.2. The procedure for listing the C sets from the compatible pairs is the following:

ALGORITHM 7.1. Given all compatible pairs for machine M, to determine all the C sets for M: (1) Let the first list consist of all compatible pairs of M and singletons consisting of states not included in any compatible pair. Let $k = 2$. (2) On each set $\{\sigma_{i_1}, \sigma_{i_2}, \ldots, \sigma_{i_k}\}$ contained in the $(k-1)$st list, carry out the following operations: Determine the

l states of M, say $\sigma_{j_1}, \sigma_{j_2}, \ldots, \sigma_{j_l}$, such that σ_{j_d} $(d = 1, 2, \ldots, l)$ is not included in the given set and such that σ_{j_d} forms a compatible pair with every state in the set. Replace $\{\sigma_{i_1}, \sigma_{i_2}, \ldots, \sigma_{i_h}\}$ with the l sets $\{\sigma_{i_1}, \sigma_{i_2}, \ldots, \sigma_{i_h}, \sigma_{j_d}\}$ $(d = 1, 2, \ldots, l)$. If $l = 0$, replace the set $\{\sigma_{i_1}, \sigma_{i_2}, \ldots, \sigma_{i_h}\}$ with itself. (3) Eliminate from the new list of sets all duplicate sets and all sets included in larger sets. Let the resulting list be the kth list. (4) (a) If the kth list differs from the $(k - 1)$st, increment k by 1 and return to (2). (b) If the kth list is the same as the $(k - 1)$st, it is the list of all C sets for machine M.

The execution of Algorithm 7.1 is facilitated by constructing a *compatibility matrix*, denoted by $[C_M]$, where the (i, j) entry is "1" if $\{\sigma_i, \sigma_j\}$ or $\{\sigma_j, \sigma_i\}$ is a compatible pair of states, and "0" otherwise. By construction, if each of the rows $\sigma_{i_1}, \sigma_{i_2}, \ldots, \sigma_{i_h}$ contains "1" in any given column σ_{j_d}, then σ_{j_d} forms a compatible pair with every state in the set $\{\sigma_{i_1}, \sigma_{i_2}, \ldots, \sigma_{i_h}\}$. Consequently, if $\{\sigma_{i_1}, \sigma_{i_2}, \ldots, \sigma_{i_h}\}$ is a set in the $(k - 1)$st list, and if rows $\sigma_{i_1}, \sigma_{i_2}, \ldots, \sigma_{i_h}$ of the compatibility matrix contain "1" in column σ_{j_d}, the set $\{\sigma_{i_1}, \sigma_{i_2}, \ldots, \sigma_{i_h}\}$ is to be replaced by the set $\{\sigma_{i_1}, \sigma_{i_2}, \ldots, \sigma_{i_h}, \sigma_{j_d}\}$.

As an example, consider machine $A32$ of Fig. 7.1. Table 7.2 displays all the compatible pairs for $A32$, from which the first list can be compiled:

$$\{1, 2\}, \{1, 3\}, \{1, 5\}, \{2, 3\}, \{2, 4\}, \{2, 5\}, \{3, 5\}, \}3, 6\}, \}4, 6\}$$

The compatibility matrix for $A32$, which can be constructed directly from the first list, is shown in (7.1). From this matrix and the first list, the second list can be found to be

$$\{1, 2, 3\}, \{1, 2, 5\}, \{1, 3, 5\}, \{2, 3, 5\}, \{2, 4\}, \{3, 6\}, \{4, 6\}$$

For example, both rows 1 and 2 in (7.1) contain "1" in columns 3 and 5; $\{1, 2\}$ of the first list, therefore, is replaced by $\{1, 2, 3\}$ and $\{1, 2, 5\}$. Since there is no column in which both rows 2 and 4 contain "1," $\{2, 4\}$ of the first list is replaced by $\{2, 4\}$. From (7.1) and the second list, the third list can be found to be

$$\{1, 2, 3, 5\}, \{2, 4\}, \{3, 6\}, \{4, 6\}$$

Since this list is the same as the fourth list, it constitutes the list of all C sets for $A32$.

$$[C_{A32}] = \begin{array}{c} \\ 1 \\ 2 \\ 3 \\ 4 \\ 5 \\ 6 \end{array} \begin{array}{c} \begin{array}{cccccc} 1 & 2 & 3 & 4 & 5 & 6 \end{array} \\ \left[\begin{array}{cccccc} 0 & 1 & 1 & 0 & 1 & 0 \\ 1 & 0 & 1 & 1 & 1 & 0 \\ 1 & 1 & 0 & 0 & 1 & 1 \\ 0 & 1 & 0 & 0 & 0 & 1 \\ 1 & 1 & 1 & 0 & 0 & 0 \\ 0 & 0 & 1 & 1 & 0 & 0 \end{array} \right] \end{array} \qquad (7.1)$$

The minimal form of $A32$, namely, $\breve{A}32$, corresponds to the smallest proper grouping constructible from the listed C sets or from subsets of the listed C sets. Since every grouping must contain all 6 states, the minimal proper grouping must be of size 2 or larger. However, since the grouping $\{1, 2, 3, 5\}$, $\{4, 6\}$ is not proper, the lower bound 2 is not realizable. With the aid of Table 7.2 it can be readily verified that $\{1, 2\}$, $\{3, 5\}$, $\{4, 6\}$ constitute a proper grouping; this grouping, therefore, is a minimal proper grouping. It can also be verified that $\{1, 5\}$, $\{2, 4\}$, $\{3, 6\}$ constitute another minimal proper grouping. The minimal proper grouping of an input-restricted machine, therefore, is not always unique. As a result, a given input-restricted machine may have a number of minimal forms which are not necessarily isomorphic to each other.

Once a minimal proper grouping for machine M is obtained, the transition table of the corresponding minimal form $\breve{M}$ can be obtained from the transition table of M, as follows:

ALGORITHM 7.2. Given the minimal proper grouping for M, namely, $\Sigma_1, \Sigma_2, \ldots, \Sigma_n$, where Σ_i is given by $\{\sigma_{i_1}, \sigma_{i_2}, \ldots \sigma_{i_{r_i}}\}$, to construct a minimal form $\breve{M}$ with the state set $\{\sigma'_1, \sigma'_2, \ldots, \sigma'_n\}$: (1) Let $k = 1$. (2) (a) If all the entries common to rows $\sigma_{k_1}, \sigma_{k_2}, \ldots, \sigma_{k_{r_k}}$ and column ξ_j in the z_ν and $s_{\nu+1}$ subtables of M are blank, let the entry common to row σ'_k and column ξ_j in the z_ν and $s_{\nu+1}$ subtables of $\breve{M}$ be blank. (b) If at least one of the entries common to rows $\sigma_{k_1}, \sigma_{k_2}, \ldots, \sigma_{k_{r_k}}$ and column ξ_j in the z_ν subtable of M is not blank, let it be the entry common to row σ'_k and column ξ_j in the z_ν subtable of $\breve{M}$. (c) If there are nonblank entries common to rows $\sigma_{k_1}, \sigma_{k_2}, \ldots, \sigma_{k_{r_k}}$ and column ξ_j in the $s_{\nu+1}$ subtable of M, find a compatible set Σ_l in which all these entries are included. Let σ'_l be the entry common to row σ'_k and column ξ_j in the $s_{\nu+1}$ subtable of $\breve{M}$. (3) (a) If $k < n$, increment k by 1 and return to (2). (b) If $k = n$, the transition table for $\breve{M}$ is completed.

Table 7.3 shows the transition table for machine $\breve{A}32_1$, the minimal form of $A32$, based on the minimal proper grouping $\{1, 2\}$, $\{3, 5\}$, $\{4, 6\}$; these sets are represented in $\breve{A}32_1$ by the states 1, 2, 3, respectively.

TABLE 7.3. MACHINE $\breve{A}32_1$

s_ν \ x_ν	z_ν				$s_{\nu+1}$			
	α	β	γ	δ	α	β	γ	δ
1	0	1	1	1	3	2	3	1
2	0	1	1	—	3	3	1	—
3	0	0	0	1	2	3	1	2

Table 7.4 shows the transition table for machine $A\breve{3}2_2$, the minimal form of $A32$, based on the minimal proper grouping $\{1, 5\}$, $\{2, 4\}$, $\{3, 6\}$; these sets are represented in $A\breve{3}2_2$ by the states 1, 2, 3, respectively. Figures 7.2 and 7.3 show the transition diagrams of $A\breve{3}2_1$ and $A\breve{3}2_2$, respectively. To illustrate the quasi-equivalence of $A\breve{3}2_1$ and $A\breve{3}2_2$ to $A32$, consider

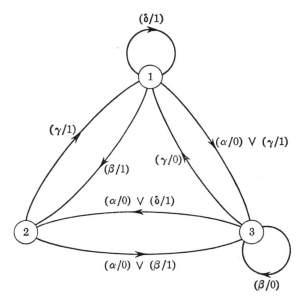

Fig. 7.2. Machine $A\breve{3}2_1$.

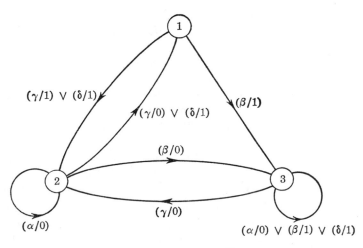

Fig. 7.3. Machine $A\breve{3}2_2$.

the input sequence $\gamma\gamma\delta\alpha\delta\gamma\alpha\beta\gamma\alpha\gamma\beta\beta\delta$, which is acceptable to state 1 of $A32$. When this sequence is applied to state 1 of $A32$, or state 1 of $A\breve{3}2_1$, or state 1 of $A\breve{3}2_2$ (the last two states being quasi-equivalent to the first state), the responses are seen to be identical and given by 10101100000111.

TABLE 7.4. MACHINE $A\breve{3}2_2$

s_ν \ x_ν	z_ν				$s_{\nu+1}$			
	α	β	γ	δ	α	β	γ	δ
1	—	1	1	1	—	3	2	2
2	0	0	0	1	2	3	1	1
3	0	1	0	1	3	3	2	3

7.5. A Reduction Method for Input-restricted Machines

As became evident in the preceding sections, the determination of the minimal form of an input-restricted machine is quite laborious. In cases where a minimal form is not insisted upon, but where a reduced state set is still desirable, a simplified method can be employed, which often yields a greatly reduced form (and sometimes a minimal form) of the given machine. The proposed method is essentially the same as the P_k-table method of minimizing nonrestricted machines, described in Sec. 3.6. The only difference between the usage of this method for nonrestricted machines and the usage for input-restricted machines is that in the latter case blank entries may be interpreted arbitrarily.

As an example, Tables 7.5 and 7.6 show the P_1 table and P_2 table, respectively, for machine $A32$ of Table 7.1. The P_1 table is obtained by interpreting the blank entries in the z_ν subtable of $A32$ in such a manner that the sets $\{1, 2, 3, 5\}$ and $\{4, 6\}$ become a 1-equivalence partition. Notice that other interpretations are also possible, but that the chosen interpretation results in the smallest number of 1-equivalence classes. The P_2 table is obtained by interpreting the blank entries in the P_1 table in such a manner that the sets $\{1, 2\}$, $\{3, 5\}$, and $\{4, 6\}$ become a 2-equivalence partition. Since this is the final P_k table, P_2 is the equivalence partition, from which the reduced form can be constructed as outlined in Algorithm 7.2. As it happens, the sets $\{1, 2\}$, $\{3, 5\}$, and $\{4, 6\}$ also constitute a minimal proper grouping, so that the reduced machine based on P_2 is also a minimal form of $A32$ (it is, in fact, $A\breve{3}2_1$ of Fig. 7.2). Notice, however, that a different interpretation of the blank entries in the P_1 table could result in the 2-equivalence partition $\{1\}$, $\{2, 3, 5\}$, $\{4, 6\}$, and hence to the 3-equivalence partition $\{1\}$, $\{2, 3, 5\}$, $\{4\}$, $\{6\}$, and finally to the equivalence partition $\{1\}$, $\{2\}$, $\{3, 5\}$, $\{4\}$, $\{6\}$. The last partition, clearly, offers a less satisfactory reduction of $A32$ than $\{1, 2\}$, $\{3, 5\}$, $\{4, 6\}$. In general, it is advisable to attempt a number of alternative interpretations at each step of the partitioning procedure and examine the influence of the various alternatives on the number of classes obtained in the final partition, or at least in the immediately following partition. The interpretation which yields the smallest number of classes is the one to be selected.

TABLE 7.5. P_1 TABLE FOR $A32$

Σ	x_ν / s_ν	$s_{\nu+1}$			
		α	β	γ	δ
a	1	—	3_a	4_b	2_a
	2	4_b	—	—	—
	3	6_b	6_b	—	—
	5	—	—	2_a	—
b	4	—	6_b	1_a	5_a
	6	3_a	—	2_a	3_a

TABLE 7.6. P_2 TABLE FOR $A32$

Σ	x_ν / s_ν	$s_{\nu+1}$			
		α	β	γ	δ
a	1	—	3_b	4_c	2_a
	2	4_c	—	—	—
b	3	6_c	6_c	—	—
	5	—	—	2_a	—
c	4	—	6_c	1_a	5_b
	6	3_b	—	2_a	3_b

The advantage of the described method is that it permits personal ingenuity and experience to be exploited in producing reduced forms in a relatively short time. The disadvantage of the method is that it does not guarantee the reduction, and certainly does not guarantee the minimization, of the given machine. It is important to point out that a minimal form is not guaranteed by this method even if all possible interpretations of blank entries are attempted at every step of the procedure. The reason is that every equivalence partition is necessarily composed of nonoverlapping equivalence classes, while a minimal proper grouping may be composed of overlapping compatible sets. For example, consider machine $A33$ of Fig. 7.4 and Table 7.7. P_1 in this case is $\{1, 2\}$,

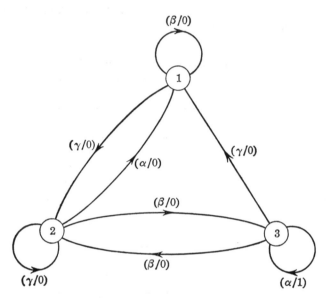

FIG. 7.4. Machine $A33$.

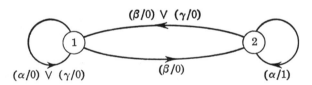

FIG. 7.5. Machine $A\breve{3}3$.

$\{3\}$, or $\{1, 3\}$, $\{2\}$. In either case, P_2 is $\{1\}$, $\{2\}$, $\{3\}$, which implies that $A33$ cannot be reduced by the proposed method. On the other hand, if the general minimization method is used, it is found that $\{1, 2\}$ and $\{1, 3\}$ are the C sets for $A33$ and that these two C sets constitute a proper grouping. $A33$, therefore, has a minimal form $A\breve{3}3$, which consists of two states only. Figure 7.5 shows this minimal form, where states 1 and 2 represent the sets $\{1, 2\}$ and $\{1, 3\}$, respectively, of machine $A33$.

TABLE 7.7. MACHINE $A33$

	z_ν			$s_{\nu+1}$		
x_ν / s_ν	α	β	γ	α	β	γ
1	—	0	0	—	1	2
2	0	0	0	1	3	2
3	1	0	0	3	2	1

PROBLEMS

7.1. Show that no set in a minimal proper grouping can be included in any other set in this grouping.

7.2. $C_1, C_2, \ldots, C_h$ are all the C sets for the input-restricted machine M. Show that $C_1, C_2, \ldots, C_h$ constitute a proper grouping, and hence that the number of states in $\hat{M}$ cannot exceed h. Show that if every C set has a state not contained in any other C set, then the number of states in $\hat{M}$ is exactly h.

7.3. The first version of the pairs table for a 6-state machine is shown in Table P 7.1. Find all the C sets and a minimal proper grouping for this machine.

7.4. Find a minimal form of the machine specified by Table P 7.2.

7.5. Determine the minimal form of the input-restricted machine shown in Fig. P 7.1.

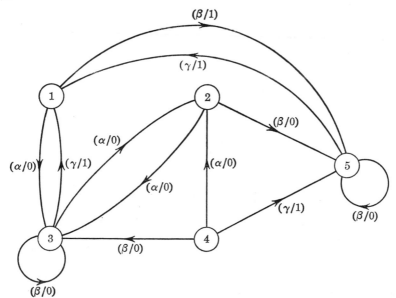

FIG. P 7.1

7.6. Reduce the machine specified by Table P 7.3, using the reduction method described in Sec. 7.5.

TABLE P 7.1

Pairs	α	β	γ	δ
1, 2	1, 4	1, 6	—	—
1, 3	1, 5	—	3, 5	—
1, 5	2, 6	—	—	3, 6
1, 6	—	4, 6	—	—
2, 3	1, 3	3, 5	—	—
2, 5	4, 5	—	1, 5	—
2, 6	1, 5	—	—	4, 6
3, 4	3, 6	2, 5	3, 6	—
3, 5	2, 3	—	—	1, 3
3, 6	—	2, 6	4, 6	—
4, 5	—	—	—	1, 2
4, 6	—	—	1, 5	1, 3

TABLE P 7.2

	z_ν				$s_{\nu+1}$			
x_ν s_ν	α	β	γ	δ	α	β	γ	δ
1	0	0	—	1	2	3	—	4
2	0	0	—	—	3	5	—	—
3	1	0	1	—	4	6	3	—
4	1	0	—	1	5	3	—	1
5	—	0	—	—	—	6	—	—
6	—	—	1	0	—	—	4	2

TABLE P 7.3

	z_ν						$s_{\nu+1}$					
x_ν s_ν	a	b	c	d	e	f	a	b	c	d	e	f
1	1	—	2	—	4	—	9	—	9	—	2	—
2	2	3	2	1	2	—	2	11	9	10	3	—
3	1	3	2	—	4	—	9	3	11	—	1	—
4	1	3	2	—	4	—	1	4	11	—	9	—
5	2	3	2	1	2	—	7	5	13	3	4	—
6	2	4	—	1	1	3	6	10	—	12	1	3
7	—	3	2	—	4	—	—	2	1	—	1	—
8	—	3	—	1	—	—	—	11	—	7	—	—
9	—	3	—	—	4	—	—	3	—	—	8	—
10	1	3	2	—	—	—	10	8	9	—	—	—
11	2	3	2	3	2	—	2	2	1	7	12	—
12	1	3	—	—	4	—	12	4	—	—	2	—
13	2	4	—	1	1	3	13	7	—	9	12	3

BIBLIOGRAPHY[1]

Aizerman, M. A., L. A. Gusev, L. I. Razoner, I. M. Smirnova, and A. A. Tal: Finite Automata, *Automation and Remote Control*, vol. 21, pp. 156–164, 1960.

Aufenkamp, D. D.: Analysis of Sequential Machines, *IRE Trans.*, vol. EC-7, pp. 299–306, 1958.

——— and F. E. Hohn: Analysis of Sequential Machines, *IRE Trans.*, vol. EC-6, pp. 276–285, 1957.

Bellman, R.: Sequential Machines, Ambiguity and Dynamic Programming, *J. Assoc. Comput. Mach.*, vol. 7, pp. 24–28, 1960.

———: "Adaptive Control Processes," pp. 119–123, Princeton University Press, Princeton, N. J., 1961.

Bennett, W. S.: Minimizing and Mapping Sequential Circuits, *Trans. AIEE*, vol. 74, pt. 1, pp. 443–447, 1955.

Blokh, A. Sh.: Equivalent Transformations of Sequential Machines, *Automation and Remote Control*, vol. 21, pp. 1057–1061, 1960.

Burks, A. W.: The Logic of Fixed and Growing Automata, Annals of the Computation Laboratory, vol. 29, pp. 147–188, Harvard University Press, Cambridge, Mass., 1959.

——— and H. Wang: The Logic of Automata, *J. Assoc. Comput. Mach.*, vol. 4, pp. 193–218, 279–297, 1957.

——— and J. B. Wright: Theory of Logical Nets, *Proc. IRE*, vol. 41, pp. 1357–1365, 1953.

Cadden, W. J.: Equivalent Sequential Circuits, *IRE Trans.*, vol. CT-6, pp. 30–34, 1959.

de Bruijn, N. G.: A Combinatorial Problem, *Proc. Ned. Acad. Wetensch.*, vol. 49, pp. 758–764, 1946.

Elspas, B.: The Theory of Autonomous Linear Sequential Networks, *IRE Trans.*, vol. CT-6, pp. 45–60, 1959.

Fitch, F. B.: Representation of Sequential Circuits in Combinatory Logic, *Phil. Sci.*, vol. 25, pp. 263–279, 1958.

Friedland, B.: Linear Modular Sequential Circuits, *IRE Trans.*, vol. CT-6, pp. 61–68, 1959.

——— and T. E. Stern: On Periodicity of States in Linear Modular Sequential Circuits, *IRE Trans.*, vol. IT-5, pp. 136–137, 1959.

Gill, A.: Comparison of Finite-State Models, *IRE Trans.*, vol. CT-7, pp. 178–179, 1960.

———: Analysis of Nets by Numerical Methods, *J. Assoc. Comput. Mach.*, vol. 7, pp. 251–254, 1960.

[1] The Bibliography is limited to articles and books which deal directly with topics covered in this book.

Gill, A.: Characterizing Experiments for Finite-memory Binary Automata, *IRE Trans.*, vol. EC-9, pp. 469–471, 1960.

――――: A Note on Moore's Distinguishability Theorem, *IRE Trans.*, vol. EC-10, pp. 290–291, 1961.

――――: Cascaded Finite-State Machines, *IRE Trans.*, vol. EC-10, pp. 366–370, 1961.

――――: State-identification Experiments in Finite Automata, *Information and Control*, vol. 4, pp. 132–154, 1961.

――――: A Theorem Concerning Compact and Cyclic Sequences, *IRE Trans.*, vol. IT-8, p. 255, 1962.

Gillespie, R. G., and D. D. Aufenkamp: On the Analysis of Sequential Machines, *IRE Trans.*, vol. EC-7, pp. 119–122, 1958.

Ginsburg, S.: On the Length of the Smallest Uniform Experiment Which Distinguishes the Terminal States of a Machine, *J. Assoc. Comput. Mach.*, vol. 5, pp. 266–280, 1958.

――――: A Synthesis Technique for Minimal-state Sequential Machines, *IRE Trans.*, vol. EC-8, pp. 13–24, 1959.

――――: On the Reduction of Superfluous States in a Sequential Machine, *J. Assoc. Comput. Mach.*, vol. 6, pp. 259–282, 1959.

――――: A Technique for the Reduction of a Given Machine to a Minimal-state Machine, *IRE Trans.*, vol. EC-8, pp. 346–355, 1959.

――――: Synthesis of Minimal-state Machines, *IRE Trans.*, vol. EC-8, pp. 441–449, 1959.

――――: Connective Properties Preserved in Minimal-state Machines, *J. Assoc. Comput. Mach.*, vol. 7, pp. 311–325, 1960.

――――: Some Remarks on Abstract Machines, *Trans. Am. Math. Soc.*, vol. 96, pp. 400–444, 1960.

――――: Compatibility of States in Input-independent Machines, *J. Assoc. Comput. Mach.*, vol. 8, pp. 400–403, 1961.

Hartmanis, J.: Linear Multivalued Sequential Coding Networks, *IRE Trans.*, vol. CT-6, pp. 69–74, 1959.

――――: Symbolic Analysis of a Decomposition of Information Processing Machines, *Information and Control*, vol. 3, pp. 154–178, 1960.

――――: On the State Assignment Problem for Sequential Machines, *IRE Trans.*, vol. EC-10, pp. 157–165, 1961.

――――: Loop-free Structure of Sequential Machines, *Information and Control*, vol. 5, pp. 25–43, 1962.

Hibbard, T. N.: Least Upper Bounds on Minimal Terminal State Experiments for Two Classes of Sequential Machines, *J. Assoc. Comput. Mach.*, vol. 8, pp. 601–612, 1961.

Hohn, F. E., S. Seshu, and D. D. Aufenkamp: The Theory of Nets, *IRE Trans.*, vol. EC-6, pp. 154–161, 1957.

Holladay, J. C., and R. S. Varga: On Powers of Non-negative Matrices, *Proc. Am. Math. Soc.*, vol. 9, pp. 631–634, 1958.

Huffman, D. A.: The Synthesis of Sequential Switching Circuits, *J. Franklin Inst.*, vol. 257, pp. 161–190, 275–303, 1954.

――――: Information Conservation in Sequence Transducers, *Proc. Symposium on Information Networks*, pp. 291–307, 1954.

――――: The Synthesis of Linear Sequential Coding Networks, pp. 77–95 in C. Cherry (ed.), "Information Theory," Academic Press, Inc., New York, 1956.

――――: A Linear Circuit Viewpoint on Error-correcting Codes, *IRE Trans.*, vol. IT-2, pp. 20–28, 1956.

————: An Algebra for Periodically Time-varying Linear Binary Sequence Transducers, Annals of the Computation Laboratory, vol. 29, pp. 189–203, Harvard University Press, Cambridge, Mass., 1959.

————: Canonical Forms for Information-lossless Finite-state Logical Machines, *IRE Trans.*, vol. CT-6, pp. 41–59, 1959.

Huzino, S.: On Some Sequential Machines and Experiments, *Mem. Fac. Sci., Kyushu Univ.*, ser. A, vol. 12, pp. 136–158, 1958.

————: Reduction Theorems on Sequential Machines, *Mem. Fac. Sci., Kyushu Univ.*, ser. A, vol. 12, pp. 159–179, 1958.

————: Some Properties of Convolution Machines and Sigma Composite Machines, *Mem. Fac. Sci., Kyushu Univ.*, ser. A, vol. 13, pp. 69–83, 1959.

————: On Some Sequential Equations, *Mem. Fac. Sci., Kyushu Univ.*, ser. A, vol. 14, pp. 50–62, 1960.

Karatsuba, A. A.: Solution of a Problem from the Theory of Finite Automata, *Uspekhi Matematiki Nauk*, vol. 15, pp. 157–159, 1960. (English translation No. K-218, Morris D. Friedman, Inc., West Newton, Mass.)

Lee, Y. Y.: Automata and Finite Automata, *Bell System Tech. J.*, vol. 39, pp. 1267–1295, 1960.

Lippel, B., and I. J. Epstein: A Method for Obtaining Complete Digital Coding Chains, *IRE Trans.*, vol. EC-6, p. 121, 1957.

McCluskey, E. J.: A Comparison of Sequential and Iterative Circuits, *Trans. AIEE*, vol. 78, pt. 1, pp. 1039–1044, 1959.

————: Introduction to State Tables, pp. 109–119 in E. J. McCluskey and T. C. Bartee (eds.), "A Survey of Switching Circuit Theory," McGraw-Hill Book Company, Inc., New York, 1962.

McNaughton, R.: The Theory of Automata, a Survey, pp. 379–421 in F. L. Alt (ed.), "Advances in Computers," vol. 2, Academic Press, Inc., New York, 1961.

Mealy, G. H.: Method for Synthesizing Sequential Circuits, *Bell System Tech. J.*, vol. 34, pp. 1045–1079, 1955.

Mezei, J. E.: Minimal Characterizing Experiments for Finite Memory Automata, *IRE Trans.*, vol. EC-10, p. 200, 1961.

Moore, E. F.: Gedanken-experiments on Sequential Machines, pp. 129–153 in C. E. Shannon and J. McCarthy (eds.), "Automata Studies," Princeton University Press, Princeton, N.J., 1956.

Narasimhan, R.: Minimizing Incompletely Specified Sequential Switching Functions, *IRE Trans.*, vol. EC-10, pp. 531–532, 1961.

Netherwood, D. B.: Minimal Sequential Machines, *IRE Trans.*, vol. EC-8, pp. 339–345, 1959.

Paull, M. C., and S. H. Unger: Minimizing the Number of States in Incompletely Specified Sequential Switching Functions, *IRE Trans.*, vol. EC-8, pp. 356–367, 1959.

Rabin, M. O., and D. Scott: Finite Automata and Their Decision Problems, *IBM J. Research Develop.*, vol. 3, pp. 114–125, 1959.

Raney, G. N.: Sequential Functions, *J. Assoc. Comput. Mach.*, vol. 5, pp. 177–180, 1958.

Reed, I. S.: Mathematical Structure of Sequential Machines, pp. 187–196 in E. J. McCluskey and T. C. Bartee (eds.), "A Survey of Switching Circuit Theory," McGraw-Hill Book Company, Inc., New York, 1962.

Runyon, J. P.: Derivation of Completely and Partially Specified State Tables, pp. 121–144 in E. J. McCluskey and T. C. Bartee (eds.), "A Survey of Switching Circuit Theory," McGraw-Hill Book Company, Inc., New York, 1962.

Schubert, E. J.: Matrix Algebra for Sequential Logic, *Trans. AIEE*, vol. 78, pt. 1, pp. 1074–1079, 1960.

Seshu, S.: Mathematical Models for Sequential Machines, *IRE Natl. Conv. Record*, vol. 7, pt. 2, pp. 4–16, 1959.

————, R. E. Miller, and G. Metze: Transition Matrices of Sequential Machines, *IRE Trans.*, vol. CT-6, pp. 5–12, 1959.

———— and M. B. Reed: "Linear Graphs and Electrical Networks," pp. 250–260, Addison-Wesley Publishing Company, Inc., Reading, Mass., 1961.

Simon, J. M.: Some Aspects of the Network Analysis of Sequence Transducers, *J. Franklin Inst.*, vol. 265, pp. 439–450, 1958.

————: A Note on the Memory Aspects of Sequence Transducers, *IRE Trans.*, vol. CT-6, pp. 26–29, 1959.

Srinivasan, C. V., and R. Narasimhan: On the Synthesis of Finite Sequential Machines, *Proc. Indian Acad. Sci.*, vol. 50, pp. 68–82, 1959.

Stearns, R. E., and J. Hartmanis: On the State Assignment Problem for Sequential Machines, *IRE Trans.*, vol. EC-10, pp. 593–603, 1961.

Stern, T. E., and B. Friedland: The Linear Modular Sequential Circuit Generalized, *IRE Trans.*, vol. CT-8, pp. 79–80, 1961.

Trakhtenbrot, B. A.: On Operators Realizable in Logical Nets, *Doklady Akad. Nauk S.S.S.R.*, vol. 112, pp. 1005–1007, 1957.

Unger, S. H.: Simplification of State Tables, pp. 145–170 in E. J. McCluskey and T. C. Bartee (eds.), "A Survey of Switching Circuit Theory," McGraw-Hill Book Company, Inc., New York, 1962.

van Aardenne-Ehrenfest, T., and N. G. de Bruijn: Circuits and Trees in Oriented Linear Graphs, *Simon Stevin*, vol. 28, pp. 203–217, 1950–1951.

Yoeli, M.: The Cascade Decomposition of Sequential Machines, *IRE Trans.*, vol. EC-10, pp. 587–592, 1961.

Zadeh, L. A.: From Circuit Theory to System Theory, *Proc. IRE*, vol. 50, pp. 856–865, 1962.

INDEX

Adjoint state, 54
Admissible set, 90
Aizerman, M. A., 199
Alphabet, input, 4
  output, 4
Alphabet finitude, 3–5
Asynchronous system, 3
Aufenkamp, D. D., 31, 49, 185, 199, 200

Bellman, R., 199
Bennett, W. S., 199
Black box, 1, 2, 4, 5
Blokh, A. Sh., 199
Branch, converging, 24, 32
  diverging, 24, 32
  reflecting, 24, 32
Burks, A. W., 199

Cadden, W. J., 199
Characterizing functions, 7
Compact sequence (p, μ), 180, 181
Compatibility, 186–188
Compatibility matrix, 191
Compatible set, 190
Complete cycle, 39, 40
Congruous finite-state machines, 29
Converging branch, 24, 32
Cycle, complete, 39, 40
  proper, 36

de Bruijn, N. G., 181, 199, 202
Decomposable finite-state machines, 28
Decomposition of machines, 27–29
  maximal, 28
Delay operator, 171

Dependent variables, 9
Determination of memory, 164, 166
Deterministic finite-state machines, 8
Diagnosing path, 102
Diagnosing sequence, 90, 102
Diagnosing tree, 100–103
Disjoint state, 54
Disjunction finite-state machines, 29–31
Distinguishability, machine, 67–69
  simple, 51
  state, 49–52
Diverging branch, 24, 32

Elspas, B., 199
Enumeration of machines, 19, 20
Epstein, I. J., 180, 201
Equivalence, machine, 67–69
  simple, 51
  state, 49–52
Equivalence class, machine, 69
  state, 58
Equivalence partition, machine, 69–72
  state, 57–60
Equivalence partitioning, machine, 69–72
  state, 60–67
  of transition matrix, 65–67
Equivalence table, 70–72
Excitation variables, 1
Exclusive class, 139
Experiments, adaptive, 88
  classification of, 87–89
  diagnosing, 89
  m-wise, 90
  multiple adaptive, 115–118, 129

203

Experiments, diagnosing, multiple
    preset, 110–115, 129
  pairwise, 90–97
  simple adaptive, 105–110, 129
  simple preset, 103–105, 129
  fault identification, 142–145
  homing, 89
    regular, 123
    regular adaptive, 125–130
    regular preset, 123–125, 129
    simple adaptive, 121–123
    simple preset, 120, 121
  machine identification, 136–149
    general problem, 137–139
    in known class, 139–142
    linear binary, 177–179
    output-independent, 182
    strongly connected (n, p, q), 148,
      149
  multiple, 89
  preset, 88
  simple, 89
  state identification, 87–131

Fault identification, 142–145
Finite-memory finite-state machines,
    156–169
Finite-memory system, 157–160
Finite-state machines, alternative
    model, 12, 13
  basic model, 7, 8
  congruous, 29
  decomposable, 28
  deterministic, 8
  disjunction, 29–31
  examples of, 8, 9
  finite-memory, 156–169
  information-lossless, 149–153
  input-restricted, 185–197
  isomorphic, 20, 21, 23, 24
  linear binary, 169–179
  minimal, 76, 81, 82
  (n, p, q), 19
    simply minimal, 19–21, 81, 82
    simply reducible, 19, 20, 81
  nonrestricted, 8

Finite-state machines, nontrivial, 8
  output-independent, 179–182
  quiescent, 170
  reversible, 147
  strongly connected, 145–149, 180
  trivial, 8
Fitch, F. B., 199
Free response of linear binary machine,
    174
Friedland, B., 199, 202

Gill, A., 87, 199
Gillespie, R. G., 199
Ginsburg, S., 87, 134, 185, 200
Ground state, 170
Grouping, 188
  proper, 188
    minimal, 190
Gusev, L. A., 199

Hartmanis, J., 200, 202
Hibbard, T. N., 126, 200
Higher-order transition matrix, 34–36
Hohn, F. E., 31, 49, 199, 200
Holladay, J. C., 200
Homing path, 118
Homing sequence, 120
Homing tree, 118–120
Huffman, D. A., 6, 49, 149, 169, 200
Huzino, S., 201

Identification, fault, 142–145
Identification experiments (see Experiments)
Impulse response of linear binary machine, 175, 176
Incompatibility, 186
Information-lossless finite-state machines, 149–153
Initial state, 14
Input alphabet, 4
Input-output pair, 22
Input-output sequence, 161

Input-restricted finite-state machines, 185–197
Input restriction, 186
Input sequence, 13
Input symbol, 5
Intermediate variables, 1
Isolated state, 25, 32
Isolated submachine, 26, 33, 34
Isomorphic finite-state machines, 20, 21, 23, 24

k-distinguishability, 52–54
k-equivalence, 52–54
k-equivalence class, 54
k-equivalence partition, 54–57
Karatsuba, A. A., 201
Kleene, S. C., 6

Lee, Y. Y., 201
Linear binary finite-state machines, 169–179
  response of, free, 174
    impulse, 175, 176
    periodic, 174
Lippel, B., 180, 201
Lossiness test table, 151, 152
Lossy state, 149

McCluskey, E. J., 201
Machine (see Finite-state machines)
Machine distinguishability, 67–69
Machine enumeration, 19, 20
Machine equivalence class, 69
Machine equivalence partitioning, 69–72
Machine minimization, 72–75, 190–194
Machine reduction, 78–81, 194–197
McNaughton, R., 201
Matrix, compatibility, 191
  partial construction of, 43, 44
  skeleton, 40–43
  transition (see Transition matrix)
Maximal decomposition of machines, 28

Maximal memory, 160
Mealy, G. H., 49, 201
Memory, 160
  determination of, 164–166
  maximal, 160
  x, 160
  z, 160
Merging, 78–81
Metze, G., 202
Mezei, J. E., 201
Miller, R. E., 202
Minimal finite-state machines, 76, 81, 82
Minimal form, 72–78, 189
Minimal grouping, 188, 190
Minimal path, 38, 39
Minimal x-z function, 166
Minimal x-z table, 169
Minimization, of machine, 72–75, 190–194
  of x-z function, 166–169
Modified skeleton matrix, 42, 43
Moore, E. F., 6, 49, 87, 136, 201
Multiple-experiment tree, 111, 112
Multiple experiments, 89

(n, p, q) finite-state machines (see Finite-state machines)
Narasimhan, R., 201, 202
Netherwood, D. B., 201
Nonrestricted finite-state machines, 8
Nontrivial finite-state machines, 8

Operator, delay, 171
Output alphabet, 4
Output-independent finite-state machines, 179–182
Output sequence, 13
Output symbol, 5

(p, μ) sequence, 180
Pairs table, 62–65, 187, 188
Partial construction of matrices, 43, 44

Path, 34
  diagnosing, 102
  homing, 118
  minimal, 38, 39
  proper, 36–38
  redundant, 37
Paull, M. C., 185, 201
Period, 174
Periodic response of linear binary ma-
    chine, 174
Permutation family, 20, 24
Persistent state, 24, 32
Persistent submachine, 26, 33, 34
P_k table, 60–62, 194–196
Prediction of machine behavior, 13–15
Preset experiments, 88
Proper cycle, 36
Proper path, 36–38

Quasi equivalence, 188–190
Quiescent finite-state machines, 170

Rabin, M. O., 201
Raney, G. N., 201
Razoner, L. I., 199
Reachability, 26, 27
Reduced form, 78–81, 189
Reduction of machine, 78–81, 194–197
Redundant path, 37
Reed, I. S., 201
Reed, M. B., 202
Reflecting branch, 24, 32
Response (see Linear binary finite-state
    machines)
Response variables, 1
Reversible finite-state machines, 147
Runyon, J. P., 201

Sampling times, 2
Schubert, E. J., 202
Scott, D., 201
Sequence, compact (p, μ), 180, 181
  diagnosing, 90, 102
    minimal, 90, 102

Sequence, homing, 120
    minimal, 120
  input, 13
  input-output, 161
  output, 13
  (p, μ), 180
Seshu, S., 31, 200, 202
Set, compatible, 190
  state, 6, 9–12
Shannon, C. E., 6
Signal, synchronizing, 2
Simon, J. M., 157, 202
Simple distinguishability, 51
Simple equivalence class, 69
Simple experiments, 89
Skeleton matrix, 40–42
  modified, 42, 43
Smirnova, I. M., 199
Source, synchronizing, 2
Srinivasan, C. V., 202
State, 6, 7
  adjoint, 54
  admissible, 90
  disjoint, 54
  ground, 170
  initial, 14
  isolated, 25, 32
  lossy, 149
  persistent, 24, 32
  transient, 24, 32
  ξ_i-mergeable, 130, 131
State distinguishability, 49–52
State equivalence class, 58
State equivalence partition, 57–60
State equivalence partitioning, 60–67
State identification experiments, 87–131
State set, 6
  determination from internal struc-
    ture, 9–12
Stearns, R. E., 202
Stern, T. E., 199, 202
Strongly connected finite-state ma-
    chines, 145–149, 180
Submachine, 25
  isolated, 26, 33, 34
  persistent, 26, 33, 34
  transient, 26, 33, 34

Subtable, $s_{\nu+1}$, 17
  z_ν, 17
Successor tree, 97–100
Symbol, input, 5
  output, 5
Synchronizing signal, 2
Synchronizing source, 2
Synchronous system, 3
System, asynchronous, 3
  finite-memory, 157–160
  synchronous, 3

Table, equivalence, 70–72
  lossiness test, 151, 152
  minimal x-z, 169
  P_k, 60–62, 194–196
  pairs, 62–65, 187, 188
  transition, 17–19
  x-z, 166–169
Tal, A. A., 199
Time discreteness, 2, 3
Trakhtenbrot, B. A., 202
Transfer ratio, 171
Transient state, 24, 32
Transient submachine, 26, 33, 34
Transition diagram, 21–24
Transition matrix, 31–34
  equivalence partitioning of, 65–67
  higher-order, 34–36
Transition table, 17–19
Tree, diagnosing, 100–103
  homing, 118–120

Tree, multiple-experiment, 111, 112
  successor, 97–100
Trivial finite-state machines, 8
Turing, A. M., 6

Unger, S. H., 185, 201, 202

van Aardenne-Ehrenfest, T., 181, 202
Varga, R. S., 200
Variables, dependent, 9
  excitation, 1
  intermediate, 1
  response, 1
von Neumann, J., 16

Wang, H., 199
Wright, J. B., 199

x memory, 160
x-z function, minimal, 166
  minimization of, 166–169
x-z table, 166–169
ξ_i-mergeable state, 130, 131

Yoeli, M., 202

z memory, 160
Zadeh, L. A., 157, 202